BATI6871 .3wks 004 CGP

Contents

Component 02 — Computational Thinking, Algorithms and Programming

Published by CGP

Editors: Sammy El-Bahrawy, Rob Harrison, Shaun Harrogate, Jack Perry.

Contributors: Colin Harber-Stuart, Shaun Whorton.

With thanks to Simon Little for the proofreading.
With thanks to Ana Pungartnik for the copyright research.

Microsoft® and Windows® are either registered trademarks or trademarks of Microsoft Corporation
in the United States and/or other countries.

Microsoft® product screenshots reprinted with permission from Microsoft Corporation.

Android is a trademark of Google Inc.

ISBN: 978 1 78294 860 5

Printed by Elanders Ltd, Newcastle upon Tyne.
Clipart from Corel®

Based on the classic CGP style created by Richard Parsons.

GCSE OCR

Computer Science

No doubt ... s are
seriously ... e...

It's ...
not to r... e.

There's als... eme,
so there'l... ing.

Complete
Revision & Practice

Everything you need to pass the exams!

Contents

Component 01 — Computer Systems

Computer Systems

As it's the first page I'll start simple. Computer Science is all about computers. What, you already knew that?

A **Computer** is a **Machine** that Processes **Data**

1) The purpose of a computer is to take <u>data</u>, <u>process</u> it, then <u>output</u> it.
   Computers were created to help process data and complete tasks <u>more efficiently</u> than humans.

2) A <u>computer system</u> consists of <u>hardware</u> and <u>software</u> that work together to process data/complete tasks.

> - Hardware is the <u>physical</u> stuff that makes up your computer system, like the CPU, motherboard, monitor and printer.
> - Software is the <u>programs</u> or <u>applications</u> that a computer system runs e.g. an operating system, a word processor or video game.

External pieces of hardware like the keyboard, mouse and printer are called peripherals.

3) There are <u>many types</u> of computer system. These range from small devices like calculators and watches, up to large <u>supercomputers</u> used by banks or for scientific applications. Computers may be <u>general purpose</u> (designed to perform <u>many tasks</u>, e.g. PCs and tablets) or <u>dedicated systems</u> (designed for <u>one particular</u> function, e.g. controlling traffic lights or an aeroplane).

Embedded Systems are Computers inside a Larger System

1) <u>Embedded systems</u> are computers <u>built into other devices</u>, like dishwashers, microwaves and TVs. They are usually dedicated systems.

2) Embedded systems are often used as <u>control systems</u> — they <u>monitor</u> and <u>control</u> machinery in order to achieve a desired result. E.g. In a <u>dishwasher</u> the embedded system could control the water pumps and water release mechanisms, manage the various dishwasher cycles and control the thermostat to keep the water at an appropriate temperature.

3) As they're <u>dedicated</u> to a single task, embedded systems are usually easier to <u>design</u>, cheaper to <u>produce</u>, and more <u>efficient</u> at doing their task than a general purpose computer.

Computers contain Components which Work Together

This section is all about the main hardware components of a computer.
As a warm-up, let's take a look inside a <u>typical desktop PC</u>.

<u>Power supply</u> — supplies power to motherboard, optical and hard drives, and other hardware.

<u>Case cooling fan</u> — extracts hot air from the computer case.

<u>CPU heat sink and cooling fan</u> — keeps the CPU at a steady temperature (CPUs generate a lot of heat).

<u>CPU</u> (hidden under the heat sink) — the most important component. Does all the processing (see p.2-3).

<u>Optical drive</u> — for read/writing of optical discs (see p.9).

<u>RAM sticks</u> (computer memory) slot in here (see p.6-7).

<u>Motherboard</u> — The main circuit board in the computer, where the hardware is connected.

<u>Hard Disk Drive</u> — Internal secondary storage (see p.8).

The <u>graphics card</u> slots in here (see p.7).

If you know your computer, you need not fear defeat...

There's a lot to take in on this first page. You should make sure you're comfortable with the components on this page before going any further, as they'll crop up a lot throughout this section.

The CPU

The CPU is very important — it's the main component of a computer, so here are two whole pages about it.

The **CPU** is the **Central Processing Unit**

1) The <u>CPU</u> is the <u>brain</u> of the computer system.

2) It processes all of the <u>data</u> and <u>instructions</u> that make the system work.

3) The processing power of a CPU depends on different characteristics, like its <u>clock speed</u>, <u>number of cores</u> and <u>cache size</u> — there's lots about this on p.7.

4) The CPU <u>architecture</u> describes the <u>main components</u> of the CPU, how they <u>interact</u> with each other, and with <u>other parts</u> of the computer system. <u>Von Neumann</u> and <u>Harvard</u> are the two main types of architecture. You will need to know about Von Neumann — see next page.

CPUs contain 1000s of gold pins — some of these transmit data, others supply power to the CPU.

The CPU has **Three Main Parts**

The Control Unit (CU)

- The control unit is in <u>overall control</u> of the CPU. Its main job is to <u>execute program instructions</u> by following the <u>fetch-decode-execute cycle</u> (see next page).
- It controls the flow of data <u>inside</u> the CPU (to registers, ALU, cache — see below.) and <u>outside</u> the CPU (to main memory and input/output devices).

The Arithmetic Logic Unit (ALU)

- The ALU basically does all the <u>calculations</u>.
- It completes simple <u>addition</u> and <u>subtraction</u>, <u>compares</u> the size of numbers and can do <u>multiplications</u> and <u>divisions</u> using repeated addition and subtraction.
- It performs logic operations such as <u>AND</u>, <u>OR</u> and <u>NOT</u> (see p.98) and <u>binary shifts</u> (see p.105) — remember, computers process <u>binary data</u>.
- It contains the <u>accumulator</u> register — see next page.

The Cache

- The cache is <u>very fast</u> memory in the CPU. It's <u>slower</u> than the <u>registers</u> (see below), but <u>faster</u> than <u>RAM</u> (see p.6).
- It stores <u>regularly used data</u> so that the CPU can access it <u>quickly</u> the next time it's needed. When the CPU requests data, it checks the <u>cache</u> first to see if the data is there. If not, it will fetch it from <u>RAM</u>.
- Caches have a very <u>low capacity</u> and are <u>expensive</u> compared to RAM and secondary storage.
- There are different <u>levels</u> of cache memory — L1, L2 and L3. <u>L1</u> is <u>quickest</u> but has the <u>lowest capacity</u>. L2 is <u>slower</u> than L1 but can <u>hold more</u>. L3 is <u>slower</u> than L2 but can <u>hold more</u>.

The CPU contains various <u>registers</u> which temporarily hold tiny bits of data needed by the CPU. They are <u>super-quick</u> to read/write to, much quicker than any other form of memory. You need to know about the <u>program counter</u>, <u>memory address register (MAR)</u>, <u>memory data register (MDR)</u> and the <u>accumulator</u> (see next page).

That's a lot to remember, for something so small...

It's important that you know all about the CU, ALU and cache. Try learning everything you can about each one, then cover up the page and write down as many notes as you can remember.

The CPU

Now let's look at the Von Neumann architecture and what the registers do in a bit more detail.
Von Neumann came up with his design in 1945 and it still describes how most computers work today.

Von Neumann's Design **Revolutionised** Computing

The Von Neumann architecture describes a system where the CPU runs programs stored in memory.
Programs consist of instructions and data which are stored in memory addresses.

The program counter (PC) holds the memory address of the instruction for each cycle.

The accumulator stores intermediate results of calculations in the ALU.

One of the main features of the Von Neumann architecture is that it only uses one memory for both the data and the instructions.

These arrows show the flow of data.

Output Device

Central Processing Unit (CPU)

Control Unit
Program Counter

Arithmetic & Logic Unit (ALU)
Accumulator

Registers
Memory Address Register (MAR)
Memory Data Register (MDR)

Input Device

Memory

The memory address register (MAR) holds any memory address about to be used by the CPU. The address might point to data or a CPU instruction.

The memory data register (MDR) holds the actual data or instruction. This may have been fetched from memory, or be waiting to be written to memory.

The memory holds the program instructions and the program data.

CPUs follow the **Fetch-Decode-Execute Cycle**

Essentially, all a CPU does is carry out instructions, one after another, billions of times a second.
The Fetch-Decode-Execute cycle describes how it does it.

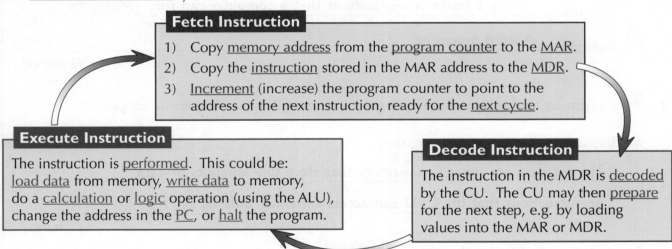

Fetch Instruction

1) Copy memory address from the program counter to the MAR.
2) Copy the instruction stored in the MAR address to the MDR.
3) Increment (increase) the program counter to point to the address of the next instruction, ready for the next cycle.

Execute Instruction

The instruction is performed. This could be: load data from memory, write data to memory, do a calculation or logic operation (using the ALU), change the address in the PC, or halt the program.

Decode Instruction

The instruction in the MDR is decoded by the CU. The CU may then prepare for the next step, e.g. by loading values into the MAR or MDR.

Learn this with the Revise-Assess-Review cycle...

To remember what each register does, look at its name to see if it stores an address or data. If you're confused about the difference between the PC and MAR, remember: the program counter just starts off the cycle by pointing to the instruction. The MAR is far busier — all addresses (data or instruction) being used must go into the MAR, meaning its value might change several times each cycle.

Warm-Up and Worked Exam Questions

There's a lot to learn on those first few pages — once you're happy with them, have a go at these questions.

Warm-Up Questions

1) Name five hardware components of a typical desktop computer.

2) Write the names of the parts of the CPU in the correct places:
   - Program Counter (PC)
   - Memory Address Register (MAR)
   - Accumulator
   - Memory Data Register (MDR)

   Central Processing Unit

Control Unit	Other Registers
ALU	

3) State the function of the following registers:
   a) Accumulator   b) MAR   c) MDR

Worked Exam Questions

1 Computer systems consist of hardware and software that work together.

a) Define what is meant by hardware. Give **one** example.

Definition: ....The physical components that make up a computer system.....................

Example: ....A mouse..

There are loads of possible examples for each of these — far too many to list.

[2 marks]

b) Define what is meant by software. Give **one** example.

Definition: ....The programs or applications that a computer can run.....................

Example: ....A word processor...

[2 marks]

2 A tech firm are testing the registers in some prototype CPUs that they are developing.

a) Explain the purpose of CPU registers.

....The registers are super fast memory that store tiny amounts of data....

....or instructions that the CPU can access extremely quickly.............

[2 marks]

b) A fault is identified in the prototype CPUs where the program counter is not incrementing with each cycle. Explain what will happen in the CPU in this case.

....The memory address of the next instruction will always be the same,....

....so the CPU will carry out the same instruction repeatedly.............

[2 marks]

Exam Questions

3 A microwave contains an embedded system which controls its cooking modes.

a) What is an embedded system?

....

[1 mark]

b) Give **two** other examples of devices that may contain an embedded system.

1. ....

2. ....

[2 marks]

c) Explain **two** benefits of using an embedded system, rather than a general purpose computer, in a microwave.

1. ....

....

....

2. ....

....

....

[4 marks]

4 The control unit, arithmetic logic unit and cache memory are all parts of the CPU.

a) State **two** functions of the Control Unit.

1. ....

2. ....

[2 marks]

b) Describe the function of the Arithmetic Logic Unit (ALU).

....

....

[2 marks]

c) Explain how cache memory is used by the CPU.

....

....

....

[3 marks]

Memory

As you'll have gathered from earlier, memory is a pretty fundamental part of a computer. It contains all the instructions that the CPU follows. Without memory, a computer wouldn't know what to do with itself.

RAM is **High Speed, Volatile** memory

1) RAM (or Random Access Memory) is used as the main memory in a computer. It can be read and written to. RAM is volatile.

- Volatile memory is temporary memory. It requires power to retain its data.
- Non-volatile is permanent memory — it keeps its contents even when it has no power.

2) The main memory is where all data, files and programs are stored while they're being used.
3) When a computer boots up, the operating system is copied from secondary storage to RAM.
4) When software applications, documents and files are opened, they are copied from secondary storage to RAM. They stay in RAM until the files or applications are closed.
5) RAM is slower than the CPU cache, but much faster than secondary storage.

Secondary storage is covered on p.8-9.

Virtual Memory is **Secondary Storage** used as extra **RAM**

1) Computers have a limited amount of RAM. As applications are opened, RAM fills with data.
2) When RAM is full, the computer needs somewhere else to put application data. It moves data that hasn't been used recently to a location on secondary storage (p.8) known as virtual memory.
3) Virtual memory may be needed if there are too many applications open at once, or if a particularly memory-intensive application is being used (or both).
4) If the CPU needs to read data stored in virtual memory, it must move the data back to RAM. This is slow as data transfer rates are much slower on secondary storage than RAM.
5) Using virtual memory can make a computer slow to respond when switching between applications (while data for one application in virtual memory is swapped with the other) or when using a memory-intensive application (due to data constantly moving between virtual memory and RAM just to keep the program running).

ROM tells the CPU how to **Boot Up**

1) ROM ('Read Only Memory') is non-volatile memory. As it says on the tin, it can only be read, not written to.
2) ROM comes on a small, factory-made chip built into the motherboard.
3) It contains all the instructions a computer needs to properly boot up. These instructions are called the BIOS (Basic Input Output System).
4) As soon as the computer is powered on, the CPU reads the instructions from ROM. This tells the CPU to perform self checks and set up the computer, e.g. test the memory is working OK, see what hardware is present and copy the operating system into RAM.
5) Although the CPU can only read ROM, it is possible to update ('flash') the BIOS on a ROM chip.

The BIOS is a type of firmware — hardware-specific software built in to a device. Embedded systems (p.1) are controlled by firmware.

ROM chips often use flash memory. This is a very common type of non-volatile memory that stores data in electrical circuits by trapping electrons. It's used in SD cards, USB sticks and solid state drives (SSDs). There's loads about flash devices on p.8.

Get all this information stored on your brain's non-volatile memory...

RAM is where the computer puts everything it's working on. Don't confuse memory with secondary storage — if a computer has a 2 TB (see p.100) hard drive, that doesn't mean it has 2 TB of memory.

Section One — Components of a Computer System

CPU and System Performance

All sorts of things affect the speed of a computer system, but the biggest factors are usually to do with the hardware. Choice of CPU, RAM and GPU (see below) can all have big effects on performance.

CPU Performance depends on Clock Speed, Cores and Cache

Clock speed

- This is the <u>number of instructions</u> a single processor core can carry out per <u>second</u> (Hz). For most desktop computers, this will be somewhere around 3.5 GHz (3.5 billion instructions per second).
- The <u>higher</u> the clock speed, the <u>greater</u> the number of instructions that can be carried out per second.
- Some CPUs can be <u>overclocked</u> to make them run at a higher clock speed than the factory-set rate. But it's risky if not done properly — it can make CPUs <u>overheat</u>, causing <u>crashes</u> or permanent <u>damage</u> to the system. High performance <u>cooling systems</u> (e.g. water cooling) are usually needed.

Number of Cores

- Each <u>core</u> in a CPU can process data <u>independently</u> of the rest.
- The <u>more cores</u> a CPU has, the <u>more instructions</u> it can carry out at once, so the faster it can process a batch of data.
- Most PCs and smartphones have 4 or more cores these days.

It's <u>not</u> quite as simple as 'doubling the number of cores doubles performance'. Software needs to be <u>designed</u> to use multicore processing. And not all processing tasks can be split evenly between cores — some steps will <u>depend</u> on others, meaning one core may end up waiting for another core to catch up.

Cache Size

- The cache (p.2) is data storage inside the CPU that's much <u>faster than RAM</u>.
- A <u>larger</u> CPU cache gives the CPU faster access to <u>more data</u> it needs to process.

Generally speaking, CPUs with <u>higher clock speeds</u>, <u>more cores</u> or <u>larger caches</u> will have better performance, but will also be more expensive.

More RAM can mean a Faster or Smoother System

1) If a computer has <u>too little</u> RAM it may run slowly due to the use of <u>virtual memory</u> (see previous page).
2) The <u>more RAM</u>, the <u>more applications</u> or more <u>memory-intensive</u> applications it can smoothly run, making it faster overall.
3) It's easy to <u>upgrade</u> RAM on a PC or laptop — it's just a matter of replacing the RAM sticks with higher <u>capacity</u> (or higher speed) ones.
4) If the computer <u>already</u> has plenty of RAM to run everything the user wants, increasing RAM may make <u>no</u> difference to performance.

RAM comes on sticks which plug into slots on the motherboard.

GPUs help CPUs process Images

1) <u>GPUs</u> (graphics processing units) are specialised circuits for handling <u>graphics</u> and <u>image</u> processing. They relieve the <u>processing load</u> on the CPU, freeing it to do other things.
2) Computers have <u>basic</u> GPUs integrated onto the <u>motherboard</u> or the <u>CPU</u>. For better graphics performance, a <u>dedicated</u> GPU (graphics card) is often used.
3) Using high-end graphics cards can greatly improve performance in graphics-intensive applications, e.g. PC <u>gaming</u> and design software.

Cooling fan

Video Outputs

PCI interface slots into motherboard

High-end hardware tends to be very expensive...

There are other factors that affect CPU performance, but you don't need to worry about them at GCSE. Using SSDs rather than traditional hard drives is another way to speed up a computer — more info on p.8.

Secondary Storage

When you think of memory, you might think of USB sticks, CDs, hard drives, etc. — these are all types of 'secondary storage'. All that RAM and ROM stuff from p.6 was actually what we call 'primary storage'.

There are **Two Main Tiers** of **Storage**

1) Primary storage refers to the memory areas that the CPU can access very quickly, like CPU registers, cache, ROM and RAM. Primary storage has the fastest read/write speeds and is mostly volatile (p.6).

2) Secondary storage is non-volatile — it's where all data (operating systems, applications and user files) are stored when not in use. It includes magnetic hard disk drives, solid state drives, CDs and SD cards. Read/write speeds are much slower compared to primary storage.

> There's also tertiary storage, which is used for long term data storage (it's mainly used for archives and back-ups of massive amounts of data).

Magnetic Hard Disks are **High-Capacity**, **Reliable Storage**

1) Hard disk drives (HDDs) are the traditional internal storage in PCs and laptops.

2) A hard disk drive is made up of a stack of magnetised metal disks spinning at a rate of between 5400 and 15000 rpm (revolutions per minute).

3) Data is stored magnetically in small areas called sectors within circular tracks. Read/write heads on a moving arm are used to access sectors on the disks.

4) Portable HDDs are popular for backing up and transporting large amounts of data.

5) Despite their moving parts, HDDs are generally very long lasting and reliable, although they could be damaged by large impacts like being dropped.

Data track
Sector
Read/Write head
Movable arm

Solid State Drives are **Fast** and **Reliable Secondary Storage**

1) Solid State Drives (SSDs) are storage devices with no moving parts. Most of them use a type of flash memory (see p.6). SSDs are used for the same purpose as HDDs — for internal storage.

2) SSDs have significantly faster read/write times than HDDs. Using a SSD rather than traditional HDD can give much quicker times for booting up and opening programs and files.

3) Hybrid drives exist which use solid state storage for the OS and programs, and a hard disk for data.

4) Like HDDs, portable SSDs can be used to back up and transport data.

Other types of flash storage

USB pen drives and memory cards (e.g. SD cards) are also flash-based, solid-state storage.

They're much slower than SSDs and have a much shorter read/write life.

They're used to expand the storage capacity of small devices like cameras, smartphones and tablets (which are too small for SSDs or HDDs). Their capacity is very high relative to their tiny size.

There are **Advantages** to using **HDDs** and **SSDs**

Advantages of HDDs	Advantages of SSDs
• HDDs are cheaper.	• SSDs are faster.
• Both are high capacity, but HDDs are higher.	• SSDs don't need defragmenting (see p.15).
• HDDs have a longer read/write life than SSDs — SSDs can only be written a certain number of times before they begin to deteriorate.	• SSDs are more shock-proof than HDDs.
	• HDDs make some noise, SSDs are silent.

Secondary Storage

Optical Discs are Cheap and Robust Secondary Storage

1) Optical discs are things like <u>CDs</u>, <u>DVDs</u> and <u>Blu-Ray</u>™ discs.

2) CDs can hold around 700 MB of data, DVDs can hold around 4.7 GB and Blu-Rays can hold around 25 GB.

3) Optical discs come in three forms:

> – <u>read-only</u> (e.g. CD-ROM / DVD-ROM / BD-ROM)
> – <u>write-once</u> (e.g. CD-R / DVD-R / BD-R)
> – <u>rewritable</u> (e.g. CD-RW / DVD-RW / BD-RW)

Data is stored as microscopic indentations on the shiny surface of the disc. Data is read by shining a laser beam on the surface and detecting changes in the position of the reflected beam.

4) Nowadays, their use is <u>declining</u>:
- As Internet speeds have increased, <u>streaming</u> and <u>download</u> services like Netflix®, iTunes® and Steam® have removed the need for optical discs.
- Modern devices like <u>phones</u> and <u>tablets</u> don't have optical drives.
- DVD-Rs and DVD-RWs used to be popular for backing up data, but they can't compete with flash storage devices due to their <u>low capacity</u> per disc, very <u>slow</u> read/write speeds and poor reliability of <u>RW</u> discs.

5) They do have some <u>advantages</u> — they're very cheap (per GB), portable, and won't be damaged by <u>water</u> or <u>shocks</u> (although they are easily <u>scratched</u>).

Magnetic Tapes are used for Archiving

1) <u>Magnetic tape</u> has much <u>greater storage capacity</u> than HDDs. It also has an extremely <u>low cost</u> per GB.

2) Magnetic tapes are often used by <u>large organisations</u> in archive libraries to store <u>huge amounts</u> of data.

3) It comes in plastic <u>cassettes</u> (containing reels of tape). Cassettes require a special tape-drive for read/writing.

4) Tape is read/written <u>sequentially</u>, meaning it is read/written from the <u>beginning</u> to the <u>end</u>, or until it is stopped by the computer. This means tape is very <u>slow</u> when <u>finding</u> specific data stored on it, but has a <u>fast</u> read/write speed once it is in the correct place to begin reading/writing.

Magnetic tapes are most suitable for businesses who do large, frequent back-ups — see p.15.

A quick Summary...

Here's a summary of the relative <u>speeds</u>, <u>costs</u> and <u>capacities</u> of all these different types of storage.

Optical disc	Memory Card		Magnetic Tape	HDD		SSD
Slowest		**Average read/write speed**				*Fastest*

Magnetic Tape		Optical disc	HDD		Memory Card	SSD
Cheapest		**Average cost (per GB)**				*Priciest*

Optical disc	Memory Card	SSD	HDD			Magnetic Tape
Lowest		**Average capacity**				*Highest*

REVISION TIP

Be sure to learn the pros and cons of all these types of storage...

Be careful with your terminology. Storage <u>media</u> refers to the actual thing that holds the data, e.g. an optical disc. Storage <u>devices</u> read/write data to media, e.g. optical drives, or HDDs.

Warm-Up and Worked Exam Questions

Once you've got all the different memory and storage terms learnt, it's time to have a go at some questions. If you're confident with the warm-up questions, then test yourself against the exam questions.

Warm-Up Questions

1) What is the difference between RAM and ROM?
2) Explain what it means for a single-core processor to have "a clock speed of 3 GHz".
3) Name a type of secondary storage that:
   a) usually comes on a reel in a cassette
   b) stores data as little pits on its surface
   c) stores data on a stack of magnetic disks
4) Give one advantage of storing data on a USB pen drive over an optical disk.

Worked Exam Questions

1 Nigella runs a piece of software to analyse the performance of her computer. It recommends that she should install more RAM in her computer.

   a) State the purpose of RAM in a computer system.

   RAM holds any data that is currently in use.

   [1 mark]

   b) Give **two** reasons why Nigella may need to install more RAM in her computer.

   1. Her computer may be running slowly.

   2. She may want to run more programs at once.

   [2 marks]

2 Shaun is on a skiing trip. Each night, he copies skiing videos to his laptop's secondary storage.

   a) Give **three** characteristics to consider when choosing a suitable type of secondary storage for a computer system.

   You could also mention how quickly they transfer data, or how portable they are.

   1. Capacity

   2. Cost

   3. Durability —— Durability is how much physical damage it can take without breaking.

   [3 marks]

   b) Shaun uses a helmet-mounted action camera while skiing, which records onto a flash memory card. Give **two** reasons why this is a suitable storage type for an action camera.

   1. Flash storage is resistant to impacts, so is unlikely to be damaged when the action camera is in use.

   2. Flash storage can be very compact and lightweight.

   [2 marks]

Exam Questions

3 Diana has bought a new laptop. The laptop contains 3 GB RAM and 128 GB secondary storage.

a) Explain why secondary storage is needed in addition to RAM.

....

....

....

[3 marks]

b) Diana wants to back up the data on her laptop twice a week.
Give **two** advantages and **two** disadvantages of storing her backup data on optical discs.

Advantages: 1. ....

2. ....

Disadvantages: 1. ....

2. ....

[4 marks]

4 Jackson is considering upgrading his PC. Will offers to sell his old CPU to Jackson.
Will's CPU is the same type as Jackson's CPU but has a different specification.

Jackson's CPU	Will's CPU
8 cores	4 cores
6 MB cache	3 MB cache
1.6 GHz clock speed	2.8 GHz clock speed

a) Explain why using a CPU with a large cache capacity may increase CPU performance.

....

....

[2 marks]

b) Do you think Jackson should buy Will's CPU? Give reasons to justify your decision.

....

....

....

....

There's no wrong answer, as long as your answer is properly justified.   *[4 marks]*

c) Jackson increases the RAM in his PC from 4 GB to 8 GB, but is disappointed to find no noticeable increase in his computer's performance. Explain why this may be the case.

....

....

[2 marks]

Systems Software — The OS

Systems software is software designed to run and maintain a computer system. By far the most important one is the operating system (OS). There's also utility software (see p.15), but that's very much the runner up.

Operating Systems manage Hardware and run Software

An Operating System (OS) is a complex piece of software found on most computer systems.

Main Functions of an OS

- Communicate with <u>internal</u> and <u>external hardware</u> via the <u>device drivers</u> (see below).

- Provide a <u>user interface</u>, allowing a user to interact with the computer (see p.13).

- Provide a <u>platform</u> for different <u>applications</u> to run (see p.13).

- Allow the computer to <u>multi-task</u> by controlling <u>memory resources</u> and the <u>CPU</u> (see p.13).

- Deal with <u>file management</u> and <u>disk management</u> (see p.14).

- Manage the <u>security</u> of the system, e.g. through <u>user accounts</u> (see p.14).

The words 'application' and 'program' can be used interchangeably to describe computer software.

Device Drivers let the OS and Hardware Talk to Each Other

Operating systems use device driver software to <u>communicate</u> with <u>internal hardware</u> or <u>peripherals</u> connected to the computer system:

- Every piece of hardware connected to the computer system requires a <u>device driver</u>. Drivers essentially act as a 'translator' for the <u>signals</u> between <u>OS</u> and <u>hardware</u>.

- When a computer is booted up, the OS will choose the correct device drivers for the hardware it <u>detects</u>. If new hardware is connected to the computer, the system will <u>install</u> the new, matching driver.

- Device manufacturers may release <u>updates</u> to device drivers in order to fix <u>bugs</u>, add <u>features</u> or improve the <u>performance</u> of their hardware. Updates may be installed <u>automatically</u> by the OS or <u>manually</u> by the user.

Some OSs will automatically find and install the drivers when you plug in a new device.

A driver lets a computer speak to a mouse? If you say so...

The OS is the boss of the computer system. It gives you a way to interact with your computer, controls hardware via drivers, and allows the computer to run applications and multi-task. There's loads more to learn about the OS, so make sure you've got your head around everything on this page before moving on.

Systems Software — The OS

One of the most recognisable functions of an OS is its user interface. It's one of the first things you imagine when you think about a particular system. But there's much more to an operating system than how it looks...

Operating Systems provide a **User Interface**

1) A User Interface allows the user to interact with a computer system.

2) Graphical User Interfaces (GUIs) are the most common type — they're designed to be easy for everyday users by making them visual, interactive and intuitive.

3) GUI systems are optimised for specific input methods. In the past, GUIs have been WIMP-based (using windows, icons, menus and pointers). Android™ and iOS® were created for touchscreen devices, using finger gestures like pinching and swiping in place of a mouse.

4) A command-line interface is text based. The user enters specific commands to complete tasks. Command-line interfaces are less resource-heavy than GUIs.

5) Command-line interfaces aren't suitable for everyday users. But for advanced users, they can be far more efficient and powerful than a GUI. They can be used to automate processes using scripts (simple programs).

©iStock.com/valio84sl

You can swipe between screens or tap an icon to open it on Android™.

You type instructions into a command-line interface.

The OS allows **Multi-Tasking** by managing **Resources**

1) Operating Systems provide a platform to run applications (by configuring hardware so they can use it, and giving access to the CPU and memory).

2) Operating Systems that can run multiple applications at the same time are called multi-tasking OSs.

3) The OS helps the CPU carry out multi-tasking by efficiently managing memory and CPU processing time:

- When an application is opened, the OS moves the necessary parts of the application to memory, followed by additional parts when they are required. The OS will decide if applications or features have been used recently — if not, they may be removed from memory.

- To run multiple applications, the OS needs to make sure that the applications don't overwrite or interfere with each other. A memory manager allocates certain applications certain memory addresses, to make sure their processes are placed into separate locations.

- Only one application is processed by the CPU at a time, so the other processes must wait. The OS divides CPU time between open applications and may prioritise certain processes in order for instructions to be executed in the most efficient order.

  > It may seem like lots of programs are processed at the same time, but in reality the CPU switches between each one extremely quickly.

- When required, the OS organises the movement of data to and from virtual memory.

REVISION TASK

Make sure you understand how multi-tasking works...

Take a look at a few different types of OS (e.g. desktop computer, smartphone, game console). What differences can you see between the GUIs? How have they been adapted to suit the device?

Systems Software — The OS

It's also the job of the OS to make sure that all your files are where they're meant to be. So when you go looking for carKeys.txt or tvRemote.exe, they'll be right where you left them.

The OS handles File and Disk Management

1) Computers store data as <u>files</u>. Images, music, videos and spreadsheets are all just collections of data. <u>File extensions</u> (for example .jpg, .mp3, .mpeg) tell the computer which <u>software</u> should be used to open the file.

2) The OS is responsible for <u>file management</u> — the organisation of data into a usable <u>hierarchical structure</u>. It also deals with the <u>movement</u>, <u>editing</u> and <u>deletion</u> of data.

3) The <u>hard disk</u> is also managed by the OS. It splits the <u>physical disk</u> into storage <u>sectors</u>, decides which sectors to <u>write data</u> to, and keeps track of <u>free space</u> on the disk. Ideally, the data for a single file would be placed in <u>adjacent</u> sectors, but this isn't always possible (see p.15).

4) The OS may also include <u>utility software</u> to help it manage files and disks. <u>File compression</u> software can reduce the <u>size</u> of individual files and <u>encryption</u> software is used to <u>secure</u> the contents of files. <u>Defragmentation</u> software can help to <u>organise</u> and <u>maintain</u> the hard disk by collecting all the free space together.

Utility software can be used for loads of different things. For example, File Explorer allows users to navigate and edit the file structure or access their files. See p.15 for more about utilities.

Operating Systems deal with User Accounts

1) Operating Systems can be <u>single-user</u> or <u>multi-user</u>.

- <u>Single-user</u> operating systems allow only <u>one user</u> to use the computer <u>at once</u>. Most common OSs, such as Windows 10® and OS X®, are single-user operating systems, even if the computer has multiple <u>user accounts</u>, or is connected to a <u>network</u> (see p.20).

- <u>Multi-user</u> OSs (e.g. UNIX server) allow <u>several users</u> to use the computer at the <u>same time</u>. They're often used on <u>mainframes</u> (huge supercomputers) and give many users <u>simultaneous access</u>. For example, <u>ATMs</u> allow thousands of people access to a large bank's mainframe at the same time.

2) The OS is also responsible for <u>user account control</u>. User accounts allow different users to be granted <u>access</u> to specific data or resources on a computer system.

3) On most desktop operating systems each user has access to <u>their own</u> <u>personal data</u> and <u>desktop</u>, but cannot access other users' personal data.

4) Operating systems may have anti-theft measures to <u>prevent</u> other users from accessing locked devices or accounts to steal information. User accounts may be <u>password</u>, or <u>pin</u> protected. Some devices also require a user to draw a specific <u>pattern</u> on the screen, or have <u>fingerprint</u> or <u>retina</u> scanners.

Two people at one computer doesn't count as a multi-user OS...

Make sure you know the difference between multi-user and single-user OSs. A single user OS may have multiple user accounts, but only a single person can use the computer at any one time.

Systems Software — Utilities

Utility system software helps to maintain or configure a computer. Many useful utilities are installed with the operating system, but extra utility software can be installed to perform additional tasks.

Defragmentation Utilities put broken up files back together

1) Files are stored on a hard disk in available spaces. Ideally, entire files would be stored together.

2) However, as files are moved, deleted and change size, lots of small gaps begin to appear on the disk. When writing files to the disk, the OS splits files into smaller blocks to fill up the gaps.

3) Over time, the disk becomes more and more fragmented. This makes reading and writing files slower as the read/write head has to move back and forth across the disk.

4) Defragmentation software reorganises data on the hard drive to put fragmented files back together. It also moves files to collect all the free space together. This helps to prevent further fragmentation.

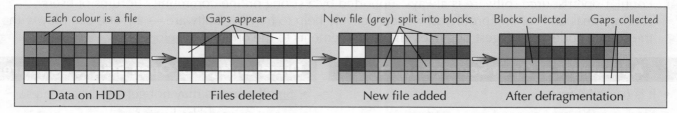

Each colour is a file — Gaps appear — New file (grey) split into blocks. — Blocks collected — Gaps collected

Data on HDD — Files deleted — New file added — After defragmentation

5) As SSDs use flash storage with no moving parts, fragmentation doesn't cause them any problems — they can access data just as quickly however it's arranged. In fact, as SSDs have a limited number of read/writes, defragmenting them can actually shorten their lifespan.

Backup Utilities help to... Backup data

1) A backup is a copy of a computer system's files and settings stored externally. This means data can be recovered in the event of data loss. Data loss can happen for many reasons: fire, theft, flood, malware, hardware failure, or even just accidentally deleting a file.

2) A backup utility is software with facilities such as scheduling of regular backups, creating rescue disks, disk images, and options for full or incremental backups:

To restore from full backups, only the latest back-up is needed.

A full backup is where a copy is taken of every file on the system. They often use a lot of storage space. A full backup can take a long time to create, but is faster to restore from.

Incremental backups are where only the files created or edited since the last backup are copied. They use less storage space and are much quicker to create. But, a full system restore is slow — the last full backup must be restored, followed by every incremental backup since that point.

Compression Software

Compression software reduces the size of files so they take up less disk space. It's used loads on the Internet to make files quicker to download. Standard file formats include .zip and .rar. Compressed files need to be extracted before they can be used.

Encryption Software

Encryption software scrambles (encrypts) data to stop third-parties from accessing it. Encrypted data can be decrypted using a special 'key'.

There's more about compression on p.113 and encryption on p.33.

There are many more examples of utility software...

EXAM TIP

Remember, utilities are bits of software that help maintain your system. You need to know the four above, but it's worth knowing some others for the exam, e.g. disk/registry cleaners, system restore, file managers, anti-virus / anti-spyware / firewalls, automatic updating, system diagnosis tools.

Open Source and Proprietary Software

Generally speaking, open source software is free and proprietary software is paid for.
But the proper definitions are to do with whether the licence lets you change and share the software.

Open Source software is given away with its Source Code

1) Open source software is software where the source code is made freely available. Users may legally modify the source code to create their own spin-off software, which can be shared under the same licence and terms as the original software.

2) Well-known examples include Apache HTTP server (runs web servers), GIMP (image editing), Mozilla® Firefox® (web browser), and VLC media player.

3) Linux is a hugely successful open source OS released in 1991. Hundreds of Linux-based OSs have been developed and shared over the years. The most popular include UBUNTU, Debian and Android™.

4) Popular open-source software is always supported by a strong online community (forums of users sharing ideas and solving problems). Users actively help to improve software — anyone can play with the source code and suggest bug fixes and improvements to the original developers.

Source code is the actual programming code behind the software. It shows exactly how the software was made.

Advantages of Open Source Software	Disadvantages of Open Source Software
• It is (usually) free. • Made for the greater good, not profit — it benefits everyone, encourages collaboration, sharing of ideas. • Software can be adapted by users to fit their needs. • Wide pool of collaborators can be more creative and innovative than the programmers of one company. • Popular software is very reliable and secure — any problems are quickly solved by the community.	• Small projects may not get regular updates... • ...and so could be buggy • ...or have unpatched security holes. • There may be limited user documentation. • No warranties if something goes wrong. • No customer support (although community forums will often make up for this). • Companies using open-source code to make custom software may not want competitors to see their source code, but they have no choice.

Proprietary Software is Closed Source Software

1) Proprietary software is software, usually paid for, where only the compiled code is released. The source code is usually a closely-guarded secret. Proprietary software licenses restrict the modification, copying and redistribution of the software.

2) Businesses often use proprietary software instead of open source as it tends to have better customer support options. Companies producing proprietary software include Microsoft® (Office®, Windows®, Outlook®, etc.) and Adobe® (Photoshop®, Illustrator®, etc.).

Compiled code is the final file (e.g. .exe file) that runs — it doesn't tell you how the program was made.

Advantages of Proprietary Software	Disadvantages of Proprietary Software
• Comes with warranties, documentation, and customer support. • Should be well-tested and reliable as the company's reputation depends on this. Fixes and updates will come regularly (open source will vary more). • Usually cheaper for companies than developing their own custom-built software.	• Can be expensive. • Software may not exactly fit a user's needs, and they can't do anything about it. • Software companies may not maintain older software after warranties expire — they'll want people to buy their latest product.

Learn the definitions of open source and proprietary software...

... as well as the pros and cons of each. Just talking about cost is unlikely to get you full marks in the exam.

Warm-Up and Worked Exam Questions

You've made it to the end of Section One, and I think that calls for a bit of a celebration. But not before having a go at these questions — better get them out of the way while it's all fresh in your mind...

Warm-Up Questions

1) Give one way in which an Operating System can help to secure a user's data.

2) What is the purpose of a 'compression utility'?

3) Put the following software into the table on the right:
   - Adobe® Photoshop®
   - Linux
   - Windows® Firewall
   - VLC Media Player
   - macOS®

	Open Source	Proprietary
OS		
Utility		
Other		

Worked Exam Questions

1   The operating system on Selina's computer has an optional command line interface.

    a) Identify **two** benefits of using a command line interface instead of a GUI.

       1. Command line interfaces give greater control than GUIs.

       2. They are less resource-heavy than GUIs.

          You could also mention scripts as a possible benefit.   *[2 marks]*

    b) The operating system includes an encryption utility that can be used to encrypt folders and files. Explain **one** reason why Selina may use the encryption utility.

       To keep her data private in the event of a third party, like a hacker,

       gaining access to her files.   It may also protect her data from malware.

            [2 marks]

2   A marketing company has the same, paid-for, proprietary software on all of its computers. The software provides facilities for word processing, presentations, spreadsheets and databases.

    a) Describe what is meant by proprietary software.

       Proprietary software is software where only the compiled code is released.

       Users are not allowed to modify, copy or redistribute the software.

            [2 marks]

    b) Give **two** advantages to the company of using proprietary software.

       1. The software is likely to include customer support.

       2. It should be well-tested and reliable.

            [2 marks]

Exam Questions

3   Ioteck has created TV-PCs. TV-PCs plug into any
    USB-compatible TV, and come packaged with a
    selection of open source software.

> **TV-PC** *Only £39.99!*
> Turn your TV into a PC for
> word processing, spreadsheets,
> slideshows, databases and photos!
> *Includes portable projector-keyboard
> — type on any surface!*
>
> NEW

   a)   Describe what is meant by open source software.

   ....

   ....

   [2 marks]

   b)   Explain **one** advantage and **one** disadvantage to Ioteck
           of using open source software on the TV-PCs.

   *Try to relate your answers
   specifically to Ioteck's needs.*

   Advantage: ....

   ....

   ....

   Disadvantage: ....

   ....

   ....

   [4 marks]

4   An accounting firm plans to introduce a new scheme for regularly backing up its data.

   a)   Define what is meant by the following types of backup.

   Full backup: ....

   ....

   Incremental backup: ....

   ....

   [2 marks]

   b)   Describe a possible backup scheme for the firm that includes:

   • full backups   • incremental backups
   • data compression   • security measures

   [4 marks]

   *Think about when they should take their backups,
   and what they should do with them afterwards.*

5   Josephine's computer has a multi-tasking operating system. Explain how the
    operating system manages memory and CPU time to allow the computer to multi-task.

   [6 marks]

Revision Questions for Section One

Sometimes the first section is the easy one — but not this time. There's lots to learn here, so:

- Try these questions and <u>tick off each one</u> when you <u>get it right</u>.
- When you've done <u>all the questions</u> for a topic and are <u>completely happy</u> with it, tick off the topic.

Computer Systems and the CPU (p.1-3) ☑

1) What is a computer? ☑
2) Define hardware and software. ☑
3) What is a) an embedded system?   b) a control system? ☑
4) Explain the role of the control unit in the CPU. ☑
5) Write down the names of three registers in the CPU. ☑
6) What does ALU stand for and what does it do? ☑
7) What is cache memory and what is it used for? ☑
8) Sketch a Von Neumann computer. ☑
9) Describe what happens at each stage of the CPU fetch-decode-execute cycle. ☑

Memory and Computer Performance (p.6-7) ☑

10) What is the difference between volatile and non-volatile memory? ☑
11) What does RAM stand for? Describe how RAM is used in a computer system. ☑
12) Could changing the amount of RAM affect the performance of the computer?
    Give reasons for your answer. ☑
13) Explain when and how virtual memory is used. ☑
14) Explain why ROM is required by a computer system. ☑
15) Name three characteristics of a processor that may affect its performance. ☑
16) State three components that could be upgraded to speed up a computer system. ☑

Secondary Storage (p.8-9) ☑

17) Define primary and secondary storage. Give an example of each. ☑
18) List four uses of flash memory. ☑
19) List the advantages and disadvantages of HDDs and SSDs. ☑
20) Why might someone choose magnetic tape as a form of storage? ☑
21) What are the pros and cons of optical discs? ☑
22) Draw a diagram to summarise cost, speed and capacity for different types of secondary storage. ☑

Types of Software (p.12-16) ☑

23) List six functions of an operating system. ☑
24) Explain how device drivers are used in a computer system. ☑
25) Briefly describe a GUI and a Command-line interface. ☑
26) Describe how the OS manages resources to allow multi-tasking. ☑
27) What is a multi-user OS? Give an example of where one might be used. ☑
28) List four types of utility software. ☑
29) Explain how defragmentation software works. ☑
30) What are incremental backups and how would they be used? ☑
31) List the advantages and disadvantages for open-source and proprietary software. ☑

Networks — LANs and WANs

When you connect a device to another one, you're creating a network — networks allow devices to share information and resources. Here we'll look at the two types of network you'll need to know for your exam.

A **LAN** is a **Local Area Network**

1) A LAN covers a small geographical area located on a single site.
2) All the hardware for a LAN is owned by the organisation that uses it.
3) LANs are either wired (e.g. with Ethernet cables) or wireless (using Wi-Fi®).
4) You'll often find LANs in businesses, schools and universities.
5) Lots of homes have a LAN to connect various devices, such as PCs, tablets, smart TVs and printers.

Why Use A LAN?

- Sharing files is easier — network users can access the same files, work collaboratively on them (at the same time) and copy files between machines.
- You can share the same hardware (like printers) on a LAN.
- The Internet connection can be shared between every device connected to the LAN.
- You can install and update software on all computers at once, rather than one-by-one.
- You can communicate with LAN users cheaply and easily, e.g. with instant messaging.
- User accounts can be stored centrally, so users can log in from any device on the network.

A **WAN** is a network that **Connects LANs**

1) WAN stands for Wide Area Network.
2) A WAN connects LANs that are in different geographical locations. For example, a business with offices in three different countries would need a WAN for all their devices to connect together.
3) Unlike a LAN, organisations hire infrastructure (e.g. communication lines) from telecommunications companies, who own and manage the WAN. This is because a WAN is much more expensive to set up than a LAN.
4) WANs may be connected using fibre or copper telephone lines, satellite links or radio links.
5) The Internet is actually one big WAN (see p.30).

Many **Factors** can affect the **Performance** of **Networks**

1) Bandwidth is the amount of data that can be transferred in a given time, e.g. 500 Mbps. The greater the bandwidth, the better the network can perform.
2) Available bandwidth is shared between users of a network — too many users or heavy use (e.g. streaming video) may cause congestion and slow the network. You can limit the bandwidth available to individual users to address this.

Mbps stands for megabits per second, a measure of bandwidth.

3) Wired connections are generally faster and more reliable than wireless. Fibre optic cables can give much better performance than copper cables (see p.21). Wireless performance depends on signal quality so is affected by the range of the device, the amount of interference from other devices and physical obstructions like thick walls in buildings (see p.22).
4) Choice of hardware other than cables (see p.21) and network topology (see p.24) also have a big effect.

Don't LANguish at the bottom of the class — learn this page...

Make sure you're absolutely clear about the differences between LANs and WANs before moving on. Remember, companies use their own cables for LANs but for WANs they almost always hire lines.

Networks — Hardware

Connecting devices doesn't magically happen. To create a network, you need certain pieces of hardware...

NICs, Switches and Routers

1) A <u>Network Interface Controller</u> (NIC) is an internal piece of hardware that allows a device to connect to a network. These used to be on separate <u>cards</u>, but nowadays they're <u>built into</u> the motherboard. NICs exist for both <u>wired</u> and <u>wireless</u> connections.

2) Switches <u>connect devices</u> on a LAN. Switches receive data (in units called <u>frames</u>) from one device and <u>transmit</u> this data to the device on the network with the correct <u>MAC address</u> (see p.27).

A typical switch with lots of Ethernet ports

3) <u>Routers</u> are responsible for transmitting data <u>between</u> networks — they're always connected to at least two different networks.

A typical office router.

4) Routers have a crucial role on the Internet, directing data (in units called <u>packets</u>) to their destination — see p.28.

Ethernet port connects to LAN

ADSL port connects to the Internet

5) Routers are used in <u>homes and offices</u> to connect the LAN to the <u>Internet</u>.

Most home 'routers' are in fact a router, switch and WAP (see p.22) <u>all-in-one</u>.

Cables — CAT 5e/6, Coaxial and Fibre-Optic

1) <u>Ethernet</u> cables are used to connect devices in a LAN. The most common Ethernet cables are <u>CAT 5e</u> and <u>CAT 6</u>. They are 'twisted pair' cables, containing four pairs of <u>copper wires</u> which are twisted together to reduce internal <u>interference</u>.

Twisted pair of copper wires

CAT 6 cable

2) <u>Coaxial</u> cables are made of a <u>single</u> copper wire surrounded by a plastic layer for insulation and a metallic mesh which provides <u>shielding</u> from <u>outside interference</u>.

Insulation   Copper wire

Metallic mesh

Coaxial cable

3) <u>Fibre optic</u> cables transmit data as <u>light</u>. They are <u>high performance</u> (and therefore expensive) cables — they don't suffer <u>interference</u> and can transmit over <u>very large distances</u> without loss of signal quality.

Fibre optic cable

Hardware — nothing to do with concrete jackets...

Make sure you understand how switches and routers are different — it might take a while to click.

Wireless Networks

If you don't like the sound of all those cables, don't worry — you can throw them all away and use wireless networking instead. You'll still have to learn about both of them for the exam though, I'm afraid.

Wireless uses Radio Waves to transmit data

1) Like mobile phones and TVs, wireless networks use <u>radio waves</u> to transmit data.

2) To set up a wireless network, you need a <u>Wireless Access Point (WAP)</u> device. The WAP is basically a <u>switch</u> that allows devices to connect wirelessly.

3) Don't confuse WAPs with <u>hotspots</u> — <u>locations</u> where you can connect to a WAP.

4) To connect, devices need <u>wireless capability</u>. Many modern devices have the necessary hardware built in, but devices that don't can often still connect to a wireless network using a <u>dongle</u>.

- <u>USB dongles</u> can be plugged into computers to allow them to connect wirelessly to the internet.

- <u>HDMI dongles</u> can use wireless networks to stream high-quality video to a TV.

Dongles come in all shapes and sizes (although most of them are roughly the same shape and size).

Wi-Fi® is the Standard for Wireless Networks

1) Wi-Fi® uses two radio <u>frequency bands</u> — <u>2.4 GHz</u> and <u>5 GHz</u>.

2) The bands are split into numbered <u>channels</u> that each cover a small frequency range. The channels in the 2.4 GHz band <u>overlap</u>.

3) Wi-Fi® performance is affected by <u>interference</u> between networks using adjacent <u>channels</u>. To avoid problems, only <u>certain channels</u> that are spaced apart tend to be used.

4) The frequency band that a network uses can also affect the Wi-Fi® <u>performance</u>:

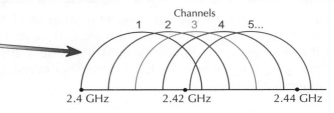

It's important that data is <u>encrypted</u> (see p.33) on Wi-Fi® networks. The security protocols for this are <u>WPA</u>™ (Wi-Fi® Protected Access) and <u>WPA2</u>™.

Advantages of 2.4 GHz	Advantages of 5 GHz
• Has a <u>greater range</u>, so can serve devices across a <u>wider area</u>.	• <u>Much faster</u> when communicating over a <u>short distance</u>.
• Better at getting through <u>solid objects</u>/<u>walls</u>.	• There are <u>more non-overlapping channels</u>, so there's <u>less chance of interference</u> from other devices.

Remember, Wi-Fi® is a separate thing from the Internet...

Wi-Fi® allows a device to wirelessly connect to a network with a WAP — that network would then need to be connected to a router in order for the device to be able to access the Internet.

Client-server and Peer-to-Peer Networks

Don't think we're finished with networks yet — we've barely started. If you want to set up a network, you need to decide what form the network is going to take — and whether you're going to need a server or not.

Client-server networks are made up of a Server and Clients

1) A client-server network is <u>managed</u> by a <u>server</u>. The devices connected to the server are <u>clients</u>.

2) Files and software are usually <u>stored centrally</u> on the server rather than on individual client devices.

3) Clients send <u>requests</u> to the server, e.g. asking for data. The server <u>processes</u> the request and <u>responds</u>. This is the <u>client-server relationship</u>.

4) The server stores <u>user profiles</u>, <u>passwords</u> and <u>access information</u> — it may <u>request a password</u> before fulfilling certain requests or <u>deny requests</u> to users without the right access level.

5) Most uses of the <u>Internet</u> work on a <u>client-server</u> relationship. E.g. <u>websites</u> are hosted on <u>web servers</u>. Web browsers are <u>client programs</u> which send requests to <u>web servers</u>. Web servers fulfil requests (e.g. by sending web pages) for thousands (or hundreds of thousands) of clients.

Pros	Cons
• Easier to <u>keep track of</u> files as they are stored centrally.	• <u>Expensive</u> to set up and needs <u>IT specialists</u> to <u>maintain</u> the network and server.
• Easier to perform <u>back-ups</u>.	• <u>Server dependence</u> — if the server goes down <u>all clients</u> lose access to their work.
• Easier to install and update <u>software</u>.	• The server may become <u>overloaded</u> if too many clients are accessing it at once.
• Easier to manage <u>network security</u> (e.g. anti-malware software and user access levels).	
• Servers are very <u>reliable</u> and are <u>always on</u>.	

Peer-to-Peer networks don't use servers

1) In Peer-to-Peer (P2P) networks all devices are <u>equal</u>, connecting <u>directly</u> to each other without a server.
2) You store files on <u>individual devices</u> and share them with <u>others</u>.
3) You may use a P2P network at <u>home</u> to <u>share files</u> between devices, or connect devices to a <u>printer</u>.

Pros
- <u>Easy</u> to <u>maintain</u> — you don't need any expertise or expensive hardware.
- <u>No dependence</u> on server — if one device fails the whole network isn't lost.

Cons
- <u>No centralised management</u> — devices need their updates and security installed individually. <u>Backups</u> are also more <u>complicated</u>.
- Copying files between devices creates <u>duplicate</u> files — it's easy to <u>lose track</u> of what's stored where and which files are <u>up-to-date</u>.
- Peer machines are <u>less reliable</u> and data may be <u>lost</u> if one <u>fails</u>.
- Machines are prone to <u>slow down</u> when other devices access them.

Although most Internet use is <u>client-server</u> based, there are some common P2P applications such as <u>video calling</u> (like Skype™) and <u>file sharing</u> (sadly this is often used for illegal sharing of copyrighted material).

Luckily, these networks are exactly what their names suggest...

Look into whether the network at home or school is client-server or peer-to-peer. Draw a diagram showing the devices and how they're connected (you can simplify it if there are a lot of devices).

Network Topologies

A <u>topology</u> is essentially the layout of the network. Networks can be arranged in lots of different topologies, but star and mesh are the two important ones you'll need to know for the exam.

In a **Star Topology** all devices are connected to the centre

In a <u>star topology</u>, all the devices are connected to a <u>central switch</u> or <u>server</u> that controls the network.

STAR — Server — Switch

The central <u>switch</u> allows many devices to access the server simultaneously.

Star networks may be <u>wired</u> or <u>wireless</u>.

Pros
- If a <u>device fails</u> or a cable is disconnected, the rest of the network is <u>unaffected</u>.
- It's simple to <u>add more devices</u> to the network.
- <u>Better performance</u> than other setups — data goes straight to the central device so all devices can <u>transmit data at once</u> (unlike ring network) and there are <u>few data collisions</u> (unlike bus network).

Cons
- In <u>wired</u> networks, every device needs a <u>cable</u> to connect to the central switch or server. This can be <u>expensive</u>, e.g. for an office building with 50 terminals.
- If there is a problem with the switch/server, the <u>whole network</u> is affected.

It's worth taking a quick look at some <u>traditional</u> network setups for comparison with star networks:

BUS — Backbone cable — Terminator — Terminator

In a bus topology, all devices are arranged in a line, connected to a single backbone cable. Devices send data in both directions. This causes data collisions, which slows the network.

RING

In a ring topology, data moves in one direction around the ring, preventing collisions. But only one device can send data at a time and data passes through many devices before reaching its destination.

In a **Mesh Topology** all devices are connected to each other

1) A <u>mesh topology</u> is a relatively <u>new</u> network layout. It is <u>decentralised</u> — networking devices are either <u>directly</u> or <u>indirectly connected</u> to every other one without the need for one central switch or server. Mesh networks work by sending data along the <u>fastest route</u> from one device to another.

2) The main advantage of a mesh topology is that there is <u>no single point</u> where the network can fail. If the central switch or server of a star network fails then the whole network fails — in a mesh network, if one device fails then the data is sent along a <u>different route</u> to get to its target.

3) The traditional problem with mesh networks has been that they were very <u>expensive</u> — you needed a lot of wire to connect so many devices together. But now more people are using <u>wireless technology</u>, mesh networks are a more practical option.

4) A <u>full mesh topology</u> is where <u>every</u> device is connected to <u>every other</u> device. In a <u>partial mesh topology</u>, not all devices are fully-connected.

Full mesh topology

Partial mesh topology

I tried to set up a star network, but it all ended up a bit of a mesh...

Don't let all this stuff about different types of network confuse you — remember, these diagrams are about the layout of a network, while the client-server/P2P diagrams showed the roles of the devices on the network.

Warm-Up and Worked Exam Questions

Now that you know what networks are made of and what they look like, test yourself against these questions. If anything catches you out, just have another read over it until you're happy.

Warm-Up Questions

1) State one piece of hardware needed in order to set up a LAN.
2) Briefly explain the relationship between client and server in a client-server network.
3) Give one type of software that uses a P2P connection across the Internet.
4) Complete the table showing different network topologies by correctly filling in the white cells:

No. of devices	Star	Partial Mesh	Full Mesh
4			
5			
6			

Worked Exam Question

1   In an office there are six computers, a scanner and a router connected together in a Local Area Network (LAN).

a)   Define the term Local Area Network (LAN).

A group of devices connected to share data over a small geographical area.

[1 mark]

b)   State **three** advantages of connecting the computers together into a Local Area Network.

1. The business' six computers can share one Internet connection.

2. The computers can share the scanner and any other hardware.

3. It is easier to install and update software.

They can also share files more easily, communicate with instant messaging and store user accounts centrally.   *[3 marks]*

Exam Questions

2   Jane connects her laptop to her home LAN using a home router.

   a)   Jane can connect her laptop to the router using either Ethernet or Wi-Fi®.
   State how an Ethernet connection is different to a Wi-Fi® connection.

   ....

   [1 mark]

   b)   Jane's home router functions as a switch, router and Wireless Access Point (WAP) all in one.
   State the function of each of these devices.

   Switch: ....

   Router: ....

   WAP: ....
   [3 marks]

3   Explain **one** advantage and **one** disadvantage of mesh topologies compared to star topologies.

   Advantage: ....

   ....

   Disadvantage: ....

   ....
   [4 marks]

4   The staff at a graphic design company work together by sharing files between their computers,
   which are connected together in a Peer-to-Peer (P2P) network. An IT consultant suggests the
   company should adopt a Client-Server network setup.

   a)   Describe what is meant by Peer-to-Peer and Client-Server networks.

   Peer-to-Peer: ....

   ....

   Client-Server: ....

   ....
   [4 marks]

   b)   Identify **two** benefits and **two** drawbacks of changing from a Peer-to-Peer (P2P) network
   to a Client-Server network.

   Benefits: 1.   ....

   2.   ....

   Drawbacks: 1.   ....

   2.   ....
   [4 marks]

Network Protocols

Moving data on a network is like going on a car journey — you need a destination, something to tell you how to get there, and rules to stop you crashing into anyone else on the road. That's where protocols come in.

Networks need **Protocols** to set the rules

1) A protocol is a set of rules for how devices communicate and how data is transmitted across a network.

2) Protocols cover how communication between two devices should start and end, how the data should be organised, and what the devices should do if data goes missing. See p.29 for more on the different types of protocol.

Communication on the same network uses **MAC Addresses**

1) Every device needs a unique identifier so it can be found on a network.

2) MAC addresses are assigned to all network-enabled devices by the manufacturer. They are unique to the device and cannot be changed.

3) MAC addresses are 48 or 64-bit binary numbers (i.e. a long string of 48 or 64 0s and 1s). To make them easier to use they're converted into hexadecimal.

| 10011000 10000001 01010101 11001101 11110010 00101111 | → | 98-81-55-CD-F2-2F |

This binary MAC address is translated into six hexadecimal numbers.

See p.106-107 for more on binary to hex conversion.

4) MAC addresses are mainly used by the Ethernet protocol on LANs. LAN switches read the MAC addresses and use them to direct data to the right device.

Communication between different networks uses **IP Addresses**

1) IP addresses are used when sending data between TCP/IP networks (see p.28-29) e.g. over the Internet.

2) Unlike MAC addresses, IP addresses aren't linked to hardware. They are assigned either manually (static) or automatically (dynamic) before the device can access the network.

3) Static IP addresses are permanent addresses. They're used to connect printers on a LAN, and for hosting websites on the Internet — companies don't want the IP address of their website changing. Static IP addresses on the Internet can be very expensive — businesses pay big money for them.

4) Dynamic IP addresses are assigned when a device logs on to a network, meaning that it may have a different address every time it connects. Internet Service Providers (ISPs) commonly use dynamic IP addresses as they are more cost effective and can be reused.

5) An IP address can either be a 32-bit or 128-bit binary number, depending on the version of IP you're using. The longer 128-bit numbers are translated into eight hexadecimal numbers, while the 32-bit ones are converted into four denary numbers, like in the example below.

| 00100101.10011001.00111110.10001000 | → | 37.153.62.136 |

This 32-bit binary IP address is translated into four denary numbers.

See p.103 for more on binary to denary conversion.

I hope this useful tIP addresses any confusion you have...

You'll find out lots more about TCP/IP and its uses on page 29. But for now, just remember: MAC addresses are wired into devices' hardware and are used to communicate within networks. IP addresses are assigned to devices and are used for communication between networks.

Network Protocols

Quick recap: inside a LAN (Ethernet), data is sent in <u>frames</u> and directed by <u>switches</u> using <u>MAC addresses</u>. Between networks (e.g. over the Internet), data is sent in <u>packets</u> and directed by <u>routers</u> using <u>IP addresses</u>.

Data is sent between networks in **Packets**

1) Data sent between networks (e.g. on the <u>Internet</u> using TCP/IP) is split into equal-sized <u>packets</u>.

2) Every data packet has a <u>header</u> — this contains the <u>control information</u>. The control information is like the envelope of a letter — it includes the packet's <u>destination address</u> (where it's going), the <u>source address</u> (where it's come from) and the <u>packet number</u> (see below).

3) The data packet's <u>payload</u> is like the letter inside the envelope — it's the thing a person is likely to read, and the whole reason the data packet has been sent in the first place. The payload might be <u>part of</u> an <u>email</u>, <u>document</u>, <u>web page</u> or <u>streamed video</u>.

4) Packets are also likely to include a <u>checksum number</u> — a form of <u>validation</u> used to check that the payload data hasn't been <u>corrupted</u> during transit. The sending and receiving devices both <u>calculate</u> a checksum value by performing a function on the payload data. If the values match then the data has been received <u>correctly</u>.

Packet Switching is used to **Direct** the data

<u>Packet switching</u> is used by <u>routers</u> to direct data packets on the Internet and other IP networks.

1) The <u>sending</u> device splits the data into <u>packets</u> to be sent across the network. Each packet is given a <u>packet number</u> to show the order of the data.

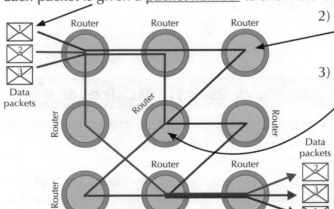

2) Each <u>router</u> reads the packet <u>header</u> and decides <u>which way</u> to send the packet next, according to the <u>IP</u> rules.

3) The way the data is sent <u>changes</u> depending on network traffic so the packets can take <u>different routes</u>. If a router receives too many packets at once, it may <u>prioritise</u> some over others.

4) As the packets take different routes, they can arrive in the <u>wrong order</u>. The receiving device uses the <u>packet numbers</u> to reassemble them in the <u>right order</u>.

5) Sometimes packets go <u>missing</u> in transit, so the receiving device checks <u>periodically</u> that all packets have been received. If it hasn't received them within a certain time, it sends a <u>timeout message</u> back to the sending device.

6) If all the data is received and the <u>checksums</u> match, a <u>receipt confirmation</u> is sent to the sending device.

> Packet switching is an <u>efficient</u> use of the network because there are so many <u>possible routes</u> that data can take — packets can reach their receiving device even if there's <u>heavy traffic</u>.

They sent me the wrong router — the packets were switched...

You need to be a packet switching master for the exam — keep going over the sequence until it sticks, and sketch the diagram if it'll help you revise. Questions can ask about any part of the process, so make sure you know how packets are sent and received, and what happens on the way.

Network Protocols

This is where we get to the protocols themselves, so it's no surprise that there's a lot of information here.

TCP/IP is the most important protocol

1) TCP/IP is the protocol which dictates how data is sent between networks. It's made up of two protocols.
2) Transmission Control Protocol (TCP) sets the rules for how devices connect on the network. It's in charge of splitting the data into packets and reassembling the packets back into the original data once they reach the receiving device. It's also responsible for checking the data is correctly sent and delivered.
3) Internet Protocol (IP) is responsible for packet switching.
4) Several other protocols build upon TCP/IP to do specific Internet-based tasks:

Protocol	Stands for...	What is it used for?
HTTP	Hyper Text Transfer Protocol	Used by web browsers to access websites and communicate with web servers.
HTTPS	HTTP Secure	A more secure version of HTTP. Encrypts all information sent and received.
FTP	File Transfer Protocol	Used to access, edit and move files between devices on a network, e.g. to access files on a server from a client computer.
POP3	Post Office Protocol — version 3	Used to retrieve emails from a server. The server holds the email until you download it, at which point it is deleted from the server.
IMAP	Internet Message Access Protocol	Used to retrieve emails from a server. The server holds the email until you delete it — you only download a copy. Used by most web-based email clients.
SMTP	Simple Mail Transfer Protocol	Used to send emails. Also used to transfer emails between servers.

Network protocols are divided into Layers

1) A layer is a group of protocols which have similar functions.
2) Layers are self-contained — protocols in each layer do their job without needing to know what's happening in the other layers.
3) Each layer serves the layer above it — it does the hidden work needed for an action on the layer above. E.g. when you send an email (on layer 4), this triggers actions in layer 3, which triggers actions in layer 2, all the way down to layer 1.

Data can only be passed between adjacent layers. E.g. Layer 2 can pass data to Layers 1 and 3 but Layer 1 can only pass data to Layer 2.

Layer Name	Protocols in this layer cover...	Protocol examples
Layer 4 — Application Layer	Turning data into websites and other applications and vice versa.	HTTP, FTP, SMTP
Layer 3 — Transport Layer	Controlling data flow — e.g. splitting data into packets and checking packets are correctly sent and delivered.	TCP
Layer 2 — Network Layer	Making connections between networks, directing data packets and handling traffic. Used by routers.	IP
Layer 1 — Data Link Layer	Passing data over the physical network. Responsible for how bits are sent as electrical signals over cables, wireless and other hardware.	Ethernet

Advantages of Using Layers

- It breaks network communication into manageable pieces. This helps developers concentrate on only one area of the network without having to worry about the others.
- As layers are self-contained, they can be changed without the other layers being affected.
- Having set rules for each layer forces companies to make compatible, universal hardware and software, so different brands will work with each other and always work in basically the same way.

Lots of layers to learn — and plenty of protocols to ponder too...

Make sure you know what the TCP/IP protocol is all about, as well as all the other protocols on this page.

Networks — The Internet

The Internet is so much a part of everyday life, it's easy to forget that it's actually just a really big network.

The **Internet** is a **Worldwide** collection of networks

1) The Internet is a <u>network of networks</u> — it's a <u>WAN</u> which connects devices and networks from all over the world. It's based around the protocol <u>TCP/IP</u>.

2) The <u>World Wide Web</u> (WWW) is a collection of <u>websites</u> that are <u>hosted</u> on <u>web servers</u> and accessed through the <u>http</u> protocol.

3) <u>URLs</u> are <u>addresses</u> used to access web servers and resources on them.

> URL: https://www.cgpbooks.co.uk/student/books_gcse_cs
>
> HTTPS is the protocol   The domain name of the website.   Path to the specific file or page.
> used (see page 29).   This is linked to an IP address.   May also contain a query for the web server.

4) A <u>Domain Name Server</u> (DNS) translates a website's <u>domain name</u> into its IP address. The Internet has a network of Domain Name Servers, meaning you don't need to remember IP addresses to access websites — you can use domain names instead.

The **Cloud** uses the Internet to store files and applications

1) <u>Hosting</u> is when a business uses its servers to <u>store</u> files of another organisation.

2) The <u>traditional</u> use for this on the Internet is the hosting of <u>websites</u>.

3) A relatively recent use of Internet hosting is for <u>general storage</u> of user files and also providing <u>online software</u> — this is cloud computing, or simply 'the cloud'. It acts like an <u>extension</u> of a traditional <u>client-server</u> network where user files are stored centrally on a network server.

Pros
- Users can access files from <u>any connected device</u>.
- Easy to <u>increase</u> how much <u>storage</u> is available
- <u>No</u> need to buy <u>expensive hardware</u> to store data.
- <u>No</u> need to pay <u>IT staff</u> to manage the hardware.
- Cloud host provides <u>security</u> and <u>back ups</u> for you.
- Cloud software will be <u>updated automatically</u>.

Cons
- Need <u>connection to the Internet</u> to access files.
- <u>Dependent on host</u> for security and back-ups.
- Data in the cloud can be <u>vulnerable</u> to hackers.
- Unclear who has <u>ownership</u> over cloud data.
- Subscription fees for using cloud <u>storage</u> and <u>software</u> may be expensive.

Virtual Networks are software-based networks

1) A <u>virtual network</u> is a network that is entirely <u>software-based</u>. Virtual networks are created by partitioning off some of a physical network's <u>bandwidth</u> to form a separate network.

2) Several virtual networks can exist on <u>the same</u> physical network. These networks all share the same <u>hardware</u>, making virtual networks more efficient than standard physical networks.

3) Each virtual network has its own <u>security</u>, including its own firewall. This means virtual networks can only be accessed by using certain <u>software</u> or <u>login information</u> — other people could be using the same physical network and not have access to the virtual network, or even know that it exists.

4) A <u>Virtual Private Network</u> (VPN) is a type of virtual network that can be used to send data <u>securely</u> over a large network, like a WAN or the Internet. E.g. a VPN can be used to send data securely between two offices on different sites, or to set up a school <u>intranet</u> that all the students can access from home.

5) A <u>Virtual LAN</u> allows you to split a LAN into several separate networks using the same hardware.

Learn the difference between the Internet and the WWW...

Don't make the mistake of thinking the WWW and the Internet are the same. The Internet is the network behind the WWW, but it also has many other uses, e.g. email, FTP and instant messaging.

Network Security Threats

Networks are great for lots of reasons, but they can also be very vulnerable to attacks by criminals. Hackers can be very imaginative when it comes to attacking and stealing data stored on networks.

Network **Attacks** come in different forms

1) A passive attack is where someone monitors data travelling on a network and intercepts any sensitive information they find. They use network-monitoring hardware and software such as packet sniffers. Passive attacks are hard to detect as the hacker is quietly listening. The best defence against passive attacks is data encryption (see p.33).

> Government agencies sometimes use data interception for cyber-security purposes — this is called Lawful Interception.

2) An active attack is when someone attacks a network with malware (see below) or other planned attacks. They are more easily detected. The main defence against them is a firewall (see p.33).

3) In an insider attack someone within an organisation exploits their network access to steal information.

4) A brute force attack is a type of active attack used to gain information by cracking passwords through trial and error. Brute force attacks use automated software to produce hundreds of likely password combinations, e.g. combining real words with predictable number sequences. Hackers may try lots of passwords against one username or vice versa. Simple measures like locking accounts after a certain number of failed attempts and using strong passwords will reduce the risk of a brute force attack.

5) A denial-of-service attack (DoS) is where a hacker tries to stop users from accessing a part of a network or website. Most DoS attacks involve flooding the network with useless traffic, making the network extremely slow or completely inaccessible.

Malware is software that can harm devices

1) Malware (malicious software) is installed on someone's device without their knowledge or consent.

2) Typical actions of malware include:

- Deleting or modifying files.
- Scareware — e.g. it tells the user their computer is infected with loads of viruses to scare them into following malicious links or paying for problems to be fixed.
- Locking files — ransomware encrypts all the files on a computer. The user receives a message demanding a large sum of money be paid in exchange for a decryption key.
- Spyware — secretly monitors user actions, e.g. key presses, and sends info to the hacker.
- Rootkits alter permissions, giving malware and hackers administrator-level access to devices.
- Opening backdoors — holes in someone's security which can be used for future attacks.

3) Malware can access your device in different ways.

- Viruses attach (by copying themselves) to certain files, e.g. .exe files and autorun scripts. Users spread them by copying infected files and activate them by opening infected files.
- Worms are like viruses but they self-replicate without any user help, meaning they can spread very quickly. They exploit weaknesses in network security.
- Trojans are malware disguised as legitimate software. Unlike viruses and worms, Trojans don't replicate themselves — users install them not realising they have a hidden purpose.

There is more than one way to attack a network...

You don't need to know every single type of malware out there, but learning all of the examples here will give you a great overview of how malware gets in to a system, and the damage it can do once it's there.

Network Security Threats

Often, security threats arise because organisations fail to secure their network properly — they might forget to encrypt their data or use bad code. Other instances are a result of hackers manipulating employees.

People are often the Weak Point in secure systems

1) <u>Social engineering</u> is a way of gaining sensitive information or illegal access to networks by <u>influencing people</u>, usually the employees of large companies.

2) A common form of social engineering takes place over the <u>telephone</u> — someone rings up an employee of a company and <u>pretends</u> to be a network administrator or somebody else within the organisation. The social engineer gains the employee's trust and persuades them to disclose <u>confidential information</u> — this might be personal (e.g. their login details) or sensitive company data.

3) Another type of social engineering is <u>phishing</u>. Phishing is when criminals send <u>emails</u> or texts to people claiming to be from a well-known business, e.g. a bank or online retailer. The emails often contain links to <u>spoof</u> versions of the company's <u>website</u>. They then request that the user <u>update</u> their <u>personal information</u> (e.g. password or bank account details). When the user inputs this data into the website they hand it all over to the criminals, who can then access their genuine account.

4) Phishing emails are often sent to <u>thousands</u> of people, in the hope that someone will read the email and believe its content is legitimate.

5) Many email programs, browsers and firewalls have <u>anti-phishing</u> features that will reduce the number of phishing emails received. There are often giveaways that you can spot, e.g. <u>poor grammar</u>. Emails asking users to follow links or update personal details should always be treated with caution.

SQL Injections give criminals easy access to insecure data

1) Networks which make use of <u>databases</u> are vulnerable to <u>SQL injection</u> attacks.

2) SQL stands for Structured Query Language — it's one of the main coding languages used to <u>access information</u> in <u>databases</u> — see p.80 for more about it.

3) SQL injections are pieces of SQL typed into a website's <u>input box</u> which then reveal sensitive information.

4) A website may allow you to view your account information, as long as you enter your password into an input box. If the website's SQL code does not have strong enough input <u>validation</u>, then someone may be able to enter a piece of <u>SQL code</u> which allows them to access other people's account information as well as their own.

> - For example, to access an online retail account you may need to put in a PIN number. When you put in your PIN number, 12345, the website's <u>SQL code</u> may be executed like this:
> - SELECT name, address, account number WHERE pin = 12345
> - However, this SQL code does not have strong <u>validation</u> because it <u>doesn't specify</u> that the PIN value has to be numerical. This can be exploited by entering the code "12345 OR 1=1". This code is an <u>SQL injection</u>. Now the SQL query looks like this instead...
> - SELECT name, address, account number WHERE pin = 12345 OR 1=1
> - <u>1=1 is always true</u> in SQL, so rather than just showing your details, the website instead shows the details of <u>everyone</u> on the website's database.

5) If a website's SQL code is <u>insecure</u>, this can be an easy way for hackers to get past a website's <u>firewall</u>.

No amount of security software can protect against human error...

The best way to prevent social engineering in the workplace is to make employees aware of the dangers — this should be part of a company's network policy, which you'll find more about on the next page. The bottom line is: don't give away any details unless you're sure of who you're giving them to.

Network Security Threats

Organisations use a <u>network policy</u> to protect themselves. A network policy is a set of rules and procedures the organisation will follow to ensure their network is protected against attacks and unauthorised access.

A good network policy will...

- Regularly <u>test</u> the network to find and fix security weaknesses and <u>investigate</u> any problems.
- Use <u>passwords</u> to prevent unauthorised people from accessing the network.
- Enforce <u>user access levels</u> to limit the <u>number</u> of people with access to sensitive information.
- Install <u>anti-malware</u> and <u>firewall</u> software to prevent and destroy malicious software attacks.
- <u>Encrypt</u> sensitive data.

Penetration Testing

- <u>Penetration testing</u> (or pentesting) is when organisations employ specialists to <u>simulate</u> potential attacks on their network.
- Pentesting is used to <u>identify possible weaknesses</u> in a network's security by trying to exploit them. The results of the pentest are then <u>reported back</u>.

Network Forensics

- <u>Network forensics</u> are investigations undertaken to find the cause of <u>attacks</u> on a network. To conduct network forensics, an organisation needs to have a system of <u>capturing</u> data packets as they enter their network.
- After the network is attacked, these packets can be <u>analysed</u> to <u>discover</u> how the network was attacked and decide how to <u>prevent</u> future attacks.

Passwords

- <u>Passwords</u> help prevent <u>unauthorised users</u> accessing the network.
- Passwords should be <u>strong</u> — they should be many characters long, use a <u>combination</u> of letters, numbers and symbols — and be <u>changed regularly</u>.

User Access Levels

- <u>User access levels</u> control which parts of the network different groups of users can access.
- E.g. business managers are likely to have a <u>higher access level</u> allowing them to access <u>more sensitive data</u>, like pay information. They may also have <u>write access</u> to files that others can only read and the ability to change employees' access levels.
- User access levels help <u>limit</u> the number of people with access to important data, so help prevent <u>insider attacks</u> on the network (see p.31).

Anti-Malware

- <u>Anti-malware software</u> is designed to find and stop <u>malware</u> from damaging a network and the devices on it. There are lots of different types of anti-malware software, including <u>antivirus</u> programs which isolate and destroy computer viruses.
- Companies use <u>firewalls</u> to <u>block unauthorised access</u>. Firewalls examine <u>all data</u> entering and leaving the network and block any potential threats.

Encryption

- <u>Encryption</u> is when data is translated into a code which only someone with the <u>correct key</u> can access, meaning unauthorised users cannot read it.
- Encrypted text is called <u>cipher text</u>, while non-encrypted data is called <u>plain text</u>.
- Encryption is essential for sending data over a network <u>securely</u>.

REVISION TASK

Learn these pages and your exam grade should be fairly secure...

Try and find a recent news article about a network attack. Identify the type of attack/malware used. See if you can find out how the attack was carried out and suggest some ways that it may have been prevented. Then try and get over the inevitable fear of ever using the Internet again...

Warm-Up and Worked Exam Questions

That's another Section down. There are lots of little things to remember, like the different protocols and types of malware, so go over them until they're secure in your mind. Then have a go at some questions.

Warm-Up Questions

1) Complete the table showing the names and functions of various network protocols:

Protocol	Function
TCP	
	Responsible for packet switching.
HTTP	
	A more secure version of HTTP.
FTP	
SMTP	
	Used to retrieve emails from a server. The user downloads a copy of the email and the server holds the original email until the user deletes it.
	Used to retrieve emails from a server. The server holds the email until the user downloads it, at which point the server deletes it.

2) Name the type of malware that:
   a) disguises itself as legitimate software.
   b) alters permissions and access levels on the user's device.
   c) spreads by self-replicating without any user help.
   d) encrypts the data on the user's device, making them pay money to the hacker in exchange for the key to decrypt it.

Worked Exam Question

1 Hannah often receives fake emails claiming to be from well-known banks and other organisations.

a) State the name given to the practice of sending fake or spoof emails.

Phishing

[1 mark]

b) Explain the purpose of these fake emails.

They are used to trick people into thinking they are from legitimate organisations

so that they give away their personal information, e.g. account login details.

[2 marks]

c) Hannah also receives suspicious emails that contain attachments, sometimes from names in her own contacts list. Explain the dangers of opening untrusted email attachments.

The email attachment could contain a virus. Opening the attachment would activate

the virus and cause it to infect the device.

[2 marks]

Exam Questions

2 The Internet offers access to a variety of services, including the World Wide Web.

    a) Explain the difference between the Internet and the World Wide Web.

    ....

    ....

[2 marks]

    b) State the function of a Domain Name Server (DNS).

    ....

[1 mark]

3 Mahindar sends an email from his smartphone to Holly, who receives it on her laptop.

    a) Explain why Mahindar and Holly's devices need IP addresses to connect to the Internet.

    ....

    ....

[2 marks]

    b) Mahindar's email is split into packets and sent over the network using packet switching.
Outline what would happen if one of the packets got lost in transit.

    ....

    ....

    ....

Start by thinking about how Holly's laptop would *[3 marks]*
find out that one of the packets was missing.

4 Kate is a network administrator at a secondary school. She has put measures in place
to prevent attacks on the school's network, including having different user access levels.

    a) Explain why the school's network needs to have different user access levels.

    ....

    ....

    ....

[3 marks]

    b) A hacker recently broke through the school's network security using a brute force attack.

       i) Explain what is meant by a brute force attack.

    ....

    ....

[2 marks]

      ii) Identify **two** steps the school can take to protect against a brute force attack.

    1. ....

    2. ....

[2 marks]

Exam Questions

5 Sally works in an office. Her computer has a MAC address, which helps Sally to access files from the company's server.

    a) Describe what is meant by a MAC address.

    ....

    ....

    [2 marks]

    b) The network managers at Sally's company work with layers of network protocols.

        i) Describe what is meant by a layer of network protocols.

        ....

        ....

        [2 marks]

        ii) State the name of **one** layer of network protocols and outline its function.

        Layer name: ....

        Layer function: ....

        [2 marks]

        iii) Identify **three** benefits of using layers when working with network protocols.

        1. ....

        2. ....

        3. ....

        [3 marks]

6 A magazine publishing company based in rural Scotland connect their computers in a LAN using a Client-Server setup. Their writers live elsewhere in the UK and either email or post their articles to the company, where they are edited in time for the weekly deadline.

Discuss the advantages and disadvantages to the company of changing from their current system to one which uses the cloud.

Make sure your answer includes both advantages and disadvantages, otherwise you won't be able to get full marks.

[6 marks]

7 A law firm has 100 members of staff in an office building in London. The firm stores confidential data about its clients on a server. The firm currently has no network policy.

Consider the threats posed to the firm's network and how a network policy could protect against them.

Discuss how a network policy could benefit the law firm.

[8 marks]

Revision Questions for Section Two

From passwords to packets to peer-to-peer to protocols — this section has been quite the mouthful...

- Try these questions and <u>tick off each one</u> when you <u>get it right</u>.
- When you've done <u>all the questions</u> for a topic and are <u>completely happy</u> with it, tick off the topic.

LANs, WANs and Hardware (p.20-22) ☑

1) What's the difference between a LAN and a WAN?
2) Give three factors that can affect the performance of a network.
3) Give one similarity and one difference between a switch and a router.
4) Give one advantage of using wired network connections over wireless.
5) What's the difference between a Wireless Access Point (WAP) and a hotspot?
6) What are Wi-Fi® channels and how are they used?

Network Types and Topologies (p.23-24) ☑

7) Draw diagrams of a Client-Server network and a Peer-to-Peer (P2P) network.
8) Compare the client-server relationship with the relationship of peers in a P2P network.
9) Give two reasons why someone might choose to set up a peer-to-peer network.
10) Give three advantages and two disadvantages of using a star network.
11) Describe the key features of a mesh network.

Protocols and The Internet (p.27-30) ☑

12) What is the definition of a protocol?
13) What is the difference between a MAC address and an IP address?
14) List three things that a data packet contains.
15) How does a receiving device know whether a packet has been corrupted or has gone missing?
16) What does each of the following stand for? Describe in a sentence what each one does:
    TCP, IP, FTP, HTTP, HTTPS, SMTP, POP3, IMAP
17) List the 4 layers of network protocols.
18) Give three reasons why we divide protocols into layers.
19) Describe how a Domain Name Server (DNS) works.
20) Give five advantages and five disadvantages of using the cloud.
21) What is a virtual network?

Network Security Threats (p.31-33) ☑

22) Describe, in a sentence each, five different types of network attack.
23) List six actions that malicious software might carry out.
24) Describe three ways that malware can access a device or network.
25) What is social engineering? Give two examples of it.
26) Explain how an SQL injection works.
27) Give five security measures a good network policy might cover.
28) Give three precautions you should take with your passwords.
29) What do organisations use firewalls for?

Ethical and Cultural Issues

Despite what you might think, computer science doesn't just exist in a well-ventilated bubble — it affects all of our lives. Computers, new technology and the Internet all impact different people in different ways.

Use of Technology can raise all sorts of Tricky Issues

1) <u>Ethical</u> issues are about what would be considered <u>right</u> and <u>wrong</u> by society.

2) <u>Legal</u> issues are about what's actually <u>right</u> and <u>wrong</u> in the eyes of <u>the law</u>.

3) <u>Cultural</u> issues are about how <u>groups of people</u> with particular beliefs, practices or languages may be affected, e.g. ethnic groups, religions, countries.

4) <u>Environmental</u> issues are about how we impact the natural world.

These categories will often overlap — many environmental and cultural questions could also be considered questions of ethics.

If a company acted <u>legally</u> but ignored all questions of ethics, it could lose <u>public trust</u>. Many companies have a <u>code of conduct</u> (a set of rules that the company and its employees will follow) to show that they take these issues seriously. A company may invent <u>its own</u> code or agree to follow a <u>standard</u> one.

New technologies affect Different Stakeholders

1) <u>Stakeholders</u> are individuals or groups of people who have an <u>interest in</u> or are <u>affected by</u> a particular <u>scenario</u> (e.g. the actions of a company or the development of a new technology.)

2) Stakeholders may include a company's <u>owners</u>, its <u>employees</u>, the <u>shop</u> that sells the company's product, <u>customers</u>, the company's hardware <u>suppliers</u> and the <u>local community</u>.

3) Each group of stakeholders has different <u>priorities</u> which may conflict with those of the others.

4) In the exam, you may be given a <u>scenario</u> and asked to discuss the ethical, legal, cultural or environmental issues it raises for the various <u>stakeholders</u>.

EXAMPLE:

Sally pays to download movies from a major on-demand streaming service. Her friend suggests that she should use a website where the movies are free but that probably isn't legal. Identify the key stakeholders and discuss the ethical and legal issues this raises for each.   *[8 marks]*

<u>Sally</u> is a stakeholder who faces ethical and legal dilemmas. If she uses the website, she would <u>save money</u>, but may be supporting <u>copyright theft</u> and, indirectly, other <u>criminal activities</u>. She may also be breaking the <u>law</u> herself and could face <u>prosecution</u>. By using a website of dubious nature, she will put herself at risk from computer <u>viruses</u> and other <u>malware</u>. She may argue that the website is <u>easily accessible</u>, the legality is a <u>grey area</u> and that the <u>government</u> or <u>film company</u> should shut down these websites if they don't want people to use them.

The movie's <u>creators, publishers and employees</u> are stakeholders. They may <u>lose money</u> as a result of people using these websites. This could affect their ability to employ staff and make films in the future. They could use copyright laws, e.g. the Copyright, Design and Patents Act to attempt to prosecute the website's <u>owners</u> or the website's <u>users</u>. If they targeted users, this could be an effective <u>scare tactic</u>, but could also create <u>bad press</u> for the company.

<u>Owners</u> of the legitimate streaming service are also stakeholders who would <u>lose money</u> which could affect their ability to <u>employ</u> staff or <u>stay in business</u>.

<u>Governments</u> could also be stakeholders. The film company's government will want to <u>protect</u> its companies and will be <u>under pressure</u> to take action. However this may be very expensive and technically difficult. If the website is hosted in a <u>different country</u> with different copyright laws, tricky <u>political negotiations</u> may be required. The government may also be concerned that money from these websites could be funding further illegal activities.

These are really common essay questions in the exam...

When you're answering questions on these issues, get in the habit of thinking about what groups are affected (stakeholders) and what issues (legal/ethical/cultural/environmental) it raises.

Ethical and Cultural Issues

It's quite concerning to think how many people have access to your social media profile. However, some people in the world don't get to access social media at all — so maybe you're the lucky one...

It's hard to keep information **Private** on the Internet

1) Many websites (e.g. social media, banking and retail) require users to provide <u>personal information</u> in order to set up an account, e.g. date of birth and address.

2) <u>Social media</u> websites actively <u>encourage</u> you to post even more <u>personal</u> information, including photographs and details of your job and social life.

3) <u>Cloud computing</u> websites allow users to upload <u>personal files</u> to their servers.

4) Companies may make your personal information, photos, etc. available to <u>other website users</u> or the <u>whole Internet</u>. They may also <u>sell</u> your <u>personal details</u>, <u>buying habits</u>, <u>likes / dislikes</u> etc. to other organisations (who might use it to send you <u>targeted adverts</u> or <u>spam</u> emails). Companies can do lots with your information as long as they stay within the bounds of the <u>privacy agreement</u>.

5) Users will <u>accept</u> a privacy agreement before using many websites and software. The trouble is that very few people actually read these so are <u>unaware</u> of what they're agreeing to. Even if they <u>do</u> read the terms, users often have <u>no choice</u> but to agree if they want to use the website or software at all.

6) Users can take steps to make the information they share more <u>private</u>, e.g. change their <u>privacy settings</u> on social media sites. Websites often have fairly relaxed privacy settings by <u>default</u>. They also can have privacy settings that are hard to <u>find</u> and hard to <u>understand</u>.

7) Users have to trust companies to keep their data <u>secure</u>. But this doesn't always happen — there have been various <u>high profile cases</u> where customer data held by large companies has been <u>leaked</u> or <u>stolen</u>.

8) There are also issues around having so much personal information accessed via <u>mobile devices</u>, which might be stolen.

Censorship and **Surveillance** are controversial issues

Censorship

1) <u>Internet censorship</u> is when someone tries to <u>control</u> what other people can access on the Internet. Some countries' governments use censorship to restrict access to certain information.

2) One of the strictest countries for censorship is <u>China</u>, where they restrict access to websites which are <u>critical</u> of the government. China also censors many major <u>foreign websites</u>, including Facebook®, Twitter and YouTube™. In <u>Cuba</u>, citizens can only access the Internet from government-controlled <u>access points</u>.

3) Many governments use <u>some form</u> of censorship. Many countries (including the UK) restrict access to pornography, gambling and other inappropriate websites in order to <u>protect children</u>.

Surveillance

1) <u>Computer surveillance</u> is when someone <u>monitors</u> what other people are accessing on the Internet.

2) Many countries use some form of surveillance. Government <u>intelligence agencies</u> may use packet sniffers and other software to <u>monitor internet traffic</u>, looking out for certain <u>key words</u> or <u>phrases</u> that might alert them to illegal activities, terrorism, etc. In some countries <u>Internet Service Providers</u> (ISPs) <u>keep records</u> of all websites visited by all its customers for a certain amount of time.

Censorship and surveillance are <u>controversial</u> topics. Some people support them in some form, e.g. to protect children or to stop terrorism. Others are completely against them, including several non-profit organisations which campaign against what they call <u>cyber censorship</u> and <u>mass surveillance</u>.

You should have seen this page before it was censored...

The weird thing about this stuff is that everyone knows it's happening but no-one does anything about it — the Internet is such a big part of modern life that for many people their loss of privacy is a price worth paying. Other people aren't so keen about losing their privacy though, which is why these issues are so controversial.

Ethical and Cultural Issues

This page might talk about trolls, but there's nothing fantastical or whimsical about it.
In fact, this page gets into some serious issues which have damaged people's lives.

New technology can impact our **Social Well-being**

1) Companies release <u>new technology</u> regularly, and pay for <u>advertisements</u> to promote it. These techniques often try to <u>influence</u> and pressure people into buying or <u>upgrading</u> to the latest device.

2) Technology has also increased <u>peer pressure</u> — children feel pressure to own the latest device for fear of being <u>bullied</u> by their peers. Parents feel pressured into buying them.

3) <u>Smartphones</u> make it easier for people's <u>work</u> to intrude into other areas of life. Employees may be expected to carry a smartphone all the time, so that they can <u>always be contacted</u> — the smartphone may beep each time they get a work <u>e-mail</u>. This can be <u>stressful</u> for employees who feel they can never really <u>switch off</u> from work.

4) Face-to-face <u>social interaction</u> can be neglected as more of our social lives move online. This is made worse by having the Internet on mobile devices — it's now almost possible to ignore real life completely.

Cyberbullying and **Trolling** are a problem on **Social Media**

Cyberbullying

- <u>Cyberbullying</u> is when somebody uses social media to deliberately <u>harm</u> someone else.
- This includes trying to <u>intimidate</u> or <u>insult</u> someone, or trying to <u>humiliate</u> or <u>defame</u> them (damage their reputation).
- Cyberbullying can cause serious <u>distress</u> — people have been driven to suicide because of these attacks.

Trolling

- <u>Trolling</u> is when somebody tries to cause <u>public arguments</u> with others online.
- For example, the <u>troll</u> may take part in a political discussion online, but only to make comments which would <u>frustrate</u> the other members of the discussion. Trolls normally do this for their own <u>amusement</u> or to gain <u>attention</u>.

1) Problems like cyberbullying and trolling may be a result of the <u>anonymity</u> that the Internet gives people. They say things online that they wouldn't say if talking to someone face-to-face.

2) The Internet has made it easier for children to access <u>inappropriate material</u>, like pornography, drugs and gambling. <u>Parents</u> and <u>schools</u> can use <u>parental-control software</u> to try to stop children seeing it.

3) <u>Sexting</u> (sending sexually explicit messages or images to other people) is more common as smartphones and <u>video messaging</u> applications have become more popular. Sexting can be <u>dangerous</u> as the person receiving the images might not be trustworthy — social media allows them to forward someone else's images onto anyone they want. There are now <u>laws</u> which try to prevent this.

Technology has enabled a lot of anti-social behaviour...

These are all sensitive topics, but they're worth mentioning in the exam if they're relevant to the question. The problems on this page can have a damaging impact on the mental wellbeing of the victim — if you ever experience any of them, the best thing to do is to tell someone about it.

Ethical and Cultural Issues

Overuse of technology isn't just dangerous to mental health — it can also cause physical conditions. But as it becomes more and more central to our lives, these problems can be harder to avoid...

Using technology too much can cause Health Problems

1) <u>Eyestrain</u> can be caused by looking at a device's screen for too long. This is a particular problem if the device is used in <u>bad lighting</u>, the screen is <u>flickering</u> or there is <u>sunlight glare</u> on the screen.

> Eyestrain can be prevented by using suitable lighting, keeping the screen a <u>good distance</u> away from your eyes and taking <u>regular breaks</u> from using your device.

2) <u>Repetitive Strain Injury</u> (RSI) is when parts of the body (normally <u>fingers</u> and <u>wrists</u>) become damaged as a result of <u>repeated movements</u> over a long period time, such as typing on a keyboard.

> RSI can be prevented by having a correct <u>posture</u>, arranging your <u>desk</u> appropriately and taking regular breaks.

3) Sitting at a computer too long can cause <u>back problems</u>. Back pains are normally caused by <u>poor posture</u>.

> You can prevent back pains by using an <u>adjustable chair</u>, a foot rest and/or an adjustable monitor, and ensuring that you aren't sitting at an awkward angle.

Technology and the Internet have shaped our Culture

<u>Selfies</u> (photos we take of ourselves) have become really <u>popular</u> because smartphone cameras and social media allow us to take them and share them easily. But could they be seen as a sign that social media is gradually making people more <u>attention-seeking</u> and <u>self-obsessed</u>...

<u>Viral</u> is a word used to describe videos, images or messages on the Internet which have <u>rapidly spread</u> over social media and have been seen by <u>millions</u> of people. Companies, politicians, celebrities and charities all try to use images and videos in their <u>promotional campaigns</u> in the hope that they will go viral.

<u>Social media</u> and <u>blogging</u> websites allow people to publish writing, art or other media. This can give a voice to groups of people who might have been ignored by mainstream media.

There are benefits and problems with all technologies...

REVISION TASK

Pick a new technology that you know quite a lot about. Think about what opportunities and conveniences it can give to its users. Try and come up with some issues that it can cause as well — think about the effects of overusing it, or of people abusing it. Are there any other stakeholders, other than the company behind it and the end user? What issues do they face?

Ethical and Cultural Issues

Computers have had a tremendous impact on our culture — it's difficult to imagine some of the things we do today without them. Just remember that many people have been left behind by this technological revolution.

New technology is changing how we do Business

1) Music and television streaming services have allowed their customers to listen and watch media for less money, usually through a subscription service. But some people aren't happy about it — e.g. musicians who feel streaming companies don't pay them enough money to use their music.

2) The sharing economy is the name given to services which use new technology to let people make money from things they already own — e.g. Uber™ lets you turn your car into a taxi service, and Airbnb™ uses the Internet to let you rent out a room in your house to tourists.

3) These services are cheap, but they draw customers away from taxi firms and hotel owners. Also, they may be more risky for sharers and customers. E.g. the sharer may not know the safety regulations they should follow, and may find their insurance policy won't cover them if there's damage or theft.

Unequal access to technology has caused a Digital Divide

1) The digital divide is created by the fact that some people have greater access to technology than others. E.g. people can use the Internet to apply for jobs or university courses, access a range of services from banking to retail, and keep in touch with friends. People who have a limited access to the Internet are therefore at a heavy disadvantage.

CAUSES OF THE DIGITAL DIVIDE

- Some people don't have enough money to buy new devices like smartphones and laptops, which can be very expensive.

- Urban areas are likely to have greater network coverage than rural areas.

- Some people don't know how to use the Internet and other new technologies, and so are shut out of the opportunities they offer. This is a problem for many older people who haven't grown up with computers and so have little experience with them.

2) The global divide is created by the fact that the level of access to technology is different in different countries. People in richer countries tend to have greater access to technology than people in poorer countries. The Internet and other technologies have created lots of opportunities for the people with access to them, so this has increased the inequality between poorer and richer countries.

3) Projects have been set up to combat the digital and global divides. There are several British community projects aimed at improving Internet coverage in rural areas. One Laptop Per Child is a charity which provides laptops to children in Africa, Central Asia and South America.

These issues have got my fingers arguing — it's a digital divide...

Technology doesn't just affect those who use it — it affects everyone, including the people who can't use it. In the exam, think about how new technology might contribute to the digital divide, as well as all the other issues covered in this section. There's often loads you can say, so don't focus too much on one single issue.

Warm-Up and Worked Exam Questions

You're probably already aware of some of the issues on these pages, but it's worth going back over any that are new to you. The more you can remember, the more marks you'll be able to bank in the exam.

Warm-Up Questions

1) Tick one box in each row to show whether it concerns censorship or surveillance.

	Censorship	Surveillance
A business monitors what their employees view online.		
A country's government blocks access to Facebook®.		
A government agency intercepts emails containing certain words.		
A school restricts access to harmful websites.		
An Internet Service Provider collects data on browsing habits.		

2) Give an example of a physical health risk caused by extended use of technology, and suggest one way that it could be prevented.

3) What is meant by the 'digital divide'?

Worked Exam Question

1   Jasmine uses several social media websites. She was recently a victim of cyberbullying.

   a) Define the terms cyberbullying and trolling.

   Cyberbullying: The use of social media to deliberately harm someone else.

   Trolling: Causing arguments or provoking anger and frustration online.

   [2 marks]

   b) Suggest **two** reasons why cyberbullying and trolling have become a problem on social media.

   1. Social media can give people greater anonymity than they would have in real life.

   2. There is often no punishment if somebody behaves badly online.

   [2 marks]

   c) Social media has also had a positive impact on how we communicate. Describe **one** way in which social media benefits its users.

   Social media allows friends to keep in touch over a long distance,

   which helps maintain and even improve our social lives.

   It also allows potentially cheap communication, and easy sharing of media such as photos.   *[2 marks]*

Exam Questions

2   A supermarket replaces all of their staffed checkouts with electronic self-service checkouts.
    This increases the company's profits, but causes some of the checkout workers to lose their jobs.

   a)   Define the term stakeholder.

   ....
   [1 mark]

   b)   Identify **two** stakeholders in the decision to replace the staffed checkouts. State whether the
   effect on these stakeholders was positive or negative and give a reason for your answer.

   Stakeholder 1: ....

   The effect on this stakeholder was: Positive / Negative

   Reason: ....

   Stakeholder 2: ....

   The effect on this stakeholder was: Positive / Negative

   Reason: ....
   [6 marks]

3   Tom works for a smartphone company. He is stressed as he feels he can't switch off from work.

   a)   Explain how new technology could have allowed work to intrude into other areas of Tom's life.

   ....

   ....
   [2 marks]

   b)   Tom's company releases a new smartphone every year.
   Outline the social pressures that can be created by the regular release of new technology.

   ....

   ....
   [2 marks]

   c)   Tom's neighbour, Jerry, is also stressed because he is finding it difficult to apply for jobs.
   All the companies he wants to apply to only accept online applications, and he has limited
   access to the Internet. Explain **one** reason why a person's Internet access might be limited.

   ....

   ....
   [2 marks]

4   In many factories robots have replaced humans for routine tasks such as cutting
   and joining materials together and retrieving products stored in a warehouse.

   Discuss the impact of robots replacing humans to carry out routine tasks in factories.
   In your answer you might consider: stakeholders, technology and ethical issues.
   Try to talk about both positive and negative effects that the robots might have.
   [6 marks]

Environmental Issues

Devices all have an environmental impact. Take a smartphone — it's made of materials that are mined from the Earth, it consumes energy when used, and when it's thrown away it could end up on a landfill site.

When we **Make** devices we use up **Natural Resources**

1) Electronic devices contain lots of raw materials.
2) Plastics (which are used for casing and other parts) come from crude oil.
3) Devices also contain many precious metals like gold, silver, copper, mercury, palladium, platinum and indium. Many of these metals only occur naturally in tiny quantities.
4) Extracting these materials uses lots of energy, creates pollution and depletes scarce natural resources.

When we **Use** devices we use **Energy**... lots of it

All the billions of devices in the world today are consuming energy in the form of electricity — a lot of it.

1) Most electricity is made using non-renewable resources like coal, oil and gas. Extracting these resources and producing electricity in power stations causes lots of pollution including greenhouse gases.
2) All computers generate heat and require cooling. The powerful servers used by businesses and the Internet are a particular problem. They're very power hungry and require special air-conditioned rooms to keep them cool. That means using even more energy and more pollution.
3) Devices also waste a lot of energy. Servers normally only use a small proportion of their processing power. People often leave their desktops, laptops and smartphones idle. This means these devices are using a lot of energy without actually doing anything.
4) There are several ways to reduce the amount of energy wasted by devices:

   - Virtual servers are software-based servers rather than real machines. Multiple virtual servers can run on one physical server, so the physical server can run at full capacity.
   - Most modern devices include sleep and hibernation modes to reduce their power consumption when they are idle.
   - Don't leave electronic devices (TVs, laptops, etc.) on standby.

When we **Throw Away** devices we create loads of **E-waste**

1) E-waste is a huge problem — the world creates 20-50 million tonnes of e-waste every year. Modern devices have a very short life before they're discarded — either because they break or because people want to upgrade.
2) Device manufacturers and retailers are part of this problem. They provide short warranties (e.g. 1 year), use marketing to convince people to upgrade and have pricing policies that make it cheaper to replace than to repair.
3) The Waste Electric and Electronic Equipment (WEEE) directive was created to tackle the e-waste problem. The WEEE has rules for disposing of e-waste safely, to promote reuse (e.g. refurbishing broken devices to use again) and recycling (e.g. extracting the devices' precious metals).
4) To cut costs a lot of e-waste is sent to certain African and Asian countries where regulations are less strict. Here, most of it ends up in landfill and can be a hazard — toxic chemicals can leak into the ground water and harm wildlife.

Don't (e-)waste your time — use your energy to learn this page...

From manufacture right through to when they're thrown away, our devices put a strain on the environment. But it's not all bad — they let us communicate without having to travel long distances in pollution-spouting vehicles, and reduce our need for paper. However, whether these make enough of a difference is debatable.

Computer Legislation

There are now lots of different laws related to computing, but fortunately you only have to learn about a select few. There's a lot of (freedom of) information here, so make sure you take your time to go over it.

The **Data Protection Act** controls the use of personal data

1) The Data Protection Act 1998 gives rights to data subjects (people whose personal data is stored on computer systems). The Act has eight principles, as shown here.

2) Before collecting personal data an organisation must register with the government, saying what data they'll collect and how they'll use it.

3) The Act gives data subjects the right to see the personal data an organisation holds about them.

4) There are some exceptions to this, e.g. organisations don't have to disclose the data they hold if it could affect national security, tax assessment, or the outcome of a court case.

5) If a data subject feels an organisation's use of their data has caused them distress, they may be entitled to compensation.

Data Protection Act
The 8 Principles

- Data must only be used in a fair and lawful way
- Data must only be used for the specified purpose.
- Data should be adequate, relevant and not excessive for the specified use.
- Data must be accurate and kept up to date.
- Data should not be kept longer than is necessary.
- The rights of the data subject must be observed.
- Data should be kept safe and secure.
- Data should not be transferred abroad without adequate protection.

The **Freedom of Information Act** allows public access to data

1) The Freedom of Information Act 2000 allows members of the public to access information held by a public organisation about that organisation's activities. The Act covers information stored in computer data files (including audio and video files), emails, and printed documents.

2) Public organisations include government departments, the Houses of Parliament, local councils, the armed forces, the National Health Service, police authorities, schools and universities.

3) The Act makes public organisations publish certain information on a regular basis so that the public have access to it. It also allows members of the public to request specific information.

4) There are some exceptions to the Act. E.g. an organisation can withhold requested information if it is intended for future publication, or if disclosing it could affect national security or cause people harm.

The **Computer Misuse Act** prevents illegal access to files

The Computer Misuse Act 1990 was introduced to stop hacking and cyber crime. It introduced three new offences:

1) Gaining unauthorised access to a private network or device, e.g. through hacking (just accessing a network could get you a fine or prison sentence).

2) Gaining unauthorised access to a network or device in order to commit a crime, like stealing data or destroying the network.

3) Unauthorised modification of computer material — e.g. deleting or changing files. The Act also makes it illegal to make, supply or obtain malware.

Some of these laws are a bit similar — don't mix them up...

The Freedom of Information Act deals with information held by organisations about themselves, and the Data Protection Act deals with people's personal data held by organisations. The Computer Misuse Act hasn't changed much since 1990, but it has been amended to give harsher punishments to offenders, and to give more power to law enforcement agencies, e.g. to carry out surveillance.

Computer Legislation

Another part of computer legislation covers intellectual property — stuff people create. Your favourite song, the essay you wrote and even this book are intellectual property, and these laws are here to help protect it.

The **Copyright, Designs and Patents Act** protects innovation

1) The Copyright, Designs and Patents Act 1988 was introduced to protect intellectual property — anything someone has created, e.g. a novel, a song, piece of software, a new invention.

2) Copyright covers written or recorded content, e.g. books, music, films, software, video games.

3) The Act makes it illegal to share copyrighted files without the copyright holder's permission, use unlicensed software or plagiarise (copy) somebody else's work. Copyright holders can make money by granting permission to use the material for a fee.

4) Patents cover new inventions — they protect ideas and concepts rather than actual content. E.g. if a company invented a new method of charging smartphone batteries, they could obtain a patent to prevent other companies from releasing smartphones that used this process. In computing, patents mostly apply to pieces of hardware.

5) The Internet has made it harder to protect copyrighted content due to the ease of file sharing. It's also difficult to enforce copyright if content is held on servers in countries with more relaxed copyright laws.

6) A lot of illegal file sharing takes place over peer-to-peer networks (p.23) using the BitTorrent® protocol to share files directly between devices. Cloud-based (p.30) file-hosting websites are also used — copyrighted content is uploaded to the website where anyone with an account can download it.

7) It's a grey area as to how much responsibility the website owners have for content that users upload. However many of the most popular Torrent and file-hosting websites used for illegal sharing have eventually been prosecuted for copyright violation and forced to shut down.

Creative Commons licences allow legal file sharing

1) Creative Commons (CC) licences allow you to legally share media and software online without having to ask for permission first. Intellectual property owners use creative commons licences when they want other people to share or build upon their work.

2) There are four main types of creative commons licence:

Type of CC licence	Conditions
Attribution	Work can be shared, copied or modified, but the copyright holder has to be credited.
Share-alike	Modified works can only be distributed with the same license terms as the original.
Non-commercial	Nobody can use the copyrighted work for profit.
No derivative works	The work can be copied and distributed, but can't be modified or built upon.

3) CC licences are often combined, e.g. attribution share-alike or attribution share-alike non-commercial.

4) Some works are in the public domain — they don't have any copyright attached to them, meaning you can copy and share them as you wish. UK copyright expires 70 years after the creator's death, at which point their creation enters the public domain — Shakespeare's plays, Beethoven's symphonies and da Vinci's paintings are all now in the public domain.

REVISION TASK

Intellectual property covers loads of different media...

Search the internet for something that has a Creative Commons licence. What kind of licence is it? What benefits does the licence give the community? What about the creator? What problems might it cause that a stricter copyright licence would avoid?

Warm-Up and Worked Exam Questions

Make sure you know those laws inside out — it'd be easy to mix them up and drop some marks. Once you're confident with the last few pages, try out these questions — then go back over anything that slips you up.

Warm-Up Questions

1) Which of the following are materials used to create electronic devices?

   copper   jupiter   platinum   plastic   cedar wood   potato   mercury   mithril   gold   silver

2) State which law the following issues relate to:
   a) A hospital holds the medical records of its patients so they can be treated.
   b) A criminal hacks into a broadband company's network
      and steals its customers' account details.
   c) A request is made to a university to release information
      regarding the amount their vice chancellor is paid.
   d) A polling company holds data on members of the public for a survey it is conducting.
   e) An employee accesses their manager's network account and deletes company data.

3) Define what each of these Creative Commons licence conditions
   means for the intellectual property that is being shared:
   a) Attribution   b) Non-commercial
   c) Share-alike   d) No derivative works

Worked Exam Questions

1   The average household can spend almost £100 a year on wasted electricity.

   a)   Identify **two** ways that electronic devices waste electricity.

   1.   Users sometimes leave devices idle / on standby.

   2.   Devices generate excess heat due to inefficiency.

   [2 marks]

   b)   Explain how hardware manufacturers can limit the amount of electricity wasted by devices.

   Manufacturers can include sleep or hibernation modes in new devices

   to reduce their energy consumption when they are idle.

   [2 marks]

2   The Data Protection Act 1998 gives rights to data subjects.

   a)   Define the term data subject.

   Someone whose personal data is stored on somebody else's computer system.

   [1 mark]

   b)   State **two** principles of the Data Protection Act.

   Any of the eight principles would be fine here.

   1.   Data must only be used in a fair and lawful way.

   2.   Data should be kept safe and secure.

   [2 marks]

Exam Questions

3   Illegal file sharers infringe upon the copyright of musicians and film makers.

    a) Define the term copyright.

    ....

    [1 mark]

    b) Some pieces of music are in the public domain. Explain what is meant by the public domain.

    ....

    ....

    [2 marks]

4   The average smartphone is only used for two years before it is discarded as e-waste.

    a) Define the term e-waste.

    ....

    [1 mark]

    b) Identify **two** reasons why smartphones are only used for a short amount of time
    before they are discarded.

    1. ....

    2. ....

    [2 marks]

    c) Outline the problems that the short life span of electronic devices has on the environment.

    ....

    ....

    ....

    ....

    [4 marks]

    d) Outline how the problem of e-waste can be managed to limit its impact on the environment.

    ....

    ....

    [2 marks]

5   A cinema collects information from customers who book seats to watch movies.
The cinema would like to store this information for the following reasons:
  • to make it easier for customers when they book seats in the future.
  • to enable the cinema to contact customers with details of future films.

Explain the measures that the cinema should take to ensure that customer data is stored legally.

    Think about what legislation they might be at risk of breaking, and what they can do to avoid this.   *[6 marks]*

Revision Questions for Section Three

Well, that section had a lot of issues — thankfully you're not here to solve its problems, just learn its content.
- Try these questions and <u>tick off each one</u> when you <u>get it right</u>.
- When you've done <u>all the questions</u> for a topic and are <u>completely happy</u> with it, tick off the topic.

Ethical and Cultural Issues (p.38-42) ☑

1) Define each type of issue in a sentence: ethical, legal, cultural, environmental ☑
2) What is a stakeholder? Identify five stakeholders in the release of a new smart phone. ☑
3) Give two reasons why someone might give their personal details to a website. ☑
4) Give two problems with many online companies' privacy agreements. ☑
5) What can you do to make the information you share online more private? ☑
6) Explain the difference between censorship and surveillance. ☑
7) Give one argument for and one against Internet censorship. ☑
8) Give one argument for and one against governments carrying out Internet surveillance. ☑
9) Give four examples of how new technology may affect social well-being. ☑
10) What is cyberbullying? ☑
11) What is an Internet troll? ☑
12) Give two reasons why cyberbullying and trolling have become so common. ☑
13) What is sexting and why is it dangerous? ☑
14) Give three examples of health problems which can be caused by using a computer. ☑
15) Give three examples of how technology and the Internet have shaped our culture. ☑
16) Give three reasons for why a digital divide exists. ☑

Environmental Issues (p.45) ☑

17) Give three examples of natural resources which are used to make computers. ☑
18) Explain how a device's need for energy impacts the environment. ☑
19) Give three ways to reduce the amount of energy devices waste. ☑
20) What is e-waste and why do we generate a lot of it? ☑
21) Describe an environmental danger caused by e-waste left in landfill sites. ☑

Computer Legislation (p.46-47) ☑

22) What are the eight principles of the Data Protection Act 1998? ☑
23) a) Which Act allows the public to see information held by a public organisation about its activities?
    b) Give two exceptions to this Act that allow organisations to withhold information. ☑
24) What were the three new offences introduced by the Computer Misuse Act 1990? ☑
25) What is intellectual property? ☑
26) Why do we use copyright? ☑
27) Give three things that the Copyright, Designs and Patents Act 1988 makes illegal. ☑
28) Give the four types of Creative Commons licence. ☑
29) Why might a creator of intellectual property want to use a Creative Commons licence? ☑

Computational Thinking

Computational thinking is all about the steps you take to find the best solution to a complex problem.

Three Key Techniques for Computational Thinking

DECOMPOSITION — breaking a complex problem down into smaller problems and solving each one individually.

Computational Thinking

ABSTRACTION — picking out the important bits of information from the problem, ignoring the specific details that don't matter.

ALGORITHMIC THINKING — a logical way of getting from the problem to the solution. If the steps you take to solve a problem follow an algorithm then they can be reused and adapted to solve similar problems in the future.

These techniques are all used in Real-Life...

Computational thinking is something you'll do all the time without even noticing.

For example, when deciding which film to watch at the cinema with your family:

Decomposition	Abstraction	
Things to look at	Details to ignore	Details to focus on
What type of films are on?	Plot details, actors and director.	Film genre and age rating.
What times are the films on?	Days other than the date you're going.	Start and end times on the date you're going.
What are the reviews like?	In depth analysis of the characters and plot.	Ratings

Algorithmic thinking may involve coming up with some logical steps to reach a decision. E.g. listing all of the films that are showing, then deleting all the age restricted films and ones with poor ratings. Getting each family member to vote for their favourite, then picking the film with the most votes.

If the family went to see a film the following week they could use the same processes of decomposition, abstraction and algorithmic thinking, but they would have to do the research and make the decisions again.

... and the Same Skills can be used in Computer Science

Computer scientists rely on decomposition, abstraction and algorithmic thinking to help them turn a complex problem into small problems that a computer can help them to solve.

Imagine the task is to sort a list of product names into alphabetical order:

See p.57-59 for more on sorting algorithms.

- One part of the decomposition might decide what alphabetical order means — letters are straightforward but what if some entries in the list contain numbers and punctuation?
- Another part of the decomposition might look at comparing the entries — this could be decomposed further into how you could compare two entries, three entries, etc.
- Abstraction will help the programmer focus on the important bits — it doesn't matter what the entries are and what they mean. The important information is the order of the characters in each entry.
- Algorithmic thinking will put the tasks into a step by step process. For example, you might compare the first two entries and order them, then compare the third entry to each of the first two and put it in the correct place, then compare the fourth entry to each of the first three, etc.

REVISION TASK

Break your big problems down into small manageable tasks...

Think about a recent decision you've made, or a problem you've solved. How did you decompose the problem? What information did you ignore/focus on? How did you reach the final solution?

Writing Algorithms — Pseudocode

Algorithms are just sets of <u>instructions</u> for solving a problem. In real-life they can take the forms of recipes, assembly instructions, directions, etc. but in computer science they are often written in pseudocode.

Algorithms can be written using **Pseudocode**

1) Pseudocode is not an actual programming language but it should follow a <u>similar structure</u> and <u>read like one</u> (roughly). The idea is that pseudocode clearly shows an algorithm's steps without worrying about the <u>finer details</u> (syntax) of any particular programming language.

2) It is <u>quick to write</u> and can be <u>easily converted</u> into any programming language.

3) There are different ways to write pseudocode — they are all <u>equally correct</u> as long as the person reading the code can <u>follow it</u> and <u>understand</u> what you mean.

EXAMPLE: **Write an algorithm using pseudocode to calculate the salary of a worker after a 10% pay increase.**

A <u>simple solution</u> to the problem would be:

```
Take worker's current salary
Multiply the salary by 1.1
Display the answer
```

This solution is perfectly adequate as the problem has been <u>split down</u> into steps and it is <u>obvious</u> to the reader what to do at <u>each stage</u>.

A more <u>useful solution</u> is shown here:

```
int salary
salary = input("Enter your salary.")
newsalary = salary * 1.1
print(newsalary)
```

This solution is better as the <u>words</u> and <u>structure</u> resemble a real <u>programming language</u>. It can be more <u>easily adapted</u> into real code.

Make sure your pseudocode isn't **Too Vague**

Even though pseudocode isn't a formal <u>programming language</u> you still need to make sure it's <u>readable</u>, <u>easy to interpret</u> and not too <u>vague</u>.

EXAMPLE: **When registering on a website, a user's password should be more than 6 characters long and it must be different from their username. Write an algorithm to check if the password is valid. If it's invalid it should say why.**

```
IF the length of the password is less than or equal
to 6 characters long OR password is the same as the
username THEN it is invalid ELSE the password is valid
```

This code is <u>too vague</u> and <u>unstructured</u>. It won't give reasons why the password is invalid and doesn't give any input variables (see p.66).

The pseudocode asks the user to <u>input</u> a username and password and stores them as <u>variables</u>.

The code gives <u>different outputs</u> depending on why the password is <u>invalid</u>.

The <u>indentation</u> of the pseudocode makes it more <u>readable</u>.

```
username = input("Enter your username.")
password = input("Enter your password.")
if length of password <= 6 then
    print("Password is too short.")
else
    if password == username then
        print("Password is the same as username.")
    else
        print("Password is valid.")
    endif
endif
```

The first IF statement checks to see if the password is <u>too short</u> and the second checks if it's the <u>same as the username</u>.

See p.70 for more on IF statements.

Pseudocode isn't always everything it appears to be...

If you have to write an algorithm in your exam, pseudocode is a great way to give your answer. You don't have to worry about the fiddly bits of syntax from a specific programming language.

Writing Algorithms — Flow Diagrams

Algorithms can also be shown using a flow diagram, and just like for pseudocode, there are different ways to write the same algorithm. You do get to draw some different shapes though, so things are looking up.

Flow diagrams use **Different Boxes** for different **Commands**

Start / Stop — The <u>beginning</u> and the <u>end</u> of the algorithm are put in boxes with <u>rounded corners</u>.

Inputs/Outputs — Anything that's <u>put into</u> or <u>taken out</u> of the algorithm goes in a <u>parallelogram box</u>.

Processes — General <u>instructions</u>, <u>processes</u> and <u>calculations</u> go in <u>rectangular boxes</u>.

Decision — <u>Decisions</u>, often a 'yes' or 'no' question, are put in <u>diamond boxes</u>.

Sub Routine — <u>Sub Routines</u> are like sub programs (p.81-82) — they reference other flow diagrams.

<u>Arrows</u> connect boxes and show the <u>direction</u> you should follow. Some boxes might have <u>multiple arrows</u> coming in or going out of them.

Algorithms can be written as **Flow Diagrams**

Flow diagrams can show <u>sequences</u>, <u>selections</u>, <u>iterations</u> or a combination of them.

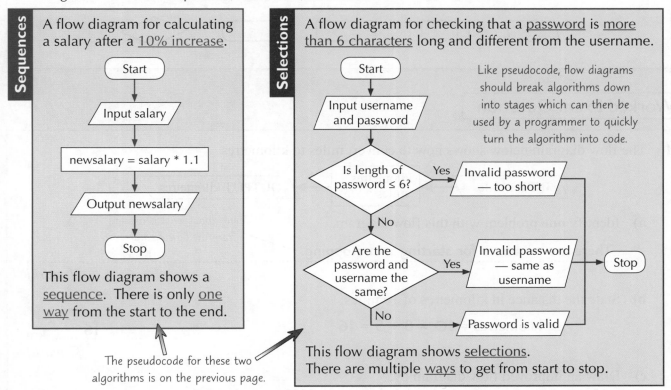

Sequences

A flow diagram for calculating a salary after a <u>10% increase</u>.

Start → Input salary → newsalary = salary * 1.1 → Output newsalary → Stop

This flow diagram shows a <u>sequence</u>. There is only <u>one way</u> from the start to the end.

The pseudocode for these two algorithms is on the previous page.

Selections

A flow diagram for checking that a <u>password</u> is <u>more than 6 characters</u> long and different from the username.

Like pseudocode, flow diagrams should break algorithms down into stages which can then be used by a programmer to quickly turn the algorithm into code.

Start → Input username and password → Is length of password ≤ 6? — Yes → Invalid password — too short; No → Are the password and username the same? — Yes → Invalid password — same as username → Stop; No → Password is valid

This flow diagram shows <u>selections</u>. There are multiple <u>ways</u> to get from start to stop.

Iterations

A flow diagram for a <u>linear search</u> (see p.56).

Start → Are there more items to search? — Yes → Check next item → Is this the right item? — Yes → Item found; No (loop back); No → Item not found → Stop

This flow diagram shows an <u>iteration</u> — it contains a <u>loop</u> that allows you to repeat a task.

EXAM TIP

Flow diagrams should show the general flow of the algorithm...

You don't need to pack flow diagrams with all the details. If you get a flow diagram question in your exam, make sure you use the correct boxes and that all paths in your diagram lead to the end.

Warm-Up and Worked Exam Questions

Now it's time to practise your computational thinking, pseudocode and flow diagram skills.
Work through these warm-up questions then have a go at the exam questions.

Warm-Up Questions

1) Give the names of the three key techniques used for computational thinking.

2) What is meant by an 'algorithm'?

3) Which of these statements are true?

> A: Pseudocode is a formal programming language.
>
> B: There are lots of different ways to write pseudocode.
>
> C: The more vague that pseudocode is the better.
>
> D: Indentation helps to make pseudocode easier to follow.

4) Draw lines matching the commands below to the correct flow diagram symbol.

Start   Output   Decision   Sub routine   Process

Worked Exam Question

1   The flow diagram below shows how to convert miles to kilometres.

INPUT miles → kilometres = miles * 8/5 → OUTPUT kilometres

a)   Identify **one** problem with this flow diagram.

   There are no boxes for starting and stopping.

   Think about what is missing from the flow diagram.

   [1 mark]

b)   State the distance in kilometres of 10 miles.

   kilometres = 10 × 8 ÷ 5 = 16

   16........ km
   [1 mark]

c)   Draw an improved flow diagram by:
   • Using a more accurate conversion factor of 1.6093 instead of 8/5.
   • Asking the user if they wish to convert another distance.
      If yes, the flow diagram performs the new calculation and if not, the flow diagram ends.

Make sure you are using the correct boxes in each part of your flow diagram.

[5 marks]

Exam Questions

2 Bernard has written the algorithm on the right using pseudocode.

```
height = input("Enter the height.")
width = input("Enter the width.")
area = height * width
print(area)
```

a) Describe what Bernard's algorithm does.

Describe what is happening on each line.

....

....

....

[3 marks]

b) State the value of `area` if `height = 5` and `width = 10`.

....

[1 mark]

3 A file uploading service won't allow two files with the same file name to be uploaded. If a file name already exists, it will ask the user to change the file name.

a) Describe with examples how abstraction can help decide how to compare the files.

....

....

....

[3 marks]

b) Describe with examples how decomposition could be used to help program this task.

....

....

....

[3 marks]

4 A robot moves on the 4 × 4 square grid shown below.
A subroutine, SqMove, is part of a flow diagram that tells the robot how to move.

Draw a flow diagram to show how the robot moves. The flow diagram should:

- Ask the user to enter which square the robot starts on.
- Run the subroutine SqMove on a loop.
- Stop when the robot reaches the top or the right of the grid.

This is when x = 4 or y = 4

[6 marks]

Search Algorithms

Computers need to follow search algorithms to find items in a list — the ones you'll need to know about are binary search and linear search. Now, if only someone could make a search algorithm to find my keys.

A **Binary Search** looks for items in an **Ordered List**

BINARY SEARCH ALGORITHM

1) Find the <u>middle item</u> in the ordered list. ← To find the <u>middle item</u> in a list of n items do (n + 1) ÷ 2 and round up if necessary.

2) If this is the item you're looking for, then <u>stop</u> the search — you've found it.

3) If not, <u>compare</u> the item you're <u>looking for</u> to the <u>middle item</u>. If it comes <u>before</u> the middle item, get rid of the <u>second half</u> of the list. If it comes <u>after</u> the middle item, get rid of the <u>first half</u> of the list.

4) You'll be left with a list that is <u>half the size</u> of the original list. Repeat steps 1) – 3) on this <u>smaller list</u> to get an even smaller one. Keep going until you find the item you're looking for.

EXAMPLE: Use the binary search algorithm to find the number 99 in the following list.

| 7 | 21 | 52 | 59 | 68 | 92 | 94 | 99 | 133 |

There are 9 items in the list so the middle item is the (9 + 1) ÷ 2 = 5th item. The 5th item is 68 and 68 < <u>99</u> so get rid of the first half of the list to leave:

| 92 | 94 | 99 | 133 |

There are 4 items left so the middle item is the (4 + 1) ÷ 2 = 2.5 = 3rd item The 3rd item is 99. You've found the item you're looking for so the search is complete.

A **Linear Search** can be used on an **Unordered List**

A linear search checks <u>each item</u> of the list in turn to see if it's the correct one. It stops when it either <u>finds the item</u> it's looking for, or has <u>checked every item</u>.

LINEAR SEARCH ALGORITHM

1) Look at the <u>first item</u> in the unordered list.

2) If this is the item you're looking for, then <u>stop</u> the search — you've found it.

3) If not, then look at the <u>next item</u> in the list.

4) Repeat steps 2) – 3) until you find the item that you're looking for or you've checked <u>every item</u>.

1) A linear search is much <u>simpler</u> than a binary search but not as <u>efficient</u>. A linear search can be used on <u>any type</u> of list, it doesn't have to be ordered. Due to it being <u>inefficient</u>, a linear search is often only used on <u>small lists</u>.

2) Once the list has been <u>ordered</u>, a <u>binary</u> search is much <u>more efficient</u> than a <u>linear</u> search. In general a binary search takes fewer steps to find the item you're looking for, which makes it more suitable for <u>large lists</u> of items.

EXAMPLE:

Use a linear search to find the number 99 from the list above.

Check the first item: 7 ≠ 99
Look at the next item: 21 ≠ 99
Look at the next item: 52 ≠ 99
Look at the next item: 59 ≠ 99
Look at the next item: 68 ≠ 99
Look at the next item: 92 ≠ 99
Look at the next item: 94 ≠ 99
Look at the next item: 99 = 99

You've found the item you're looking for so the search is complete.

Write out every step of a search algorithm, don't skip ahead...

The binary and linear search algorithms might seem like a faff for you to follow when you can just look at a list and pick out the item you want. Sadly computers are more systematic and they need to follow every step of an algorithm — in your exam you'll need to show every step too.

Sorting Algorithms

I'm sure you all know how to sort things into numerical or alphabetical order but try telling a computer that. You'll need to be able to follow and carry out the three sorting algorithms on the next three pages.

A **Bubble Sort** compares **Pairs** of items

The <u>bubble sort algorithm</u> is used to sort an unordered list of items.
The algorithm is <u>very simple</u> to follow but can often take a while to actually sort a list.

BUBBLE SORT ALGORITHM

1) Look at the <u>first two items</u> in the list.
2) If they're in the <u>right order</u>, you don't have to do anything.
   If they're in the <u>wrong order</u>, <u>swap them</u>.
3) Move on to the <u>next pair</u> of items (the 2nd and 3rd entries) and repeat step 2).
4) Repeat step 3) until you get to the <u>end</u> of the list — this is called one <u>pass</u>.
   The <u>last item</u> will now be in the correct place, so <u>don't include</u> it in the next pass.
5) Repeat steps 1) – 4) until there are <u>no swaps</u> in a pass.

Each pass will have one less comparison than the one before it.

 EXAMPLE: **Use the bubble sort algorithm to write these numbers in ascending order.**

| 66 | 21 | 38 | 15 | 89 | 49 |

First pass:

<u>66 21</u> 38 15 89 49	Compare 66 and 21 — swap them.
21 <u>66 38</u> 15 89 49	Compare 66 and 38 — swap them.
21 38 <u>66 15</u> 89 49	Compare 66 and 15 — swap them.
21 38 15 <u>66 89</u> 49	Compare 66 and 89 — no swap.
21 38 15 66 <u>89 49</u>	Compare 89 and 49 — swap them.
21 38 15 66 49 89	End of first pass.

After the <u>2nd pass</u> the order of the numbers will be: 21   15   38   49   66   89
After the <u>3rd pass</u> the order of the numbers will be: 15   21   38   49   66   89
There are <u>no swaps</u> in the 4th pass so the list has been sorted: 15   21   38   49   66   89

The bubble sort is considered to be one of the simplest sorting algorithms as it only ever focuses on <u>two items</u> rather than the whole list of items.

Pros
- It's a <u>simple algorithm</u> that can be easily implemented on a computer.
- It's an <u>efficient way</u> to <u>check</u> if a list is <u>already in order</u>. For a list of <u>n items</u> you only have to do one pass of $n - 1$ comparisons to check if the list is ordered or not.
- Doesn't use very much <u>memory</u> as all the sorting is done using the <u>original list</u>.

Cons
- It's an <u>inefficient</u> way to <u>sort a list</u> — for a list of <u>n items</u>, the <u>worst case scenario</u> would involve you doing $\frac{n(n-1)}{2}$ comparisons.
- Due to being <u>inefficient</u>, the bubble sort algorithm does not cope well with a <u>very large list</u> of items.

 EXAM TIP

In the bubble sort, items bubble up to the end of the list...

A common mistake is to forget the final pass because you realise that the list is already in order, remember that you should always show a pass when <u>nothing changes</u> to complete the algorithm.

Sorting Algorithms

The next sorting algorithm you'll need to learn is the merge sort — it splits a list apart and then magically merges it back together in the correct order. I really hope you're ready to see something special.

A **Merge Sort Splits** the list apart then **Merges** it back together

The merge sort algorithm is an example of a <u>divide-and-conquer</u> algorithm and takes advantage of two facts:

- Small lists are <u>easier to sort</u> than large lists.
- It's easier to merge <u>two ordered lists</u> than two unordered lists.

> **MERGE SORT ALGORITHM**
>
> 1) <u>Split</u> the list in <u>half</u> (the smaller lists are called <u>sub-lists</u>) — the second sub-list should start at the <u>middle item</u> (see p.56).
> 2) Keep repeating step 1) on each sub-list until <u>all the lists</u> only contain <u>one item</u>.
> 3) <u>Merge pairs</u> of sub-lists so that each sub-list has twice as many items. Each time you merge sub-lists, <u>sort the items</u> into the right order.
> 4) Repeat step 3) until you've merged <u>all the sub-lists</u> together.

EXAMPLE: **Use the merge sort algorithm to write these letters in alphabetical order.**

1) <u>Split</u> the original list of 8 items into <u>two lists</u>, the second list should start at the $(8 + 1) \div 2 = 4.5 = $ <u>5th item</u>.

2) Carry on <u>splitting</u> the sub-lists until each list only has <u>one item</u> in it.

3) <u>Merge</u> and <u>order</u> sub-lists back together. E.g.

> Compare <u>F</u> and <u>A</u> — <u>move A</u> to the new list.
> Compare <u>F</u> and <u>L</u> — <u>move F</u> to the new list.
> Compare <u>P</u> and <u>L</u> — <u>move L</u> to the new list.
> <u>P</u> is the <u>last item</u> in the new list.

Note that merging is always performed on <u>two ordered lists</u> and is <u>very simple</u> to do.

4) Keep <u>merging</u> sub-lists until you only have <u>one list</u>.

You'll often be unable to <u>split</u> or <u>merge</u> lists <u>evenly</u>. For example, sometimes you'll have to merge a list containing <u>two items</u> with a list containing <u>one item</u> to make a list of <u>three items</u>.

Pros	Cons
• In general it's much <u>more efficient</u> and <u>quicker</u> than the bubble sort (p.57) and insertion sort algorithms (p.59) for <u>large lists</u>. • It has a very <u>consistent running time</u> regardless of how ordered the items in the original list are.	• It's slower than other algorithms for <u>small lists</u>. • Even if the list is <u>already sorted</u> it still goes through the whole <u>splitting</u> and <u>merging</u> process. • It uses <u>more memory</u> than the other sorting algorithms in order to create the separate lists.

Due to its efficiency the merge sort algorithm or variations of it are used in many programming languages such as Java™, Python and Perl as the primary sorting algorithm.

EXAM TIP

To do the merge sort, split things down before sorting them...

When doing a merge sort it's important that you show the splitting process <u>and</u> the merging process — if you only show the merging process then you've only shown half the algorithm.

Sorting Algorithms

Here it comes, the final sorting algorithm you'll need to know for your exams.
It's called the insertion sort — have a look below to see how it's done.

An **Insertion Sort** orders the items as it goes

The insertion sort algorithm is the simplest sorting algorithm to understand — it just takes
each item in turn and puts it in the right place using the first item in the list as a starting point.

INSERTION SORT ALGORITHM

1) Look at the second item in a list.

2) Compare it to all items before it (in this case just the first item)
and insert the number into the right place.

3) Repeat step 2) for the third, fourth, fifth, etc. items until the
last number in the list has been inserted into the correct place.

EXAMPLE: Use the insertion sort algorithm to write these words in alphabetical order.

| Ball | Stamp | Post | Tackle | Scrum | Kick | Rugby |

Ball	Stamp	Post	Tackle	Scrum	Kick	Rugby	No insertion.
Ball	Stamp	Post	Tackle	Scrum	Kick	Rugby	Insert post between ball and stamp.
Ball	Post	Stamp	Tackle	Scrum	Kick	Rugby	No insertion.
Ball	Post	Stamp	Tackle	Scrum	Kick	Rugby	Insert scrum between post and stamp.
Ball	Post	Scrum	Stamp	Tackle	Kick	Rugby	Insert kick between ball and post.
Ball	Kick	Post	Scrum	Stamp	Tackle	Rugby	Insert rugby between post and scrum.
Ball	Kick	Post	Rugby	Scrum	Stamp	Tackle	All items are sorted into the correct order so the sorting is complete.

Insertion sorts have many advantages over the other sorting algorithms:

- It's an intuitive way of sorting things and can be easily coded.

- It copes very well with small lists — for this reason, an insertion/merge
hybrid sort is often used to take advantage of the strengths of each algorithm.

- All the sorting is done on the original list so, like the bubble sort,
it doesn't require very much additional memory.

- It's very quick to add items to an already ordered list.

- It's also very quick at checking that a list is already sorted.

However, like the bubble sort, its main disadvantage is that it doesn't cope well with very large lists.
For a list containing *n* items:

- Best case scenario (when the list is already ordered) requires $n - 1$ comparisons.

- Worst case scenario requires $\frac{n(n-1)}{2}$ comparisons.

Take the items one by one and put them into the right position...

The insertion sort is pretty straightforward but don't fall into the trap of just taking the list and rewriting
it in order, that's not how a computer would do it. You should always show every step of the algorithm.

Warm-Up and Worked Exam Questions

There are lots of searching and sorting algorithms for you to learn, so here are some questions to test your knowledge. Start off with the warm-up questions then have a go at the exam questions.

Warm-Up Questions

1) Here is a list of the ages of Julie's sons and daughters:

3	6	8	11	13	15	18

   a) Use a binary search to find "8" in the list.
   b) Use a linear search to find "11" in the list.

2) Describe how a bubble sort works.

3) Here are the names of the four pupils who attend chess club.

Chris	Beth	Dalia	Ahmed

   a) Show the steps of a bubble sort to put the names in ascending alphabetical order.
   b) Show the steps of a merge sort to put the names in descending alphabetical order.
   c) Show the steps of an insertion sort to put the names in ascending alphabetical order.

4) Which sorting algorithm is best to use on large lists of items?

Worked Exam Questions

1   Nicola has a list of numbers: 2, 3, 7, 5, 13, 11.
   a) She says, "I can't use a binary search to find 13." Why is this the case?

   A binary search only works on ordered data.
   ....
   [1 mark]

   b) Show the steps of a linear search to find 13 in the list above.

   Check the first item: 2 ≠ 13.

   Check the second item: 3 ≠ 13.

   Check the third item: 7 ≠ 13.

   Check the fourth item: 5 ≠ 13.

   Check the fifth item: 13 = 13.

   Stop searching as the item has be found.

   The linear search is straightforward but make sure you show every single step of the algorithm to get full marks.

   [2 marks]

2   Use the insertion sort algorithm to put these European cities into alphabetical order.

Underlining the item that you're looking at will help you keep track of where you're up to.

Riga	Paris	Oslo	Baku	Minsk
Paris	Riga	Oslo	Baku	Minsk
Oslo	Paris	Riga	Baku	Minsk
Baku	Oslo	Paris	Riga	Minsk
Baku	Minsk	Oslo	Paris	Riga

   [4 marks]

Exam Questions

3 Six athletes compete in a long jump competition. Their best jumps are shown below.
Show the stages of a bubble sort to list these jumps in order from shortest to longest.

| 5.32 m | 5.50 m | 5.39 m | 6.50 m | 6.28 m | 6.14 m |

[4 marks]

4 Sonia has a sorted list of ice cream flavours that she sells in her shop.

a) Show the stages of a binary search to find the word 'butterscotch' in the list below.

| butterscotch | chocolate | mint | strawberry | vanilla |

Always check that lists are ordered before doing a binary search.

[4 marks]

b) Give **one** advantage of using a binary search over a linear search.

....

....

[1 mark]

5 Kim has a hand of playing cards, all of the same suit: 3, 7, 6, 2, 5.
a) Arrange the cards in order from highest to lowest using:

i) An insertion sort.   **ii)** A merge sort.

[4 marks]   *[4 marks]*

b) Explain **one** benefit of using an insertion sort over a merge sort on a computer.

....

....

[2 marks]

Revision Questions for Section Four

Well that's <u>algorithms</u> all <u>done</u> and <u>dusted</u>. Or so you thought — just wait until you start <u>Section 5</u>.

- Try these questions and <u>tick off each one</u> when you <u>get it right</u>.
- When you've done <u>all the questions</u> for a topic and are <u>completely happy</u> with it, tick off the topic.

Computational Thinking (p.51) ☑

1) What is meant by: a) decomposition? b) abstraction? ☑

2) Why is using algorithmic thinking useful when solving a problem? ☑

3) Outline the decomposition, abstraction and algorithmic processes for choosing a film at the cinema. ☑

Pseudocode and Flow Diagrams (p.52-53) ☑

4) What is pseudocode? Give three features of well-written pseudocode. ☑

5) What are the benefits of writing algorithms in pseudocode rather than a programming language? ☑

6) Draw the five box types used on flow diagrams and say what each one is used for. ☑

7) What do sequences, selections and iterations look like on a flow diagram? ☑

8)* Draw a flow diagram to check if a new username is valid. Usernames should be at least 5 characters long and unique. If it's invalid, the algorithm should give the reason why and get the user to enter another username. ☑

Search Algorithms (p.56) ☑

9) What are the four steps of the binary search algorithm? ☑

10) What are the four steps of a linear search algorithm? ☑

11)* Here's a fascinating list of British towns and cities:

| Ashington | Brecon | Chester | Dagenham | Morpeth | Usk | Watford |

a) Use a binary search to find "Morpeth" in the list above.
b) Now do the same using a linear search. ☑

12) What are the benefits and drawbacks of using a linear search over a binary search? ☑

Sorting Algorithms (p.57-59) ☑

13) a) What are the five steps of the bubble sort algorithm?
b)* Use the bubble sort algorithm to sort these fruit into alphabetical order:

| Orange | Banana | Apple | Peach | Grape | Lime |

☑

14) What are the four steps of the merge sort algorithm? ☑

15) And the three steps of the insertion sort algorithm? ☑

16)* Here is a list of numbers: | 8 | 7 | 5 | 1 | 3 | 6 | 4 | 2 |

a) Use the merge sort algorithm to sort this list into descending order.
b) Use the insertion sort algorithm to sort this list into ascending order. ☑

17) Outline the strengths and weaknesses of the following sorting algorithms:
a) bubble sort b) merge sort c) insertion sort ☑

*Answers on p.143

Programming Basics — Data Types

It's been a long wait of 62 pages, but <u>finally</u> we've got to the headline act, the <u>programming</u> section...

Everything we cover in this section will work slightly differently in different programming languages, but the <u>principles</u> are the same and <u>that's</u> what you need to learn for the exam.

In this section, examples of code will be given in these boxes and will be written in pseudocode (p.52).

The output of the code will be shown in this box.

Programming languages have **Five Main Data Types**

1) Programming languages store data as different <u>types</u>. You need to learn the ones in this table...

Data type	Pseudocode	Characteristics	Examples
Integer	int	Whole numbers only.	0, 6, 10293, –999
Real (or float)	real	Numbers that have a decimal part.	0.15, –5.87, 100.0
Boolean	bool	Can only take one of two values, usually true or false.	True/False, 1/0, yes/no
Character	char	A single letter, number, symbol.	"A", "k", "5", "–", "$"
String	string	Used to represent text, it is a collection of characters.	"FsTmQ2", "$money$"

2) Each data type is allocated a different amount of <u>memory</u>.

3) Using the correct data types makes code more <u>memory efficient</u>, <u>robust</u> (hard to break) and <u>predictable</u>.

Programming languages can be <u>weakly typed</u> or <u>strongly typed</u>.

- Weakly typed languages will try to <u>convert</u> data types to <u>avoid errors</u>, however this can lead to <u>unpredictable results</u>.

- Strongly typed languages won't try to convert data types and so will produce <u>more errors</u> but more <u>predictable results</u>.

Data type	Typical amount of memory taken up
Integer	2 bytes or 4 bytes.
Real	4 bytes or 8 bytes.
Boolean	1 bit is needed but 1 byte is usually used.
Character	1 byte
String	1 byte for every character in the string.

Using the **Correct Data Type** for different **Variables**

You should be able to choose the best data type to use in different situations.

EXAMPLE: Give the appropriate data type for each of the categories in this registration form.

Initial of first name:	N
Surname:	Chapman
Age (in whole years):	27
Height (in metres):	1.64
Male or Female:	Female

Initial of first name should be stored as a character.

Surname should be stored as a string.

Age (in whole years) should be stored as an integer.

Height (in metres) should be stored as a real data type.

Male or Female could be stored as boolean.

Using the wrong data type can lead to unexpected results...

Using the correct data types is a fundamental part of programming — sometimes a piece of data could take different data types and you'll have to decide which is best based on the context of the question.

Programming Basics — Casting and Operators

A mixed bag coming up on this page. First up is casting, which allows you to convert from one data type to another. Then it's arithmetic operators — you'll already be familiar with most of them from maths.

Casting is used to change the Data Type

1) Languages have <u>functions</u> (p.81) that let you manually convert between data types — this is known as <u>casting</u>. This can be done using the <u>int()</u>, <u>float()</u>, <u>bool()</u> and <u>str()</u> commands.

`int("1")` ◄— Converts the <u>string "1"</u> to the <u>integer 1</u>.

`float(1)` ◄— Converts the <u>integer 1</u> to the <u>float 1.0</u>.

The int() and float() functions will only work on numbers.

`bool(1)` ◄— Converts the <u>integer 1</u> to the Boolean value <u>True</u>.

`str(True)` ◄— Converts the <u>Boolean value</u> <u>True</u> to the <u>string "True"</u>.

2) It's important to realise that the <u>integer 1</u>, the <u>real 1.0</u> and the <u>strings "1"</u> and <u>"1.0"</u> are all different.

3) You can also find the <u>ASCII number</u> (see p.110) of <u>characters</u> and vice versa using the <u>ASC()</u> and <u>CHR()</u> functions.

`ASC("b")` ◄— Converts the <u>character "b"</u> into its <u>ASCII number 98</u>.

`CHR(98)` ◄— Converts the <u>ASCII number 98</u> into its equivalent <u>character "b"</u>.

The **Basic Arithmetic Operators** are straightforward

1) The arithmetic operators take <u>two values</u> and perform a maths <u>function</u> on them.

2) <u>Addition</u>, <u>subtraction</u>, <u>multiplication</u> and <u>division</u> operators do what you'd expect.

3) The <u>exponentiation</u> operator is used to raise a number to a <u>power</u>.

4) The <u>DIV operator</u> returns the <u>whole number part</u> of a division and the <u>MOD operator</u> gives the <u>remainder</u>.

Dividing integers might behave oddly in some programming languages, e.g. 5 / 2 may give the answer 2 instead of 2.5...

...using DIV and MOD can avoid these issues.

Function	Typical Operator	Example	Result
Addition	+	5 + 5	10
Subtraction	−	3 − 10	−7
Multiplication	*	4 * 8	32
Division	/	42 / 6	7
Exponentiation	^ or **	$2\char`\^3 (= 2^3)$	8
Quotient	DIV	20 DIV 3	6
Remainder (modulus)	MOD or %	20 MOD 3	2

5) These operators work on <u>integers</u> and <u>real</u> data values or a combination of the two.

6) Computers follow the rule of <u>BODMAS</u> (Brackets, Other, Division, Multiplication, Addition & Subtraction) — so <u>take care</u> when using operators to make sure your code is actually doing what you want it to. E.g. 2 + 8 * 2 will give 18. To do the addition first, use brackets: (2 + 8) * 2 will give 20.

Arithmetic Operators only work on integers and reals...

Get your head around these basic things now and you'll have a better chance of understanding the trickier stuff later on. The DIV and MOD operators might seem strange but they're really useful.

Programming Basics — Operators

Programming languages have other types of operator too —
this page covers the assignment operator and the comparison operators.

The **Assignment Operator**

The <u>assignment operator</u>, =, is used to <u>assign values</u> to <u>constants</u> or <u>variables</u> (see next page).

Here are some <u>examples</u> of how the assignment operator works.

The name of the constant or variable should be on the <u>left hand side</u> of the =.

```
total = 25
cost = total * 3
cost = cost + 5
```

Whatever you're assigning to it should be on the <u>right hand side</u>.

This multiplies the value of total by 3 and assigns it to the variable cost.

This increases the value of cost by 5.

The **Comparison Operators**

<u>Comparison operators</u> compare the expression on their <u>left hand side</u> to the expression on their <u>right hand side</u> and produce a <u>Boolean value</u> (either true or false).

Comparison operator	What it means	Evaluates to True	Evaluates to False
==	Is equal to	5 == 5	5 == 8
<> or !=	Is not equal to	6 != 7	6 != 6
<	Is less than	4 < 10	3 < 2
>	Is greater than	15 > 9	10 > 12
<=	Is less than or equal to	7 <= 8	11 <= 10
>=	Is greater than or equal to	3 >= 3	9 >= 12

Don't get mixed up between **=** and **==**...

1) A common mistake is to get the <u>assignment operator =</u> and the <u>comparison operator ==</u> mixed up.

2) You'll know you've used them <u>incorrectly</u> because your code won't behave as intended.

3) Have a look at the examples below to see the <u>impact</u> using the <u>wrong operator</u> in an IF statement (p.70) can have.

```
if age = 25 then
```

This piece of code just <u>assigns</u> 25 to the variable "age" — the IF statement will consider this condition as <u>always true</u>.

```
if age == 25 then
```

This piece of code checks if <u>age is equal to 25</u> and will only run if the condition is true.

Comparison operators are used to compare two expressions...

Knowing what all the different operators are and what they do is essential to learning how to write simple programs. Close the book and see if you can write down all the arithmetic and comparison operators, explain what each operator does and give an example of it being used.

Constants and Variables

Now that you know about the different data types and operations it's time to look at constants and variables. As you can probably tell by the names, constants remain the same and variables can be changed.

Data Values can be **Constants** or **Variables**

1) Data values can be stored as constants or variables.

2) The name of the constant or variable is linked to a memory location that stores the data value. The size of the memory location depends on the data type (see p.63).

3) A constant is assigned a data value at design time that can't be changed. If you attempt to change the value of a constant in a program then the interpreter or compiler (see p.92) will return an error.

4) Variables on the other hand can change value which makes them far more useful than constants.

5) Constants and variables often need to be declared (at the start of the program) before you can use them. This can be done in different ways:

'pressure' declared as a constant with integer type

'temperature' and 'weight' declared as variables with real type

```
const pressure as int = 30
var temperature as real = 20.5
var weight as real
```

Constants are assigned values when they're declared.

Initial values can be assigned to variables (but they don't have to be).

These lines of code do exactly the same as the lines above — temperature and weight are still variables.

```
const pressure = 30
real temperature = 20.5
real weight
```

To make code easier to follow, programmers usually follow standard naming conventions for constants and variables. E.g. 'lower case for the first letter, followed by a mixture of letters, numbers and underscores.'

Identifying **Constants** and **Variables** in Programs

In a multi-event athletics competition, athletes get 5 points for winning an event and 2 points for coming second. Otherwise they get 0 points. This program calculates the total number of points that an athlete has.

```
firsts = input("Number of 1st places.")
seconds = input("Number of 2nd places.")
print(5 * firsts + 2 * seconds)
```

a) **Rewrite the program so that all the variables are declared with data types and initial values.**

The two variables are firsts and seconds. They should both be declared as integers as there are a whole number of events.

```
int firsts = 0
int seconds = 0
firsts = input("Number of 1st places.")
seconds = input("Number of 2nd places.")
print(5 * firsts + 2 * seconds)
```

The initial value of each variable is set to 0.

b) **Give two reasons for assigning the values 5 and 2 to constants.**
- They don't need to be changed during the running of the program.
- If the points awarded for each event was changed you'd only need to change the value given in the declaration of the constant.

This is an example of improving the maintainability (p.89) of the program.

A constant, a variable... and finally a constant. Time starts now...

You can't change the data type of a variable, only the value. But as you saw on p.64 you can use a casting function to return a different data type, which you can then assign to a new variable:

```
int cost = 50
string cost_string
cost_string = str(cost)
```

Strings

Remember from page 63 that strings are a data type made up of characters — these characters are <u>alphanumeric</u> (letters, numbers, spaces, symbols, etc.). Now you'll see how you can manipulate them.

Strings are written inside **Quotation Marks**

Strings are usually written inside <u>double quotation marks</u> ", but sometimes <u>single quotes</u> are used '.

```
string1 = "Print me, I'm a string."
print(string1)
```
```
Print me, I'm a string.
```

Strings can be <u>joined together</u> to form new strings — this is called <u>concatenation</u>. It's often done using the <u>+ operator</u>.

```
string1 = "My favourite colour is"
string2 = "purple."
new_string = string1 + " " + string2
print(new_string)
```
```
My favourite colour is purple.
```

The + operator joins the strings together.

A space character has been added between the two strings.

Programs let you **Manipulate Strings** in a variety of ways

1) Before getting started on string manipulation you should know that the <u>characters</u> in a string are usually numbered <u>starting at 0</u>.

```
0 1 2 3 4 5
S P Y I N G
```

2) Here are some common <u>string manipulation</u> functions that you'll need to learn for your exam.

Typical function	Operation	Effect on x = "Hello"
x.upper	Changes all characters in string x to upper case.	HELLO
x.lower	Changes all characters in string x to lower case.	hello
x.length	Returns the number of characters in string x.	5
x[i]	Extracts the character in position i from string x.	x[1] = "e"
x.subString(a, b)	Extracts a string starting at position a with length b from string x.	x.subString(3, 2) = "lo"

upper, lower, length and subString are special functions called <u>methods</u>. They act on a particular object (in this case strings) and are called using the object's name followed by a dot "." and the method's name.

EXAMPLE: **An electricity company generates a customer's 7 character username from:**
- **the first 3 letters of their town as uppercase letters.**
- **the customer's age when they sign up (2 digits).**
- **the first and last letters of the customer's surname as lowercase letters.**

Write an algorithm to generate a username for any customer given that their data is stored under the variables town, age and surname.

Start by working out how to <u>extract</u> the information from <u>each variable</u>...

1) ```town.subString(0, 3).upper``` — This extracts the <u>first 3 characters</u> from the customer's town and makes them uppercase.

2) ```str(age)``` — <u>Casts</u> (p.64) the customer's age as a <u>string</u>.

3)
```
int n = surname.length
surname[0].lower + surname[n-1].lower
```
Finds the <u>length</u> of the <u>surname</u> so that it can take the <u>first</u> and <u>last characters</u> and make them <u>lowercase</u>.

... then combine the code into a <u>single algorithm</u> at the end.

```
string username
int n = surname.length
username = town.subString(0, 3).upper + str(age) + surname[0].lower + surname[n-1].lower
```

68

Warm-Up and Worked Exam Questions

That's the first part of programming done — have a go at these questions to see how much you've understood.

Warm-Up Questions

1) What is the most appropriate data type for each of these items?
   a) The nickname of your best friend.
   b) The number on a rolled dice.
   c) The exact length of a car in metres.
   d) The answer to a yes/no question.

2) Work out the results of the following arithmetic operations:
   a) `5 * 8`
   b) `10 MOD 3`
   c) `28 DIV 6`
   d) `3 + 2 * 8`

3) Will the following pieces of code return true or false?
   a) `6 <= 10`
   b) `5 == 5`
   c) `14 > 15`
   d) `12 < 8 + 5`

4) What's the difference between a variable and a constant?

5) Given that `fish = "lobster"`, state what would be returned from the following methods:
   a) `fish.length`
   b) `fish.subString(0, 3)`
   c) `fish.upper`
   d) `fish.subString(2, 3)`

Worked Exam Questions

1 The program below calculates the cost of a burger in pounds at a fast food restaurant.
A standard burger costs £6.50 with additional costs for toppings and eating in the restaurant.

```
const standard = 6.5
int toppings = 0
bool eat_in = false
toppings = input("How many toppings?")
eat_in = input("Are they eating in?")
if eat_in == true then
    print(standard + 0.5*toppings + 1)
else
    print(standard + 0.5*toppings)
endif
```

a) List **all** the variables in this program.

   <u>toppings and eat_in</u>

   [2 marks]

b) How much extra does it cost to eat your burger inside the restaurant?

   <u>£1</u>

   [1 mark]

c) The restaurant manager says that 0.5 should have been declared as a constant.
Give **two** reasons for declaring this value as a constant.

   1. <u>It doesn't need to be changed as the program is running.</u>

   2. <u>Updating the value of a constant once will update it everywhere in the program.</u>

   You could also mention that giving the value a name, e.g. toppingsCost will make the code more meaningful.

   [2 marks]

2 A digital radio stores the date as a string under the variable name `date`. The radio is stuck on the date: `8 January 2016`. State the output from each of the following pieces of code:

a) `date.subString[0] + date.subString(10,4)`

   "8" + "2016"   *They are strings so use string concatenation instead of adding them.*   <u>82016</u>

   [1 mark]

b) `date.subString(2,3).upper`

   <u>JAN</u>

   [1 mark]

Section Five — Programming

Exam Questions

3 A pedestrian crossing uses a button to request the traffic to stop. State the data type that you would use to record each of these variables and give a reason for your answer.

  a) A variable to record whether the button has been pressed or not.

  Data type: ....

  Reason: ....
  [2 marks]

  b) A variable to record how many whole seconds it's been since the button was pressed.

  Data type: ....

  Reason: ....
  [2 marks]

4 The program below calculates the value of an investment at the end of one year.

```
const investment
real rate
int interest
input investment
input rate
for x = 1 to 12
  interest = rate * investment
  investment = investment + interest
next x
print(investment)
```

Identify **two** problems with the constants or variables in the program.

1. ....

....

2. ....

....
[2 marks]

5 A juice company generates a product ID for each of its fruit juices. The product ID is generated using string concatenation on the first three letters of the fruit (in uppercase) and the volume of fruit juice in ml. E.g. a 500 ml carton of apple juice would be APP500.

  a) Define what is meant by string concatenation.

  ....
  [1 mark]

  b) What would the product code be for a 2000 ml carton of orange juice?

  ....
  [1 mark]

  c) Complete the algorithm below so that line 05 reassigns the uppercase name of the fruit to the `fruit` variable and line 06 assigns the final product ID to the `prodID` variable.

```
01 string fruit, prodID
02 int volume
03 fruit = input("Enter the name of the fruit.")
04 volume = input("Enter the volume of the juice.")

05 fruit = .................................................................................

06 prodID = ................................................................................
07 print(prodID)
```
[3 marks]

Program Flow

The flow of a program is the order that the steps are carried out in. You can control the program flow using <u>selection statements</u> — there are two main types to learn, <u>IF statements</u> and <u>SWITCH-CASE statements</u>.

IF Statements usually have an **if-then-else** structure

1) <u>IF statements</u> allow you to check if a <u>condition</u> is true or false, and carry out different actions depending on the outcome. You can think about them as a <u>flow diagram</u>.

2) Here is a program that can verify if the user knows a certain passcode before granting access.

The first part of the <u>IF statement</u> is the condition that must be checked.

Indenting the actions for each condition makes the code more readable.

```
string x
x = input("Enter the passcode.")
if x == "GO" then
    Allow unrestricted access.
else
    Deny all access.
endif
```

The part after 'then' tells the program what to do if the condition is true.

The part after 'else' tells the program what to do if the condition is false.

3) If there is <u>nothing</u> for the program to do when the <u>condition is false</u>, <u>leave out</u> the 'else' part.

Nested IF Statements allow multiple outputs

1) More complex IF statements can be made by putting one IF statement <u>inside</u> another one — this type of selection statement is called a <u>nested IF statement</u>.

2) Nested IF statements allow you to <u>check more conditions</u> once you've established that the <u>previous condition</u> is <u>true</u>.

If the <u>first condition</u> is <u>true</u>, it will check the <u>second condition</u>...

If the <u>first condition</u> is <u>false</u>, it will run this <u>else statement</u> — all access is denied.

<u>Indentation</u> lets the reader see where each IF statement begins and ends.

```
string x
x = input("Enter the passcode.")
if x == "GO" then
    if usertype == "Teacher" then
        Allow unrestricted access.
    else
        Allow restricted access.
    endif
else
    Deny all access.
endif
```

If the <u>second condition</u> is <u>true</u> then unrestricted access is allowed.

If the <u>second condition</u> is <u>false</u> then restricted access is allowed.

3) <u>IF-ELSEIF statements</u> can also be used to check <u>multiple conditions</u>. They are different from nested IF statements as they only <u>check more conditions</u> if the <u>previous condition</u> is <u>false</u>.

The conditions are all indented to the <u>same level</u>.

If <u>all conditions</u> are false then the program will deny all access.

```
if usertype == "Teacher" then
    Allow unrestricted access.
elseif usertype == "Parent" then
    Allow level 1 restricted access.
elseif usertype == "Pupil" then
    Allow level 2 restricted access.
else
    Deny all access.
endif
```

The <u>first condition</u> is always checked — if it's <u>true</u> then it will allow unrestricted access.

The <u>second condition</u> is checked if the <u>first condition</u> is <u>false</u> — if it's <u>true</u> then it will allow level 1 restricted access.

The <u>third condition</u> is checked if the <u>first</u> and <u>second conditions</u> are <u>false</u> — if it's <u>true</u> then it will allow level 2 restricted access.

If you understand IF statements then make yourself a brew...

One good thing about IF-ELSEIF statements is they're very neat, everything is indented to the same line. Lots of nested IF statements with many levels of indentation can cause readability problems in your code.

Program Flow

Here are the SWITCH-CASE statements and the first type of iteration statement — FOR loops.

SWITCH-CASE Statements check the value of a **Variable**

1) Instead of checking to see if a statement is true or false, SWITCH-CASE statements can check if a <u>variable</u> has <u>specific values</u>.

2) They're used when you want a program to perform <u>different actions</u> for <u>different values</u> of the <u>same variable</u>.

3) Here is a program that can be used to <u>count votes</u> in an election.

The number of votes for each person starts at O.

```
int johnvote = 0, suevote = 0, alanvote = 0
string vote
vote = input("Please cast your vote")
switch vote:
    case "John":
        johnvote = johnvote + 1
        print("You've voted for John.")
    case "Sue":
        suevote = suevote + 1
        print("You've voted for Sue.")
    case "Alan":
        alanvote = alanvote + 1
        print("You've voted for Alan.")
endswitch
```

If John is selected, add 1 to his vote and print "you've voted for John."

Each 'case' should be indented to the same place.

The statement starts with 'switch vote' which uses the parameter 'vote' to decide which case to use.

If Sue is selected, add 1 to her vote and print "you've voted for Sue."

If Alan is selected, add 1 to his vote and print "you've voted for Alan."

4) SWITCH-CASE statements have a <u>similar structure</u> to IF-ELSEIF statements but they give a <u>neater</u> way to test <u>different values</u> of a variable — this makes them easier than ELSEIF statements to <u>maintain</u>.

5) The <u>drawback</u> of SWITCH-CASE statements is that they can <u>only check</u> the value of <u>one variable</u>. IF-ELSEIF statements can check if <u>multiple conditions</u> are true.

FOR Loops are an example of a **Count-Controlled Loop**

1) <u>FOR loops</u> will repeat the code inside them a fixed number of times. The number of times that the code repeats will depend on an <u>initial value</u>, <u>end value</u> and the <u>step count</u>.

2) For example, for k = 1 to 10 step 3 will count up from 1 to 10 in steps of 3, so k = 1, k = 4, k = 7 and k = 10. If no step count is given the count will <u>increase by 1</u> each time.

The FOR loop repeats the code between 'for' and 'next'.

3) The <u>number of times</u> the loop repeats can also be set as the <u>program runs</u> — e.g. for k = 1 to x, where x is a variable.

4) FOR loops can also use the count <u>within the loop</u> — in the example on the right, k is used to keep track of how many votes have been cast.

Many programming languages don't use 'next' but it's used in pseudocode to make the code more readable.

```
int johnvote = 0, suevote = 0, alanvote = 0
string vote
for k = 1 to 100
    vote = input("Please cast your vote.")
    switch vote:
        case "John":
            johnvote = johnvote + 1
            print("You've voted for John.")
        case "Sue":
            suevote = suevote + 1
            print("You've voted for Sue.")
        case "Alan":
            alanvote = alanvote + 1
            print("You've voted for Alan.")
    endswitch
    print(str(k) + " votes have been cast.")
next k
```

Allows 100 votes to be cast.

The value of k can be used anywhere within the loop.

EXAM TIP

Use FOR loops when you know the number of repetitions...

In your exam a SWITCH-CASE statement might include a "default:" case. This tells the program what to do if none of the other cases are correct — it helps to make the statement more robust.

Program Flow

Here are a few other loops that you need to know about — the <u>DO UNTIL loop</u>, the <u>WHILE loop</u> and the <u>DO WHILE loop</u>. Like FOR loops, they are all <u>iteration statements</u> — they repeat a part of the program.

All these **Loops** are controlled by **Conditions**

<u>DO UNTIL</u>, <u>WHILE</u> and <u>DO WHILE</u> loops are easy to get mixed up — they're very similar but with subtle differences that you need to know:

You might also see a <u>REPEAT UNTIL loop</u> — this does the same thing as a <u>DO UNTIL loop</u>.

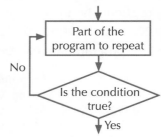

DO UNTIL LOOPS
- Controlled by a condition at the <u>end of the loop</u>.
- Keep going <u>until</u> the condition is <u>true</u> (i.e. while it is false).
- <u>Always run</u> the code inside them <u>at least once</u>.
- You get an <u>infinite loop</u> if the condition is <u>never true</u>.

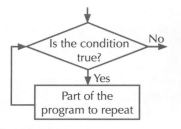

WHILE LOOPS
- Controlled by a condition at the <u>start of the loop</u>.
- Keep going <u>while</u> the condition is <u>true</u> (i.e. until it is false).
- <u>Never run</u> the code inside them if the condition is initially <u>false</u>.
- You get an <u>infinite loop</u> if the condition is <u>always true</u>.

DO WHILE LOOPS
- Controlled by a condition at the <u>end of the loop</u>.
- Keep going <u>while</u> the condition is <u>true</u> (i.e. until it is false).
- <u>Always run</u> the code inside them <u>at least once</u>.
- You get an <u>infinite loop</u> if the condition is <u>always true</u>.

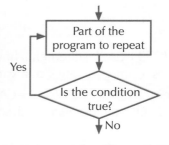

EXAMPLE: **Write an algorithm that a supermarket self-scan machine could use to check if enough money has been fed into it and output the right amount of change.**

DO UNTIL Loop:
```
int total = 0
int cost, coin, change
cost = total cost in pence
do
  coin = input("Value of coin")
  total = total + coin
until total ≥ cost
change = total - cost
output change
```
The loop starts at '<u>do</u>' and ends when the '<u>until</u>' condition is <u>true</u> — when the total is greater than or equal to the cost.

WHILE Loop:
```
int total = 0
int cost, coin, change
cost = total cost in pence
while total < cost
  coin = input("Value of coin")
  total = total + coin
endwhile
change = total - cost
output change
```
The loop starts by checking the '<u>while</u>' condition is <u>true</u> and keeps repeating until it is <u>false</u> — when the total is greater than or equal to the cost.

DO WHILE Loop:
```
int total = 0
int cost, coin, change
cost = total cost in pence
do
  coin = input("Value of coin")
  total = total + coin
while total < cost
change = total - cost
output change
```
The loop starts at '<u>do</u>' and repeats until the '<u>while</u>' condition is <u>false</u> — when the total is greater than or equal to the cost.

All of these loops in the example above work exactly the same when cost > 0.
If the cost is 0, the <u>WHILE loop</u> won't expect an input, whereas the <u>DO UNTIL</u> and <u>DO WHILE loops</u> will.

Keep looping through this page until it's stuck in your head...

As well as learning what each loop does, you should learn the difference between the different loops. The key thing is recognising exactly when the loop will start or stop.

Boolean Operators

Boolean operators work with Boolean values to produce a Boolean answer.

AND, OR and NOT are the only Boolean Operators you'll need

1) It doesn't make sense to use the arithmetic operators on things that are either true or false so instead you use the Boolean operators AND, OR and NOT.

Boolean operator	Examples that return true	Examples that return false
AND	3 < 5 AND 2 > 1	4 <= 5 AND 10 > 20
OR	1 > 8 OR 2 == 2	1 == 8 OR 2 < 2
NOT	NOT(5 > 8)	NOT(10 > 6)

In some code you might see AND written as &&, OR written as || and NOT written as !

2) Just like with numerical operators, you can combine Boolean operators — it's important that you use brackets in long Boolean expressions to let the computer know which part to do first. Boolean operations are carried out in the following order: brackets, NOT, AND then OR.

Boolean Operators can be used in Conditions

Boolean operators can be used to make all the different selection statements and iteration statements (p.70-72) more efficient and versatile.

1. Karen and Stu are playing a 'best out of 10' game. The game should end when one of them wins 6 rounds or they both win 5 rounds. Write an algorithm to keep score in the game.

```
int karenrounds = 0, sturounds = 0
string roundwinner
do
    switch roundwinner:
        case "Karen":
            karenrounds = karenrounds + 1
        case "Stu":
            sturounds = sturounds + 1
    endswitch
until karenrounds == 6 OR sturounds == 6 OR (karenrounds == 5 AND sturounds == 5)
```

There is a SWITCH-CASE statement within the loop. This is where good indentation in your pseudocode is key.

The DO UNTIL loop stops when one of these three conditions is met.

2. In a computer game a character's status depends on three variables: hunger, hydration and comfort. If any of the conditions on the right are met then the character dies, otherwise they are alive.

- Any of the variables are equal to 0.
- Any two of the variables are less than 20.
- All three of the variables are less than 40.

Write an algorithm to work out the status of the character.

```
bool alive
if hunger == 0 OR hydration == 0 OR comfort == 0 then
    alive = false
elseif (hunger < 20 AND hydration < 20) OR (hunger < 20 AND comfort < 20)
        OR (hydration < 20 AND comfort < 20) then
    alive = false
elseif hunger < 40 AND hydration < 40 AND comfort < 40 then
    alive = false
else
    alive = true
endif
```

The Boolean operators are AND, OR and NOT...

Using Boolean operators can save lots of work by letting you check lots of conditions at the same time.

Warm-Up and Worked Exam Questions

Time to see if all that information is sinking in. Have a go at these warm-up questions then read through the worked exam questions before having a go at the questions on the next page yourself.

Warm-Up Questions

1) For each of the following, say if it is selection or iteration:
   a) DO UNTIL
   b) IF-THEN-ELSE
   c) SWITCH-CASE
   d) DO WHILE
   e) IF-ELSEIF
   f) WHILE

2) Give one difference between a SWITCH-CASE statement and an IF-ELSEIF statement.

3) a) Name a type of a count-controlled loop and a type of condition-controlled loop.
   b) Explain the difference between the two loops given in part a).

4) Decide whether the following Boolean expressions are true or false:
   a) 12 > 4 AND 8 == 5
   b) NOT(11 == 3)
   c) 12 <= 4 OR 10 != 5
   d) NOT(9 > 4 AND 5 < 2)

Worked Exam Questions

1 A garden centre has a climate monitoring system that gives warnings if the temperature and humidity aren't at suitable levels. The climate monitoring system contains this algorithm.

```
if humidity == 50 AND (temperature > 16 AND temperature < 25) then
    print("Humidity and temperature at acceptable levels.")
elseif temperature <= 16 OR temperature >= 25 then
    print("Warning — Please alter the temperature.")
else
    print("Warning — Please alter the humidity.")
endif
```

a) What will the output be if humidity = 30 and temperature = 16?

"Warning — Please alter the temperature."

[1 mark]

b) What will the output be if humidity = 30 and temperature = 20?

"Warning — Please alter the humidity."

[1 mark]

2 Salik needs a program that will ask users to create a password and then check if the password contains at least six characters. If it contains fewer than six characters the user must try again, otherwise the user is informed that their password is valid. Write an appropriate program for Salik.

string password

do

        password = input("Please enter a password")

until password.length >=6

print("Your password is valid")

> Using a DO UNTIL or DO WHILE loop will mean that the code in the loop always runs through at least once.

[4 marks]

Exam Questions

3 Jasminda has written the following program to convert minutes into hours and minutes.

```
int minutes, hours, mins
minutes = input("Enter a number of minutes")
hours = minutes DIV 60
mins = minutes MOD 60
print(str(hours) + " hours and " + str(mins) + " minutes")
```

a) Is this an example of a sequence, selection or iteration? Tick the correct box.

Sequence ☐   Selection ☐   Iteration ☐

[1 mark]

b) What would the program print if the input was 150?

....

[1 mark]

4 An electric heater has four temperature settings (0, 1, 2 and 3).
The code below controls the temperature of the heater.

```
int setting, temperature
switch setting:
    case 3:
        temperature = 50
    case 2:
        temperature = 30
    case 1:
        temperature = 20
    case 0:
        temperature = 0
endswitch
```

a) Rewrite this program using a different selection statement.

> An ELSEIF statement will help you check lots of conditions.

[3 marks]

b) Give **two** reasons why a SWITCH-CASE statement is appropriate for this program.

1. ....

2. ....

[2 marks]

5 A tumble dryer will only be allowed to start if all of the following conditions are met:
- the real variable `weight` is more than 1.5 and less than 15.0
- the boolean variable `doorClosed` is true.

Write an algorithm that checks these conditions before allowing the tumble dryer to start.

[3 marks]

6 Karl and John are playing snap. Write an algorithm that:
- Asks for the name of the winner of each game.
- After ten games checks who has won more and displays
  the winner's name or tells them that it's a draw.

[6 marks]

Arrays

When you need to store data within a program you can do it using variables. But if you have lots of similar data to store, then using variables for each one is inefficient and that's where arrays come in.

Arrays are used to store multiple Data Values

1) An array is a <u>data structure</u> that can store a collection of data values all under <u>one name</u>.

2) Each piece of data in an array is called an <u>element</u> — each element can be <u>accessed</u> using its <u>position</u> (or <u>index</u>) in the array.

3) Arrays are <u>most helpful</u> when you have lots of <u>related data</u> that you want to store and it doesn't make sense to use <u>separate variables</u> — e.g. the names of pupils in a class, marks in a test, etc.

4) Just like variables, some languages require you to <u>declare arrays</u> before you use them.

A data structure is a format for storing data — other data structures include records, files and databases.

One-Dimensional Arrays are like Lists

The easiest way to get your head around <u>one-dimensional arrays</u> is to picture them as <u>lists</u>.
Different languages have lots of fancy ways to <u>create</u> and <u>update arrays</u>.
Here are the ones you'll need to learn for your exam:

1) Creating arrays — the first line of the code on the right creates the array 'rowers' and makes it <u>size 4</u> (it can only contain <u>4 elements</u>). The other lines assign the strings "<u>Mark</u>", "<u>Adam</u>", "<u>Shelly</u>" and "<u>Tobias</u>" in positions <u>0</u>, <u>1</u>, <u>2</u> and <u>3</u>.

```
array rowers[4]
rowers[0] = "Mark"
rowers[1] = "Adam"
rowers[2] = "Shelly"
rowers[3] = "Tobias"
```

2) Retrieving elements from an array can be done by using the <u>name</u> of the array and the <u>element's position</u>. Remember that positions are numbered <u>starting at 0</u>.

```
print(rowers[0])
print(rowers[2])
```
```
Mark
Shelly
```

3) Changing elements is done by reassigning the array position to a different data value.

Replaces the rower in position O with "Tamal".

```
rowers[0] = "Tamal"
print(rowers)
```
```
["Tamal", "Adam", "Shelly", "Tobias"]
```

Notice that "Mark" has been completely removed from the array.

Combining these <u>array functions</u> with <u>FOR loops</u> (see p.71) will give you a <u>systematic way</u> of accessing and changing all of the <u>elements</u> in an array. Amongst other things, FOR loops can be used to <u>search</u> for specific elements, or make a similar change to <u>lots of elements</u>.

EXAMPLE: **The numbers below are stored in an array called scores[ ].**
Write an algorithm that will add 3 to each number of the scores[ ] array.

| 4 | 12 | 32 | 18 | 21 | 11 | 9 | 14 | 24 |

```
for k = 0 to 8
    scores[k] = scores[k] + 3
next k
```

For loop will run on each element of the array.

Adds 3 to the element in position k of the array.

Think of one dimensional arrays as lists of similar objects...

In some languages (e.g. C, C++, Java™) you'll find that arrays can only store one data type and that you can't change their size once they've been declared. For the programming language you're using, check if it uses arrays and look at what properties they have in that language.

Arrays

Now that you've covered one-dimensional arrays, the only way is up — that's right, two-dimensional arrays. Arrays can have even more dimensions, but luckily the examiners have decided that two is enough for now.

Two-Dimensional Arrays are like a List Of Lists

You can think of two-dimensional arrays as <u>one-dimensional arrays</u> where <u>each element</u> is also a <u>one-dimensional array</u>.

	0	1
0	oak	ash
1	beech	cedar
2	pine	elm

You can visualise arrays as tables or grids.

```
trees = [["oak", "ash"], ["beech", "cedar"], ["pine", "elm"]]
```

The <u>position</u> of an element is usually written as [a, b] or [a][b], where <u>a</u> represents the position of the one-dimensional list that the element is in and <u>b</u> represents its position within that one-dimensional list.

```
print("Ceara's favourite tree is" + trees[0, 0])
print("Shaun's favourite tree is" + trees[2, 1])
```

```
Ceara's favourite tree is oak
Shaun's favourite tree is elm
```

You can also <u>change elements</u> in exactly the same way as you saw for <u>one-dimensional arrays</u> (p.76).

EXAMPLE:

The 'scores' array has been used to store four test scores for five pupils, as shown. E.g. scores[2, 0] will return the test 2 score for pupil 0, which is 5.

		Pupils				
		0	1	2	3	4
Tests	0	15	5	13	12	7
	1	2	14	11	14	9
	2	5	4	12	7	13
	3	6	8	18	19	15

a) **What will each of these return?**

(i) **scores[1, 3]**

The entry in row 1 and column 3 is 14.

(ii) **scores[3, 2] / scores[1, 0]**

scores[3, 2] = 18 and scores[1, 0] = 2 so scores[3, 2] / scores[1, 0] = 18/2 = 9

b) **Write an algorithm to count the total score of any given pupil.**

As there aren't very many scores you could just add them together. E.g. for pupil 0 you could do scores[0, 0] + scores[1, 0] + scores [2, 0] + scores [3, 0]. But it's <u>better practice</u> to use a <u>loop</u> as it is easier to edit.

```
int total = 0
int pupil
pupil = input("Enter the number of the pupil.")
for i = 0 to 3
    total = total + scores[i, pupil]
next i
print total
```

c) **The pass mark on every test was 9 or above. Write an algorithm to count the number of passes in the original array.**

The passtotal variable keeps track of <u>how many values</u> are passes.

The <u>i FOR loop</u> searches each row and the <u>j FOR loop</u> searches each column.

The IF statement checks if the value in position [i, j] is a pass and <u>adds 1</u> to passtotal if it is.

Finally <u>passtotal</u> is printed.

```
int passtotal = 0
for i = 0 to 3
    for j = 0 to 4
        if scores[i, j] >= 9 then
            passtotal = passtotal + 1
        endif
    next j
next i
print str(passtotal) + " marks were passes."
```

This is an example of a nested FOR loop.

Two-dimensional arrays are really just an array of arrays...

Two-dimensional arrays can be used to store information about a digital image — each pixel's information can be stored as an element in the array. Programmers can then manipulate the image using array commands, e.g. changing the values of pixels, cutting rows and columns out of the image, etc.

File Handling

File handling is all about how a program can access data and change data stored in an external file.

Always start by Opening the External File

This page will focus on how text is stored and accessed from ".txt" files. Other text files that are commonly used are ".csv" and ".dat".

1) Before you can do anything with a file you need to <u>open it</u>.
   This is done by using an <u>open command</u> and assigning it to a <u>variable</u>.

openRead will open the file in <u>read mode</u> — this allows you to <u>read data</u> from the <u>file</u> into your <u>program</u>.

This is the <u>name</u> of the <u>file</u> you want to open. Sometimes you'll have to give the <u>whole file path</u>.

```
newFile = openRead("newFile.txt")
newFile = openWrite("newFile.txt")
```

Some programming languages have other modes that allow you to do things like read and write at the same time.

openWrite will open the file in <u>write mode</u> — this allows you to <u>write data</u> from your <u>program</u> to the <u>file</u>.

2) Once a file is opened the program will start reading or writing <u>from the beginning</u>. As you read from or write to the file, the program <u>keeps its place</u> in the file (think of it like a cursor).

3) When you're finished <u>reading</u> or <u>writing</u> to a file you should always <u>close it</u> using <u>close()</u>. If you forget to close it then the file can remain <u>locked</u> and prevent others from <u>editing it</u>.

Read or Write to a file after it is Opened

1) After you have opened a file you can <u>read</u> or <u>write</u> to it depending on what mode it's in.

2) You can <u>write lines</u> of text to a file using <u>writeLine()</u>. If the file already contains some text then writeLine() will <u>overwrite</u> what is currently there.

The writeLine command is called on the variable that stores the external file.

```
winners = openWrite("victory.txt")
names = ["Jenny", "Carlos", "Matty", "Anna"]
for i = 0 to 3
    winners.writeLine(str(i) + " " + names[i])
next i
winners.close()
```

The text file will look like this.

```
0 Jenny
1 Carlos
2 Matty
3 Anna
```

The writeLine command will automatically move onto the next line after it is called.

3) You can <u>read lines</u> of text from a file using <u>readLine()</u>.

Reads the first line of the text file as programs always start reading from the start of the file. After this command is called, the 'cursor' will be at the beginning of the second line.

```
winners = openRead("victory.txt")
first_line = winners.readLine()
second_line = winners.readLine()
winners.close()
```

Reads the second line of the file as that's where the program is up to. After this command is called, the 'cursor' will be at the beginning of the third line.

4) <u>endOfFile()</u> is another useful command that you'll have to know for your exams. It returns TRUE when the 'cursor' is at the end of the file. It's main use is to signify when a program should <u>stop reading</u> a file (like in this example).

```
array champions[]
int n = 0
winners = openRead("victory.txt")
while NOT winners.endOfFile()
    champions[n] = winners.readLine()
    n = n + 1
endwhile
print(champions)
```

```
["0 Jenny", "1 Carlos", "2 Matty", "3 Anna"]
```

Learning to read and write, it's like being back at primary school...

Data is stored externally so that it's not lost when the program is closed. E.g. a computer game will save your progress externally — if it was saved internally you'd lose your progress when the game was closed.

Storing Data

Records aren't just those big black round things that look like burnt CDs, they're also a useful data structure...

Records can contain Different Data Types

1) A record is a type of data structure (like an array — see p.76), which means that it is used to store a collection of data values.

2) One of the things that makes records so useful is that, unlike arrays, they can store values with different data types (see p.63), such as strings, integers and Booleans.

3) Each item in a record is called a field, and each field is given a data type and a field name when the record is created. The field name can help to describe the data stored in that field of the record.

4) Records are fixed in length, which means that you can't add extra fields to them once they've been created.

In the context of a database table, a record is just a row of data (see next page).

Different programming languages have slight variations on record data structures. E.g. Python has dictionaries, and C has structures.

Records can keep Related Information in one place

1) When you create a record structure, you can assign a data type and a name to each field:

```
record recipes
    int recipe_number
    string recipe_name
    bool tested
    int score
endrecord
```

The record is called 'recipes'.

'recipe_number', 'recipe_name', 'tested' and 'score' are the fields of the record.

Each field has its own data type.

2) Once you've created the structure of your record, you can assign it to variables:

```
recipe1 = recipes(1, "Chocolate Cake", True, 3)
recipe2 = recipes(2, "Lemon Slice", False, 0)
recipe3 = recipes(3, "Coconut Cookies", True, 8)
```

'recipe1', 'recipe2' and 'recipe3' are all variables with the 'recipes' record structure.

The data in each field needs to have the correct data type. E.g. the last one, 'score', should be an integer.

3) You can use the variable name to access a whole record. Alternatively, you can use the variable name along with a field name to access a particular item of a record.

```
print(recipe1)
print(recipe3.recipe_name)
```
```
(1, "Chocolate Cake", True, 3)
Coconut Cookies
```

Individual items in a record can be accessed and changed.

```
recipe2.tested = True
recipe2.score = 6
print(recipe2.recipe_name + " has a
      score of " + str(recipe2.score))
```
```
Lemon Slice has a score of 6
```

Arrays are handy if you want to Group Records together

If you have multiple variables with the same record structure, you can collect them in an array.

```
array recipeBook = [recipe1, recipe2, recipe3]
for i = 0 to 2
    if recipeBook[i].score >= 7 then
        print(recipeBook[i].recipe_name)
    endif
next i
```
```
Coconut Cookies
```

This will print the names of all recipes with a score ≥ 7.

You can visualise the recipeBook array as a table:

	recipe_number	recipe_name	tested	score
0	1	Chocolate Cake	True	3
1	2	Lemon Slice	True	6
2	3	Coconut Cookies	True	8

Well, we got through all that in record time...

EXAM TIP

You might see records presented differently to this, but the key concepts will be the same. You'll still need to understand what records and fields are, and how they are used in programming.

Searching Data

Structured Query Language (SQL) can be used to search tables (usually in a database) for specific data. When we talk about the <u>records</u> and <u>fields</u> of a database table we just mean the <u>rows</u> and <u>columns</u>.

SELECT and FROM are the most important keywords

In SQL, the <u>SELECT</u> keyword is followed by the names of the <u>fields</u> (columns) you to want to <u>retrieve</u> and <u>display</u>. Then the <u>FROM</u> keyword is followed by the name of the <u>table</u> (or <u>tables</u>) you want to search.

Table: hotels

ID	hotel_name	hotel_rating	rooms	bathroom	price_in_pounds
1	Water Lodge	2.3	50	En-suite	42
2	Fire Inn	4.2	64	Shared	42
3	Earthen House	4.4	215	En-suite	39
4	Windy Hotel	3.5	150	Shared	57
5	River Hotel	3.8	180	Shared	46

```
SELECT hotel_name
FROM hotels
```
This returns hotel_name for all the records in the table hotels.

```
SELECT hotel_name, hotel_rating
FROM hotels
```
This returns hotel_name and hotel_rating for all the records in the table hotels.

```
SELECT *
FROM hotels
```
*If you want to return all the fields, you can use * as a wildcard.*

You can use WHERE to filter the results

1) The <u>WHERE</u> statement is used to specify <u>conditions</u> that a record must satisfy before it is returned.

```
SELECT * FROM hotels WHERE hotel_rating >= 4.1
```
This condition looks for records with a hotel_rating greater than or equal to 4.1.

* is the wildcard character and will return all the fields.

Look in the table hotels.

ID	hotel_name	hotel_rating	rooms	bathroom	price_in_pounds
2	Fire Inn	4.2	64	Shared	42
3	Earthen House	4.4	215	En-suite	39

2) The boolean operators <u>AND</u> and <u>OR</u> can be used with <u>WHERE</u> to make more <u>specific searches</u>.

```
SELECT hotel_name FROM hotels WHERE bathroom = "En-suite" AND price_in_pounds < 45
```

Will only select the hotel_name.

Look in the table hotels.

This condition uses a Boolean operator to check if a hotel room has an en-suite bathroom AND is less than £45.

hotel_name
Water Lodge
Earthen House

3) The <u>LIKE</u> statement can also be used with <u>WHERE</u> to search for a <u>pattern</u>. In LIKE statements, the <u>% character</u> is used as a <u>wildcard</u> to represent any combination of letters and numbers.

```
SELECT hotel_name, price_in_pounds FROM hotels WHERE hotel_name LIKE "%Hotel"
```

Will only select hotel_name and price_in_pounds.

Look in the table hotels.

This will look for all hotel names ending with Hotel. The % character is used to show that it doesn't matter what comes before it.

hotel_name	price_in_pounds
Windy Hotel	57
River Hotel	46

EXAMPLE: **Stacey is searching for a hotel that has more than 100 rooms but she doesn't want to stay in the Windy Hotel. Write a search query for Stacey that returns the name and price of the hotels that match her requirements.**

```
SELECT hotel_name, price_in_pounds FROM hotels
WHERE rooms > 100 AND hotel_name != "Windy Hotel"
```

hotel_name	price_in_pounds
River Hotel	46
Earthen House	39

This condition finds hotels with more than 100 rooms AND not called "Windy Hotel".

EXAM TIP

Tables of data can be searched using SQL...

There are lots of other SQL commands — in the exam you'll only have to know how to use the SELECT, FROM, WHERE and LIKE keywords and the wildcard characters * and %.

Sub Programs

Sub programs can be used to save time and to simplify code. By now you'll definitely have come across procedures and functions even if you don't know what they are yet — all is explained on the next two pages.

Procedures and Functions help to avoid Repeating Code

1) Procedures are sets of instructions stored under one name — when you want your program to do the whole set of instructions you only need to call the name of the procedure.

2) Functions are similar to procedures — the main difference is that functions always return a value.

3) Procedures and functions are very useful when you have sets of instructions that you need to repeat in different places within a program. They give your program more structure and readability whilst cutting down on the amount of code you actually need to write.

4) High-level programming languages (see p.92) have common procedures and functions built into them. If you want one that does something more specific you can create them yourself.

5) In most sub programs you'll encounter parameters and arguments so it's important that you know what they are and the difference between them:

- Parameters are special variables used to pass values into a sub program. For each parameter you can specify a name, a data type and a default value.
- Arguments are the actual values that the parameters take when the sub program is called.

Procedures carry out a Set Of Instructions

1) Procedures don't have to take parameters...   ...but they sometimes will.   'name' is a parameter.

```
procedure welcome()
    print("Hello and welcome.")
    print("Let's learn about procedures.")
endprocedure
```

```
procedure betterwelcome(name)
    print("Hello " + name + " and welcome.")
    print("Let's learn about procedures.")
endprocedure
```

2) Procedures are called by typing their name (and giving an argument if necessary).

```
welcome()
```
```
Hello and welcome.
Let's learn about procedures.
```

```
betterwelcome("Pablo")
```
```
Hello Pablo and welcome.
Let's learn about procedures.
```
The betterwelcome procedure requires one argument.

3) Note that procedures don't return a value.

Functions will always Return a Value

1) Functions take at least one parameter and they must always return a value.

2) When a function is called it should be assigned to a variable or used in a statement otherwise the value that it returns will not be stored anywhere and will be lost.

EXAMPLE: **Write a function to join two strings together with a space between them and show it working on the strings "computer" and "science".**

See p.67 for a reminder on string manipulation.

A function should always return a value.

The result is stored as the variable 'subject'.

```
function join_strings(x, y)
    return x + " " + y
endfunction
subject = join_strings("computer", "science")
print(subject)
```
```
computer science
```

x and y are parameters.

"computer" and "science" are the arguments.

Functions will always return a value, procedures will not...

Even though they're similar, it's important that you don't get mixed up between functions and procedures.

Sub Programs

Make sure that you know your procedures from your functions and your parameters from your arguments.

Sub Programs can contain anything covered in this Section

 Orla has been given a maths problem to add together all of the numbers between two integers (including the integers themselves) and work out if the total is divisible by 7. Write a function that Orla could use to solve the maths problem for any pair of integers.

The sub program is a function as it returns a value.

The variable 'total' is defined inside the function so it's a local variable (see below).

The IF statement checks if the total is divisible by 7. Remember % will give the remainder of a division (p.64).

x and y are the parameters of the function.

The FOR loop is used to add up all the integers from x to y.

```
function add_integers(x, y)
    int total = 0
    for i = x to y
        total = total + i
    next i
    if total % 7 == 0 then
        return true
    else
        return false
    endif
endfunction
```

Variables can be local or global

1) All variables have a <u>scope</u> (either local or global) — the scope of a variable tells you <u>which parts</u> of the program the variable can be used in.

All parameters have local scope to the sub program.

<u>Local variables</u> can only be used <u>within the structure</u> they're declared in — they have a <u>local scope</u>.
<u>Global variables</u> can be used <u>any time</u> after their declaration — they have a <u>global scope</u>.

2) Variables declared inside a <u>sub program</u> are <u>local variables</u>. They are <u>invisible</u> to the rest of the program — this means that they can't be used <u>outside</u> the function.

3) The <u>advantage</u> of local variables is that their scope only extends to the sub program they're declared in. They <u>can't affect</u> and are <u>not affected</u> by anything outside of the sub program. It also doesn't matter if you use the <u>same variable name</u> as a local variable defined elsewhere in the program.

4) Variables in the <u>main body</u> of a program can be made into global variables using the 'global' keyword — these variables can then be used anywhere in the program. It can be difficult to keep track of the <u>value</u> of global variables in <u>larger programs</u>.

5) The example below shows how <u>global variables</u> are used to store data outside of the sub program.

x and y are defined <u>globally</u> — if they were declared inside the sub program then they'd <u>reset to 0</u> each time the sub program was called.

The sub program is a <u>procedure</u> as it <u>doesn't</u> return a value.

The <u>parameters</u> a and b are added to the <u>global variables</u> x and y.

The program <u>keeps track</u> of the position after the first move and then applies the second move from that position.

a and b are parameters so they have <u>local scope</u> to this procedure — they're <u>invisible</u> elsewhere in the program.

```
// A sub program to keep track of a character's x and y position.
global x = 0
global y = 0
procedure move(a, b)
    x = x + a
    y = y + b
    print("You're in square (" + str(x) + ", " + str(y) + ").")
endprocedure
move(3, 5)
move(4, 7)
```

```
You're in square (3, 5).
You're in square (7, 12).
```

It's considered good practice to use local variables wherever possible...

You should be able to identify the local and global variables in a program and use them in your own programs.

Warm-Up and Worked Exam Questions

That's all the learning done for the programming section — perfect time for some practice. Here are some warm-up questions to get you started, followed by a whole bunch of exam questions on the next two pages.

Warm-Up Questions

1) Explain what the following commands will do with the array `footballers`.
   a) `player = footballers[3]`   b) `footballers[5] = "Pele"`

2) Write the pseudocode command that will:
   a) Open a file in read mode.   b) Open a file in write mode.
   c) Close a file.   d) Read a line of text from a file.

3) Give two reasons why a programmer may choose to use a record to store data.

4) Explain what each of these SQL keywords should be immediately followed by:
   a) SELECT   b) FROM   c) WHERE   d) LIKE

5) Give three benefits of using sub programs when you are writing code.

6) What is the difference between arguments and parameters?

Worked Exam Question

1   Frances has written a list of jobs she has to do and stored it in the ToDoList.txt file shown on the right.

   1. Clean my room.
   2. Computer Science homework.
   3. Organise my stamp collection.

   a) Describe what each line of the code below does.

   openRead(), readLine() and close() are three commands you'll need to be familiar with for your exams.

   ```
   01 myList = openRead("ToDoList.txt")
   02 print(myList.readLine())
   03 myList.close()
   ```

   Line 01 .....Opens the file in read mode and stores it under the variable myList.....

   Line 02 .....Prints the first line of the file, i.e. 1. Clean my room.....

   Line 03 .....Closes the file.....

   [3 marks]

   Frances writes the following code to add an extra job to the bottom of her list.

   You'll also need to know what the openWrite() and writeLine() commands do.

   ```
   myList = openWrite("ToDoList.txt")
   myList.writeLine("4. Make lunch for parents.")
   myList.close()
   ```

   b) Explain why the code Frances has written will not work as intended.

   .....The openWrite command will start writing from the start of the file so.....

   .....the first line of the text file will be overwritten with this text instead of.....

   .....it being added to the end......

   [2 marks]

Exam Questions

2 Write a function that takes an integer as a parameter and returns the difference between the integer's cube and its square.

[3 marks]

3 A 2D array is used to store the names of the top 3 pupils in each event of a sports day.
a) What data type should each element of the array be assigned?

....

[1 mark]

b) Give **three** reasons for using a 2D array to store this data.

1. ....

2. ....

3. ....

[3 marks]

4 The `cars` table below shows some data on the used cars that a car dealership has in stock.

CarID	Registration	Make	Type	Price	Engine_size
1	NF09 APY	Stanton	Hatchback	2500	1.4
2	SZ15 LUY	Fenwick	Saloon	4800	1.8
3	FQ55 ALW	Stanton	Hatchback	1700	2.1
4	SQ57 TTW	Fenwick	Estate	2300	2.8
5	NZ12 MBE	Stanton	Saloon	5200	1.8

a) How many records does this table have?

....

[1 mark]

b) Explain the difference between a record and a field.

....

....

....

[2 marks]

c) Draw a table showing what would be returned by the following SQL command:
```
SELECT Make, Type FROM cars WHERE Registration LIKE "N%"
```

[2 marks]

Exam Questions

5 John and three of his friends are training to run a marathon. John records how many miles he and three friends ran each day last week. John stores the data in a 2D array called `distanceRun`.

		Days of the week						
		0	**1**	**2**	**3**	**4**	**5**	**6**
Runner	**0**	9	10	8	12	0	6	9
	1	10	12	15	15	0	0	10
	2	15	14	13	16	0	8	9
	3	6	8	9	10	12	12	0

The distance run on day 0 by runner 2 is given by `distanceRun[0, 2]`.

a) Write the code to display the distance run on day 4 by runner 3.

....

[1 mark]

b) Write an algorithm that takes a runner number as an input and outputs the total number of miles that they ran over the week.

[4 marks]

c) John has written the function `milesConvert()` which takes a distance in miles and returns the equivalent distance in km. E.g. `milesConvert(5)` would return 8. Write an algorithm to convert all distances in the array to km.

[3 marks]

6 Omar has written an adventure story in the file adventure.txt.
Write an algorithm that allows a user to print Omar's adventure story one line at a time.
- Each time the user presses the "y" key the next line of the story should be printed.
- The algorithm should end when it's at the end of the text file.

       You'll need to use the endOfFile() command.

[5 marks]

7 The function `roll(n)` simulates the outcome of one random roll of an n-sided dice.
E.g. `roll(6)` will randomly return either 1, 2, 3, 4, 5 or 6.

a) Noel has declared a local variable inside the function.
Explain **two** differences between local variables and global variables.

    1. ....

....

    2. ....

....

[4 marks]

b) Noel wants to use his function in a dice game where two identical dice are rolled together.
- The player can choose the number of sides that the dice have.
- The player's score is the number of rolls it takes until both dice land on the same number.

Write a sub program that takes the number of sides of the dice as a parameter and returns a player's score.

[5 marks]

Revision Questions for Section Five

Well, that just about wraps up the programming section, perfect time to try some revision questions I think.

- Try these questions and <u>tick off each one</u> when you <u>get it right</u>.
- When you've done <u>all the questions</u> for a topic and are <u>completely happy</u> with it, tick off the topic.

Data Types, Operators, Constants, Variables and Strings (p.63-67) ☐

1) Define the following data types: integer, real, boolean, character and string.

2) a) What does casting mean?
   b) Explain what each of these functions do:
      (i) int()   (ii) float()   (iii) str()   (iv) ASC()   (v) CHR()

3) What do each of these operators mean?
   a) ==   b) !=   c) <=   d) =   e) ^

4) What is meant by: a) a constant?   b) a variable?

5) a) Define string concatenation and give an example of it being used.
   b) Explain what the following string manipulation methods do:
      (i) x.upper   (ii) x.lower   (iii) x.length   (iv) x.subString(a, b)

Program Flow and Boolean Operators (p.70-73) ☐

6) In 20 words or less, outline what each of these statements does:
   a) IF statement   b) SWITCH-CASE statement.

7) What is the main difference between IF-ELSEIF statements and nested IF statements?

8) Compare the features of the three condition-controlled loops, DO UNTIL, WHILE and DO WHILE.

9)* Write an algorithm that outputs the number of Mondays in a 30-day month
    when the user inputs the day of the week that the month started on.

Arrays (p.76-77) ☐

10) Why are arrays useful?

11)* Write commands to perform the following operations on this array. The name of the array is 'chars'.
    ["3", "T", "P", "2", "M", "e", "4", "q", "s", "3"].
    a) Print the character "M".
    b) Print the chars array with "P" changed to "D".
    c) Print the chars array with every element changed to "N".

12)* Write an algorithm to create a two-dimensional array with 10 rows and 10 columns where each
    element is an integer and its value is given by the row number multiplied by the column number.
    (Hint: Remember that rows and columns are numbered starting at 0.)

File Handling, Storing Data and Searching Data (p.78-80) ☐

13) Briefly describe what each of the following functions do:
    a) openRead()   b) openWrite()   c) endofFile()   d) writeLine()   e) readLine()

14) In programming, data can be stored in records:
    a) What is a record?   b) Give two differences between a record and an array.

15)* Outline what the SQL query given below will do:

```
SELECT * FROM world_records WHERE sport = "athletics" AND surname LIKE "M%"
```

Sub programs (p.81-82) ☐

16) What is the difference between a function and a procedure?

17) Define these terms:
    a) parameter   b) argument   c) local variable   d) global variable

*Answers on p.145

Defensive Design

On p.32 you saw that insecure databases can be a security threat — unfortunately, <u>every program</u> that interacts with a user can be a risk. To keep programs safe from tampering you need to use defensive design.

Defensive Design helps to ensure programs Function Properly

1) When programs are <u>functioning correctly</u> they should <u>never break</u> and <u>never produce errors</u>. In practice this is <u>difficult</u> to achieve — even the biggest software companies need to <u>update</u> and <u>patch</u> their programs regularly.

2) Programmers try to <u>protect</u> their programs through <u>defensive design</u>. They will try to:

- Anticipate how users might <u>misuse</u> their program, then attempt to <u>prevent it</u> from happening.
- Ensure their code is <u>well-maintained</u> (see p.89).
- Reduce the number of <u>errors</u> in the code through testing (see p.90-91).

Misuse refers to the user doing things that you don't expect them to.

Make sure the Inputs can't be Exploited

1) The easiest way for a user to <u>accidentally</u> or <u>intentionally misuse</u> a program is when entering data.

2) There are two ways that you can <u>prevent</u> users from entering something you don't want them to:

INPUT SANITISATION

Removing any <u>unwanted characters</u> before passing data through the program.

INPUT VALIDATION

Checking if data meets <u>certain criteria</u> before passing it into the program. E.g. checking that an email address contains an @ symbol and has a suitable ending (.com, .co.uk, etc).

3) Here are a few types of <u>input validation check</u> you can use:

Range check	Checks the data is within a <u>specified range</u>.
Presence check	Checks the data has actually been <u>entered</u>.
Check digit (see p.100)	Checks <u>numerical data</u> has been entered accurately.
Format check	Checks the data has the <u>correct format</u> (e.g. a date).
Look-up table	Checks the data against a table of <u>acceptable values</u>.
Length check	Checks the data is the <u>correct length</u>.

4) Programs can use a <u>mixture</u> of input sanitisation and validation to verify that the inputted data has an <u>acceptable format</u> before passing it into the program.

The best defence is — well, a good defence...

Defensive design is something that you need to consider whenever you are writing a program. A well-designed program shouldn't just stop working if it experiences something that it doesn't expect — it should continue running and inform the user about what they've done wrong or how to correct it.

Defensive Design

It would be nice if input sanitisation and validation happened by magic, but I'm afraid that it usually requires some tricky coding to get right. Make sure you can still remember everything from Section Five...

You can **Sanitise** and **Validate Inputs** in your programs

 Karen is designing a program that she can use to create a database of file names. She has written the following function to check an inputted file name. The removeChar(x) method returns a new string with the character in position x removed.

a) **Explain what the function formatName() does.**

It goes through each character of a string and deletes the character if it's "(" or ")" and returns the amended string.

b) **Is this an example of input sanitisation or input validation?**

It gets rid of unwanted characters from the file name so this is an example of input sanitisation.

c) **Give two validation checks Karen could use to check that a file name has been entered and that it isn't too long.**

• Presence check to make sure data has been entered.

• Length check to make sure the data is not greater than the maximum length allowed.

```
function formatName(file)
    int x = 0
    while x < file.length
        switch file[x]:
            case "(":
                file = file.removeChar(x)
            case ")":
                file = file.removeChar(x)
            case default:
                x = x + 1
        endswitch
    endwhile
    return file
endfunction
```

Authentication can help **Protect** your programs

1) <u>Authentication</u> can <u>confirm the identity</u> of a user before they're allowed to access certain pieces of data or features of the program. A common way that programs do this is using <u>passwords</u>.

2) <u>Passwords</u> are usually associated with a <u>username</u>. When someone tries to access a protected part of the program, it should ask them for their password to check that they are who they claim to be.

3) Here are some common ways to <u>increase the security</u> of a password-based authentication system:

• Force users to use <u>strong passwords</u> (see p.33) and get them to change their passwords <u>regularly</u>.

• Limit the number of <u>failed authentication attempts</u> before access to an account is lost.

• Ask for a <u>random selection of characters</u> from the password on each authentication.

4) It's important that programmers get the <u>level of authentication</u> correct — too much authentication can affect a program's <u>functionality</u> and put people off using it.

Authentic revision materials, available to all users of this book...

When you're writing programs you should think about what you do and don't want a user to enter, but you can put too many restrictions on the data inputted to your program. When validation, sanitisation and authentication start to negatively impact the user's experience, then you've got too much defensive design.

Defensive Design

Programmers working on large projects might often have to work with code that somebody else wrote. Keeping your code tidy is like keeping your handwriting neat — it makes it easier for people to read it.

Good code should be **Well-Maintained**

1) As part of the defensive design of a program, programmers should make sure that it is <u>well-maintained</u>.

2) A well-maintained program makes it <u>easy</u> for other programmers to understand what the code does. They should also be able to <u>change</u> parts of the source code without the risk of causing problems elsewhere in the code (e.g. knock on effects).

3) The following features can <u>improve</u> the maintainability of source code:

- <u>Comments</u> (usually written after // or #) are useful for <u>explaining</u> what the <u>key features</u> of a program do — <u>well written</u> and <u>clear</u> comments are fundamental for helping other programmers <u>understand your programs</u>.

  Too many comments can leave your programs looking cluttered and unreadable.

- <u>Indentation</u> can be used to separate <u>different statements</u> in a program. This allows other programmers to see the flow of the program more <u>clearly</u> and pick out the <u>different features</u>.

- <u>Variables</u> and <u>sub programs</u> should be named so that they refer to what they actually are. This helps programmers to <u>keep track</u> and <u>recognise</u> what the variables are all the way through your program.

- Only use <u>global variables</u> (see p.82) when <u>necessary</u> as they could affect the rest of your code. Variables with a <u>local scope</u> will only affect the sub programs that they are <u>declared in</u> — other programmers will know that <u>changing these variables</u> won't affect <u>other parts</u> of the program.

Well-maintained code is **Easy To Understand**

1) The example below shows some features of <u>well-maintained code</u>.

The sub program and variables have names which tell you what they are and what they do.

Comments are used to tell the reader what the function does and what the FOR loop does.

The code is indented so that you can see which bit of code falls within each statement.

```
// Converts a list of temperatures in °C to °F.
function convert_C_to_F(list_celsius)
    int list_length
    list_length = list_celsius.length
    array list_fahrenheit[list_length]
    // Converts each temperature in turn and adds them to a new list.
    for i = 0 to list_length - 1
        list_fahrenheit[i] = list_celsius[i] * 1.8 + 32
    next i
    return list_fahrenheit
endfunction
```

2) If a good amount of <u>useful comments</u> are put into the source code then it's very easy to produce a <u>summary</u> of what the program code actually does using <u>auto-documentation</u> (see p.93).

Keep your revision notes well-maintained, too...

Keeping code well-maintained isn't rocket science but sometimes programmers can get lazy and their code ends up in a bit of a mess. Have a look back at some code you've written. Write down some ways that you could have improved the maintainability of your code.

Testing

When you're writing programs, remember that the testing is just as important as the programming itself. Have a look at these pages to test your knowledge of testing — they'll prepare you for being tested in the tests.

Programming Errors can be **Syntax Errors** and **Logic Errors**

1) It's quite typical for a program to contain <u>errors</u> during its development — these errors need to be <u>found</u> and <u>corrected</u> as soon as possible.

2) The first task is to figure out what <u>type of error</u> has occurred:

> SYNTAX ERRORS — when the compiler or interpreter <u>doesn't understand</u> something you've typed because it doesn't follow the <u>rules</u> or <u>grammar</u> of the programming language.
>
> LOGIC ERRORS — when the compiler or interpreter is able to <u>run the program</u>, but the program does something <u>unexpected</u>.

3) <u>Syntax errors</u> can be <u>diagnosed</u> by compilers and interpreters (see p.92) — they'll be unable to turn the <u>source code</u> into <u>machine code</u> and a syntax error (with its location) will be returned.

4) <u>Logic errors</u> are more <u>difficult to diagnose</u> and <u>track down</u> — compilers and interpreters <u>won't</u> pick them up. Logic errors are found through general use of the program and by systematically <u>testing</u> it using a <u>test plan</u> (see p.91).

 Jerry has written the following function. It multiplies a given positive integer by all the positive integers less than it (e.g. if the integer was 5 it should do $1 \times 2 \times 3 \times 4 \times 5$). Identify two logic errors in Jerry's function and suggest how he should fix them.

Error 1: *In line 3 the count variable is declared (and set to 1) <u>within the loop</u>, so each time the loop repeats, the count value will be set back to 1. The declaration of the count variable should be moved <u>before the loop</u>.*

Error 2: *In line 4 the count variable is multiplied by n, whereas it should be multiplied by i. It should read count = count * i.*

```
function multiplier(n)
    for i = 1 to n
        int count = 1
        count = count * n
    next i
    return count
endfunction
```

Programs should be **Tested** before being released

1) <u>Functionality testing</u> is an essential part of the <u>development process</u> and a good way to spot <u>logic errors</u>.

2) The <u>main aim</u> of this testing is to see if the program actually meets your <u>initial requirements</u>, i.e. it does exactly what you wanted it to do without breaking or producing errors.

3) Functionality testing <u>shouldn't</u> be left until the <u>end</u> of the process — it's much better to spot errors and fix them as <u>early as possible</u> during development of the program.

4) Other types of testing will depend on what the program or system will be used for. For example:

Performance Test	Tests how quickly certain features run and their impact on computer resources.
Usability Test	Tests how user-friendly the interface and features are.
Security Test	Tests vulnerability to attacks and how securely data is stored.
Load/Stress Test	Tests how it copes under extreme conditions, e.g. lots of users at the same time.

There are more testing times ahead...

Syntax errors are usually easy to fix as the compiler should point you to the exact line that contains the error. On the other hand, it's often difficult for computers to help you out with logic errors — as far as they're concerned, if the program is running, everything is hunky-dory and working as it should.

Testing

So now that you know why programs are tested and what you're actually looking for, it's time to have a closer look at how they're tested. Often testing is planned out before development is even begun.

Testing is a key part of the Software Development Cycle

1) When <u>developing</u> a piece of software or a program you would <u>traditionally</u> follow this flow diagram.

2) The <u>type of testing</u> will impact the software development cycle.

- <u>Final testing</u> — the program only goes through the development cycle <u>once</u>. All the <u>required features</u> of the program are added at the <u>same time</u>. The program is tested against the <u>initial requirements</u> of the customer — if it meets them then the program is signed-off. The customer will get what they <u>asked for</u> but it won't necessarily be what they <u>really want</u>.

- <u>Iterative testing</u> — the program will go through the development cycle <u>a few times</u>. The idea is to try and get the program to match what the customer <u>really wants</u>. The <u>requirements</u> in the <u>first cycle</u> might only include the <u>main features</u> of the program. At the start of each <u>new cycle</u> the <u>requirements</u> will be <u>adjusted</u> (e.g. by adding new details and features).

A Test Plan should be made Before Implementation

1) A <u>test plan</u> will outline exactly what you're going to test and how you're going to test it. It should cover all the <u>possible paths</u> through a program and anticipate potential issues.

2) A <u>good test plan</u> will select appropriate <u>test data</u> to test for these issues. The <u>test data</u> that you use should fall into one of three categories:

Possible paths are all the branches of the flow diagram (p.53) for your program.

- <u>Normal data</u> — things that a user is <u>likely</u> to input into the program.
- <u>Extreme (boundary) data</u> — values at the <u>limit</u> of what the program should be able to handle.
- <u>Erroneous data</u> — inputs that the program <u>should not accept</u>.

3) The table below shows an example of a test plan for setting an alarm system. Users should be able to set their own 3-5 digit alarm code.

Type of data	Test data	Reason for testing	Expected outcome
Normal	2476	To see how the alarm copes with normal usage.	Code accepted.
Normal	No input	To see if the alarm prompts an input.	Prompt to enter a code.
Extreme	000	To see if the smallest code is accepted.	Code accepted.
Extreme	99999	To see if the largest code is accepted.	Code accepted.
Erroneous	23aY	To see if the system accepts non-digits.	Error: The code contains non-numeric data.
Erroneous	12	To see if the alarm accepts inputs shorter than 3 digits.	Error: The code is too short.
Erroneous	632191	To see if the alarm accepts inputs longer than 5 digits.	Error: The code is too long.

4) During testing the tester can add "<u>actual outcome</u>" and "<u>pass or fail</u>" columns to the table.

Luckily for you, this page flew through its testing stage...

In the exam, you'll need to be able to design suitable testing procedures for a given scenario. This could include coming up with your own test plan and test data.

Translators

For computers to process any computer language it needs to be <u>translated</u> into <u>machine code</u>.

Computer Languages can be **High-Level** or **Low-Level**

1) Most of the programming languages that you'll be familiar with (e.g. Python, C++, Java™) are <u>high-level languages</u>. The source code is <u>easy</u> for humans to write, but computers need to <u>translate it</u> into <u>machine code</u> before they can read and run it.

2) On the other hand, <u>low-level languages</u> are <u>tricky</u> for humans to read and write but are <u>easier</u> for a computer to run. They consist of <u>machine code</u> and <u>assembly languages</u>:

   000000 00010 00011 00100 00000 100000 ⟵ Binary machine code is very tricky for humans to understand.

   ADD r4, r2, r3 ⟵ Assembly code is more readable for humans and easier to remember — the first bit (ADD) is the operation code and the rest tells you what to perform that operation on.

3) High-level languages are popular with programmers, but low-level languages have their uses too:

High-Level Languages	Low-Level Languages
• <u>One instruction</u> of high-level code represents <u>many instructions</u> of machine code.	• <u>One instruction</u> of assembly code usually only represents <u>one instruction</u> of machine code.
• The same code will work for <u>many different</u> machines and processors.	• Usually written for <u>one type of machine</u> or <u>processor</u> and won't work on any others.
• The programmer can easily <u>store data</u> in lots of different structures (e.g. lists and arrays) <u>without knowing</u> about the <u>memory structure</u>.	• The programmer needs to know about the <u>internal structure</u> of the CPU (see p.2-3) and how it manages the memory.
• Code is easy to <u>read</u>, <u>understand</u> and <u>modify</u>.	• Code is very difficult to <u>read</u>, <u>understand</u> and <u>modify</u>.
• <u>Must be translated</u> into machine code before a computer is able to understand it.	• Commands in <u>machine code</u> can be executed <u>directly</u> without the need for a translator.
• You <u>don't have much control</u> over what the CPU actually does so programs will be <u>less memory efficient</u> and <u>slower</u>.	• You <u>control</u> exactly what the CPU does and how it uses memory so programs will be <u>more memory efficient</u> and <u>faster</u>.

Translators convert programming languages into **Machine Code**

1) Computers only understand instructions given to them as <u>machine code</u>, so high level languages and assembly languages need to be <u>translated</u> before a computer is able to <u>execute</u> the instructions.

2) There are <u>three types of translator</u> that you need to know about: <u>assemblers</u>, <u>compilers</u> and <u>interpreters</u>.

3) Assemblers are used to turn <u>assembly language</u> into <u>machine code</u>. There are many different assembly languages (to support different CPU types) and each one needs its own <u>unique assembler</u>.

4) Compilers and interpreters are both used to turn <u>high-level code</u> into <u>machine code</u>.

Compiler	Interpreter
Translates <u>all</u> of the source code at the <u>same time</u> and creates <u>one executable file</u>.	<u>Translates</u> and <u>runs</u> the source code <u>one instruction at a time</u>, but doesn't create an executable file.
Only needed <u>once</u> to create the executable file.	Needed <u>every time</u> you want to run the program.
Returns a <u>list of errors</u> for the entire program once compiling is <u>complete</u>.	The interpreter will return the <u>first error</u> it finds and then <u>stop</u> — this is useful for <u>debugging</u>.
Once compiled the program <u>runs quickly</u>, but compiling can take a <u>long time</u>.	Programs will <u>run more slowly</u> because the code is being translated as the program is running.

5) The <u>type of translator</u> used will depend on which <u>programming language</u> and <u>IDE</u> (p.93) you're using.

6) If the program is stored over multiple source code files then a <u>linker</u> is used to join all of the <u>separate compiled codes</u> into one executable program.

"Cette page est incroyable!" — call in the translators...

You should know the key features of low- and high-level languages, assemblers, compilers and interpreters.

Integrated Development Environments

Integrated development environments (IDEs) provide programmers with lots of handy tools when they're coding. If there's one thing I know about programmers, it's that they'll do anything to make life a bit easier.

IDEs have lots of Features to help Programmers

An integrated development environment is a piece of software that provides features to help a programmer to develop their program. Most IDEs will have similar features — the example below shows some of the features from the Microsoft® Visual Studio® IDE:

The code editor is the main part of an IDE, it's where the code is written. Most code editors will have line numbering and auto-colour coding for things like strings, functions, variables and comments. Good code editors will also have other automatic features like auto-correct, auto-indentation and auto-complete.

A run-time environment allows the code to be run quickly within the IDE — this is done using a start or run button. The run-time environment can also help to identify logic errors in the program as the programmer can see which part of the code is running when errors occur.

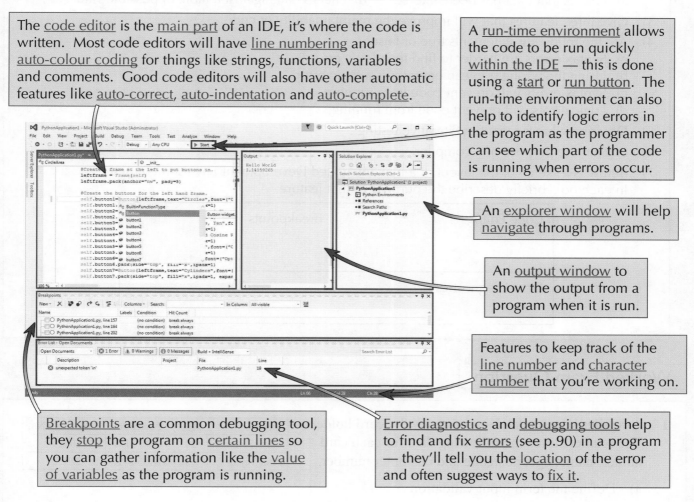

An explorer window will help navigate through programs.

An output window to show the output from a program when it is run.

Features to keep track of the line number and character number that you're working on.

Breakpoints are a common debugging tool, they stop the program on certain lines so you can gather information like the value of variables as the program is running.

Error diagnostics and debugging tools help to find and fix errors (see p.90) in a program — they'll tell you the location of the error and often suggest ways to fix it.

Here are some other common features of an IDE:

- A translator (compiler, interpreter or both) which will translate the source code into machine code (see p.92). If the IDE has both then you can take advantage of each translator's best features.
- Auto-documentation helps with the maintenance of programs. It can extract certain features of a program, like the names of variables, names of sub programs and comments. This information is stored in a separate document to give a summary of what the code does.
- A Graphical User Interface (GUI) builder helps the programmer design a user interface by building it up graphically rather than having to design it using source code. It allows you to drag and drop different objects and customise them, so you can make the interface look exactly how you want it to.

IDEs can make developing programs much quicker and easier...

Each IDE has advantages and disadvantages so it's all about choosing one that meets your needs. For example, certain IDEs will have features that support multiple programming languages and others will specialise in one programming language — both types of IDE can be helpful in different situations.

Warm-Up and Worked Exam Questions

A whole section in one go — that's no mean feat. Make sure all of it has sunk in by having a go at these warm-up questions. Then, once you're happy, try the exam questions for some serious practice.

Warm-Up Questions

1) What is the difference between input validation and input sanitisation?

2) Name the type of input check that:
   a) checks that data has been entered.   b) checks data against a table of possible values.

3) Give three features that will improve the maintainability of code.

4) Are the following statements true or false?
   a) Syntax errors are harder to find than logic errors.
   b) Using the wrong boolean operator is a logic error.
   c) Syntax errors will prevent code from running.
   d) Logic errors will prevent code from running.

5) Describe what is meant by 'iterative testing'.

6) Explain the purpose of a compiler.

7) Below is a sketch of the layout of a new Integrated Development Environment (IDE). In each box, briefly describe the purpose of that feature.

Code Editor	Breakpoints
Error Diagnostics	

Worked Exam Question

1   A retailer keeps a database of its loyalty card holders. The retailer stores the following data for each card holder: name, age, postcode and customer number.

Name	Age	Postcode	Customer No.
Carol Foreman	20	NE85 3TW	100278
Peter Taylor	55	HA55 8PZ	223327

a) Define the term input validation.

   Checking data meets certain criteria before passing it through a program.

   [1 mark]

b) Describe **two** suitable types of validation for an entry in the age field.

   1. Format check to make sure the input is an integer.

   2. Range check to make sure the age is sensible, e.g. between 0 and 120.

   [2 marks]

c) Describe **two** suitable types of validation for an entry in the postcode field.

   1. Length check to make sure the input has a valid number of characters.

   2. Format check to make sure the input contains only letters and numbers.

   A format check could also do things like check that the postcode ends with a number and two letters. *[2 marks]*

Exam Questions

2 Cynthia is writing code for a tablet computer application aimed at children.
Explain how each of the following tools in the Integrated Development Environment (IDE)
could help Cynthia write her application.

Translator: ....

....

....

Error Diagnostics: ....

....

....

Code editor: ....

....

....

[6 marks]

3 A holiday company has written a simple program to calculate the price of its group holiday
packages. The program asks the user to input the group size — if the group size is smaller
than two or greater than 10 the program displays an error message. If not, the price (in £s)
is calculated by multiplying the group size by 50 and then adding 10.

a) Describe how the company can use a test plan to check for logic errors in the program.

....

....

....

[3 marks]

b) Complete the test plan below by filling in the missing spaces.

Test Data	Expected Outcome	Reasons for test
Group_Size = 4		
	460	
Group_Size = 12		Check what happens if input too large.

[5 marks]

Exam Questions

4 A company specialises in writing programs using low-level languages.

   a) Identify **two** reasons why some programmers might use low-level languages.

     1. ....

     2. ....
[2 marks]

   b) Explain why programmers might prefer to use an assembly language over machine code.

     ....

     ....
[2 marks]

   c) State the type of translator used to translate assembly languages into machine code.

     ....
[1 mark]

5 Tiffany writes some code to check if an entered pincode is between 4 and 6 characters long.

```
string pincode = input("Enter pincode")
if pincode.length >= 4 OR pincode.length <= 6 then
    print("Valid pincode"
else
    print("Not a valid pincode, please try again")
endif
```

   a) Identify the syntax error in Tiffany's code and suggest how she could correct it.

     Error: ....

     Correction: ....
[2 marks]

   b) Identify the logic error in Tiffany's code and suggest how she could correct it.

     Error: ....

     Correction: ....
[2 marks]

6 A website's payment form requires users to input their credit card details, e.g. name, card number, expiration date, security code, etc. Evaluate the impact of only using input validation to check the details.

Think about problems that input validation can prevent, and those it can't.

[6 marks]

7 An exam board is developing automated software to calculate students' final exam grades. Evaluate the extent to which the different features of an IDE can help the exam board to develop a well-maintained program.

[6 marks]

Revision Questions for Section Six

And just like that it's the end of section six — but before you put the book down you've got one more task.

- Try these questions and <u>tick off each one</u> when you <u>get it right</u>.
- When you've done <u>all the questions</u> for a topic and are <u>completely happy</u> with it, tick off the topic.

Defensive Design (p.87-89) ☑

1) Why is it important for your programs to have a defensive design?

2) Define the terms input sanitisation and input validation.

3) Give six types of input validation check and explain what each check does.

4)* The program below checks which year the user was born in.
   Does this program use input sanitisation or input validation? Explain your answer.

```
int year
do
    year = input("Enter the year you were born.")
until year > 1900 AND year <= 2016
```

5) What is authentication and why is it used?

6) Give three things that can be done to make a password-based authentication system more secure.

7) a) Give four features of maintainable source code.
   b) Explain how each feature can help other programmers to maintain your code.

Testing (p.90-91) ☑

8) Define the following terms: a) Syntax Error   b) Logic Error

9) Explain why logic errors are more difficult to diagnose than syntax errors.

10)* This algorithm should take the user's age and always print one of the two strings.
    Find two errors in the code and suggest ways that you could fix them.

```
int x = input("Enter your age")
if x > 16 then
    print("At the age of " + x + " you must be a computer science genius.")
elseif x < 16 then
    print("Practice makes perfect!")
endif
```

11) Why is testing important?

12) Give five types of testing that you might carry out on a program.

13) What is meant by: a) iterative testing?   b) final testing?

14) What are the three different types of test data?

15)* A software company is designing an anagram application. It will take a string
    of letters and return all of the words that can be spelt using all of the letters exactly once.
    Come up with five pieces of test data that the company could use to test their program.

Translators and IDEs (p.92-93) ☑

16) Define and give an example of the following: a) Machine code   b) Assembly Language

17) Give six differences between high-level languages and low-level languages.

18) What are the three types of translator?

19) Compare the functionality and uses of a compiler and an interpreter.

20) IDEs have lots of different features. Explain what each of these features are:
   a) Code Editor   b) Run-time environment   c) Error diagnostics
   d) GUI builder   e) Auto-documentation   f) Breakpoints

*Answers on p.146

Logic

Logic gates are pretty clever stuff. They take binary information and give an output based on the Boolean operations (p.73). Each Boolean operator (<u>NOT</u>, <u>AND</u> and <u>OR</u>) has its own logic gate.

Logic Gates apply Boolean Operations to Inputs

1) Logic gates are special circuits built into computer chips.
   They receive <u>binary data</u>, apply a <u>Boolean operation</u>, then <u>output</u> a binary result.

2) Logic <u>diagrams</u> are often drawn to show logic gates and circuits.
   Each type of logic gate is shown by a different <u>symbol</u>.

3) Each type of logic gate also has a corresponding <u>truth table</u>.
   Truth tables show <u>all</u> possible input combinations of 1s and 0s, and the corresponding <u>outputs</u>.

NOT gate

1) NOT gates take a <u>single input</u> and give a <u>single output</u>.

2) The output is always the <u>opposite</u> value to the input.
   If <u>1</u> is input, it outputs <u>0</u>. If <u>0</u> is input, it outputs <u>1</u>.

It can help to think of 1s as TRUE and 0s as FALSE.

<u>NOT gate symbol</u>

Input ──────▷○──── Output

<u>NOT truth table</u>

Input	Output
0	**1**
1	**0**

AND gate

1) AND gates take <u>two inputs</u> and give <u>one output</u>.

2) If both inputs are 1, the output is <u>1</u>,
   <u>otherwise</u> the output is <u>0</u>.

<u>AND gate symbol</u>

Input A ────┐
            ├─── Output
Input B ────┘

<u>AND truth table</u>

Input A	Input B	Output
0	0	**0**
0	1	**0**
1	0	**0**
1	1	**1**

OR gate

1) OR gates take <u>two inputs</u> and give <u>one output</u>.

2) If <u>one or more</u> inputs are 1, then the output is <u>1</u>,
   <u>otherwise</u> the output is <u>0</u>.

<u>OR gate symbol</u>

Input A ────┐
            ├─── Output
Input B ────┘

<u>OR truth table</u>

Input A	Input B	Output
0	0	**0**
0	1	**1**
1	0	**1**
1	1	**1**

Logic isn't as scary as it looks...

These basic logic gates are the building blocks for bigger logic circuits. You should be able to draw each logic gate and the corresponding truth table — you'll also need to learn the equivalent expression and notation from this table:

Gate	Expression	Notation
NOT	NOT A	¬A
AND	A AND B	A ∧ B
OR	A OR B	A ∨ B

Logic

You can make more interesting logic diagrams by <u>combining</u> logic gates. If you know the truth tables from the previous page you'll be able to create truth tables for much more complicated logic diagrams.

Logic Gates are Combined for More Complex Operations

1) <u>Multiple</u> logic gates can be added to the <u>same</u> logic circuit to carry out different operations.

2) You can work out the <u>truth tables</u> by working through each gate in order.
   For every <u>input</u> combination, follow them through each gate <u>step-by-step</u>, then write down the <u>output</u>.

3) By using brackets and the terms AND, OR and NOT, circuits can be written as <u>logical statements</u>, like NOT(A AND B) below. Operations in <u>brackets</u> should be completed <u>first</u>, just like in normal maths.

This circuit shows <u>AND</u> followed by <u>NOT</u>.

The <u>truth table</u> looks like this:

A	B	A AND B	P = NOT(A AND B)
0	0	0	1
0	1	0	1
1	0	0	1
1	1	1	0

This circuit shows <u>OR</u> followed by <u>NOT</u>.

The <u>truth table</u> looks like this:

C	D	C OR D	Q = NOT(C OR D)
0	0	0	1
0	1	1	0
1	0	1	0
1	1	1	0

4) The two logic circuits shown above are examples of <u>two-level logic circuits</u> — they require the inputs to pass through a <u>maximum</u> of <u>two</u> logic gates to reach the output.

Logic Circuits can have More than Two Inputs

This is a <u>two-level logic</u> circuit with <u>3 inputs</u>.

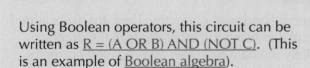

Using Boolean operators, this circuit can be written as <u>R = (A OR B) AND (NOT C)</u>. (This is an example of <u>Boolean algebra</u>).

To cover <u>every</u> input combination, extra rows are needed in the truth table. There are <u>3</u> inputs and each can take one of 2 values, so $2 \times 2 \times 2 = \underline{8}$ rows are needed.

In general, the number of rows is 2^n, where n is the number of different inputs.

A	B	C	A OR B	NOT C	R = (A OR B) AND (NOT C)
0	0	0	0	1	0
0	0	1	0	0	0
0	1	0	1	1	1
0	1	1	1	0	0
1	0	0	1	1	1
1	0	1	1	0	0
1	1	0	1	1	1
1	1	1	1	0	0

To be OR NOT to be — literally covering all forms of being...

Once you've learned each gate's truth table, you can work out the truth tables of much more complicated circuits. If you take the inputs through each gate one step at a time you'll be fine — it's only logical...

Units

Just like you have units like centimetres, metres and kilometres for measuring distance, computers need units for measuring <u>digital information</u>. You'll need to learn all of the unit names on this page and their sizes.

Bits are the **Smallest Measure** of **Data**

1) Computers use 1s and 0s to represent the flow of electricity.
   <u>1</u> is used to show that electricity <u>is</u> flowing, and <u>0</u> shows that it is <u>not</u> flowing.

2) All the data we want a computer to process must be converted into <u>binary code</u> (1s and 0s).

3) Each 1 or 0 in a binary code is a <u>bit</u> (<u>b</u>inary dig<u>it</u>). For example, 1010 is 4 bits.

4) The table below shows <u>the size</u> of other units of data:

A <u>byte</u> is big enough to store one <u>character</u> (like x, e, M or £). See p.110 for more info.

Most <u>files</u> (like <u>songs</u>, <u>pictures</u> and <u>documents</u>) are measured in <u>kB</u> or <u>MB</u>.

High definition <u>videos</u> and complex <u>applications</u> are often measured in <u>gigabytes</u>.

<u>Secondary storage</u> capacity is measured in <u>gigabytes</u> or <u>terabytes</u>.

Name	Size
Bit (b)	A single binary digit (1 or 0)
Nibble	4 bits
Byte (B)	8 bits
Kilobyte (kB)	1000 bytes
Megabyte (MB)	1000 kilobytes
Gigabyte (GB)	1000 megabytes
Terabyte (TB)	1000 gigabytes
Petabyte (PB)	1000 terabytes

You might see each unit defined to be 1024 (not 1000) times bigger than the previous unit. The main reason is that 1024 is a power of 2 which is helpful when dealing with binary data.

5) Each <u>bit</u> can take one of <u>two different values</u> (either 1 or 0). This means that a <u>nibble</u> (4 bits) can take 2^4 = <u>16 different values</u>, and a <u>byte</u> (8 bits) can take 2^8 = <u>256 different values</u>.

Parity Bits are used to check for **Errors**

1) <u>Check digits</u> are a way of checking that data has been <u>entered</u> and <u>read</u> correctly. They are <u>digits</u> added to the <u>end</u> of numbers (e.g. ISBNs on books) and are calculated using the other digits in the number. If the check digit is <u>correct</u> when data is <u>read</u>, then it's likely the data has been <u>entered/read</u> correctly.

2) For binary data, the check digit is called a <u>parity bit</u>. You can have <u>even</u> and <u>odd</u> parity bits:

   • An <u>even</u> parity bit is added to make a binary string have an <u>even</u> number of 1s.
   • An <u>odd</u> parity bit is added to make a binary string have an <u>odd</u> numbers of 1s.

   > The 7-bit string 1010010 has three 1s, so the even parity bit is <u>1</u>. This is sent as 1010010<u>1</u>.
   > The 7-bit string 1100101 has four 1s, so the even parity bit is <u>0</u>. This is sent as 1100101<u>0</u>.

3) If <u>one bit</u> of the binary string is <u>read incorrectly</u> then the computer will pick up on the error. E.g. if an even parity bit is used and 1010110<u>1</u> is read.

4) If <u>two bits</u> within the same binary string are read incorrectly then <u>no error</u> will be detected. For example, if an even parity bit is used and the binary string 10<u>1</u>00<u>0</u>00 is read as 10<u>0</u>00<u>1</u>00 then no error will be picked up.

If <u>odd parity bits</u> were used then these strings would be 1010010<u>0</u> and 1100101<u>1</u>.

This page has me in bits...

Keep working your way through that unit table until the size order is clear in your head — it might just show up on your exam. A bit is smaller than a nibble, and a nibble is less than a full byte. I know, hilarious.

Warm-Up and Worked Exam Questions

Try these warm-up questions on logic and units — if there is anything you're unsure about, have a look back through the first part of this section before having a go at the exam questions on the next page.

Warm-Up Questions

1) Look at the three logic expressions in the box below:

> (NOT A) AND B   C OR (NOT D)   (E AND F) OR G

   a) Draw a logic circuit for each expression.
   b) Construct a truth table for each expression.

2) Put these units in order of size: Gigabyte, Kilobyte, Nibble, Megabyte, Byte

3) Look at the three strings below:

> String A: 0110101   String B: 0100101   String C: 011010010100101

   a) Add an even parity bit to each string.
   b) Add an odd parity bit to each string.

Worked Exam Questions

1 A logic gate can be written as P = A AND B.
  a) State the value of input B when input A is 1 and output P is 0.

$$B = \underline{\quad 0 \quad}$$
[1 mark]

  b) A NOT logic gate is placed after the AND logic gate to make the logic diagram below. State the input values when output P is 0.

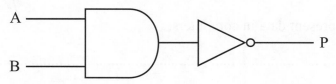

For the NOT gate to output 0, the input of the NOT gate must be 1.

$$A = \underline{\quad 1 \quad} \quad B = \underline{\quad 1 \quad}$$
[1 mark]

2 Misha wants to save some music files onto a solid state drive (SSD).
  a) State which SSD has the largest capacity:
    250 gigabyte (GB), 200 000 megabyte (MB) or 0.3 terabyte (TB).

Convert all the values to the same unit — then compare them.

0.3 Terabyte = 300 GB
200 000 MB = 200 GB

$$\underline{\text{0.3 Terabyte}}$$
[1 mark]

  b) Calculate how many 5 MB music files Misha could save onto a 250 GB SSD.

1 GB = 1000 MB

So 250 GB = 250 × 1000 = 250 000 MB

250 000 ÷ 5 = 50 000 songs

$$\underline{\text{50 000}}$$
[2 marks]

Exam Questions

3   A series of transistors make the two-level logic circuit (NOT A) AND (B AND C).

a)   Complete the truth table below.

A	B	C	NOT A	B AND C	(NOT A) AND (B AND C)
0	0	0			
0	0	1			
0	1	0			
0	1	1			
1	0	0			
1	0	1			
1	1	0			
1	1	1			

[3 marks]

b)   Draw the logic diagram that represents (NOT A) AND (B AND C).

Have a look at p.98 for a reminder of what the gates should look like.

[3 marks]

4   Computers process data in binary code and often use check digits.

a)   Outline what is meant by a check digit.

....

....

[2 marks]

b)   Describe how binary is used to represent data in computers.

....

....

[2 marks]

c)   An even parity bit has been added to the end of three 7-bit binary codes to create
     the 8-bit binary codes below. Identify and explain which code contains an error.

Code 1	Code 2	Code 3
10101011	10100101	10010011

....

....

[2 marks]

d)   Explain how a binary code containing a parity bit can be
     read incorrectly without any errors being detected.

....

....

[2 marks]

Binary Numbers

As computers only understand 1s and 0s, all data must be converted into binary to be processed.
Binary can be used to represent all numbers in our standard number system.

Counting in Binary is a bit like Counting in Denary

1) In our standard number system we have ten different digits (0, 1, 2, 3, 4, 5, 6, 7, 8, 9).
This is called denary, decimal or base-10.

2) Binary only uses two different digits (0 and 1) — we call this base-2.

3) Counting in binary is similar to counting in denary, but the place values from right to left
increase by powers of 2 (e.g. 8, 4, 2, 1), instead of powers of 10 (e.g. 1000, 100, 10, 1).

4) The following table shows the binary equivalents of the denary numbers 0-15:

0 = 0	4 = 100	8 = 1000	12 = 1100
1 = 1	5 = 101	9 = 1001	13 = 1101
2 = 10	6 = 110	10 = 1010	14 = 1110
3 = 11	7 = 111	11 = 1011	15 = 1111

Binary Numbers are easier to Convert using Tables

Drawing a table with binary place values in the first row makes binary to denary conversion easier.

EXAMPLE: **Convert the 8-bit binary number 0011 0101 to a denary number.**

Each column is just a power of 2. i.e. 2^3, 2^2, 2^1, 2^0.

1) Draw up a table with binary place values in the top row. Start with 1 at the right, then move left, doubling each time.

128	64	32	16	8	4	2	1
0	0	1	1	0	1	0	1

2) Write the binary number 0011 0101 into your table.

3) Add up all the numbers with a 1 in their column:

32 + 16 + 4 + 1 = 53. So 0011 0101 is 53 in denary.

This works with all binary numbers — just draw as many columns as you need, doubling each time.

8-bit numbers can represent the denary numbers 0 to 255. 16-bit numbers can show
the numbers 0 to 65 535, and 32-bit can show the numbers 0 to 4 294 967 295.

Convert Denary to Binary by Subtracting

When converting from denary to binary, it's easier to draw a table of binary place
values, then subtract them from largest to smallest. Have a look at this example:

EXAMPLE: **Convert the denary number 79 into an 8-bit binary number.**

1) Draw an 8-bit table.

2) Move along the table, only subtracting the number in each column from your running total if it gives a positive answer.

128	64	32	16	8	4	2	1
0	1	0	0	1	1	1	1

79 – 128 = 49   79 – 64 = 15   15 – 32 = 17   15 – 16 = 1   15 – 8 = 7   7 – 4 = 3   3 – 2 = 1   1 – 1 = 0

3) Put a 1 in every column that gives a positive answer, and a 0 in the rest.

So 79 converted to an 8-bit binary number is 0100 1111.

There are other methods to convert denary to binary, so just choose the one you are most comfortable with.

Use powers of 2 to convert between binary and denary...

There's a really easy way to test yourself on this stuff. Write down a denary number between 0 and 255 and convert it to binary. Then write down an 8-bit binary number and convert it to denary.

Binary Numbers

Add **Binary Numbers** using **Column Addition**

As binary only uses 1s and 0s we <u>can</u> comfortably do $0 + 0 = 0$, $1 + 0 = 1$ and $0 + 1 = 1$.
Using binary we <u>can't</u> write $1 + 1 = 2$. Instead, we have to write $\underline{1 + 1 = 1\,0}$.

EXAMPLES:

1. Add the following 8-bit binary numbers together: 1000 1101 and 0100 1000

1) First, put the binary numbers into columns.

2) Starting from the right, add the numbers in columns.

3) When doing $1 + 1 = 10$, carry the 1 into the next column.

So 1000 1101 + 0100 1000 = 1101 0101

```
   1 0 0 0 1 1 0 1
 + 0 1 0 0 1 0 0 0
   1 1 0 1 0 1 0 1
                 1
```

2. Add the two 8-bit binary numbers below:

```
     0 0 1 1 0 0 1 1
   + 0 1 1 1 1 0 0 1
     1 0 1 0 1 1 0 0
     1 1 1   1 1
```

1) Start at the right-hand side and add each column.

2) Sometimes you'll get something like $1 + 1 + 1 = 11$, so you need to write 1, then carry 1 to the next column.

So 0011 0011 + 0111 1001 = 1010 1100

You can check your answer by converting the numbers and answer to denary, to make sure it still works.

Overflow Errors occur when a **Number** has **Too Many** bits

1) Sometimes, during binary arithmetic you will get a result that requires <u>more</u> bits than the CPU is expecting — this is called <u>overflow</u>.

2) For example, in binary the <u>8-bit</u> calculation 1111 1111 + 0000 0001 gives the <u>9-bit</u> answer <u>1 0000 0000</u>. Computers will see the 1 as an <u>overflow error</u> and just output 0000 0000, which is nonsense.

3) Computers usually deal with these extra bits by <u>storing</u> them elsewhere.

4) Overflow <u>flags</u> are used to show that an overflow error has occurred.

EXAMPLE: **a) Add the 8-bit binary numbers below, giving your answer as an 8-bit binary number.**

1) <u>Add</u> the binary numbers in the usual way.

2) The final calculation is $1 + 1 = 10$, so <u>carry the 1</u>.

3) You are left with a <u>9-bit answer</u> — this is an <u>overflow error</u>.

4) <u>Ignore</u> the overflow to give your 8-bit answer. 0110 0101

```
     1 1 0 1 0 0 0 1
   + 1 0 0 1 0 1 0 0
   1 0 1 1 0 0 1 0 1
   1           1
```

b) Identify any problems that could be caused by giving your answer as an 8-bit number.

There is an overflow error which can lead to a loss of data and a loss of accuracy in your answer. It could also cause software to crash if it doesn't have a way of dealing with the extra bit.

Binary, binary, quite contrary, how do you overflow...

Overflows occur when a calculation gives a result with more bits than are available to store it. This can be a real problem — programmers must make sure that they can't occur, or that they are dealt with.

Binary Numbers

Binary Shifts can be used to Multiply or Divide by 2

1) A binary shift (also known as a logical shift) moves every bit in a binary number left or right a certain number of places.

2) Gaps at the beginning or end of the number are filled in with 0s.

3) The direction of the binary shift indicates whether it multiplies or divides the binary number:

> **Left shifts MULTIPLY a binary number.**
> For every place shifted left, the number is doubled.

> **Right shifts DIVIDE a binary number.**
> For every place shifted right, the number is halved.

4) If a number is shifted 3 places right, it would be halved three times (i.e. divided by $2^3 = 8$).
   If a number were shifted 4 places left, it would be doubled four times (i.e. multiplied by $2^4 = 16$).

5) Left shifts can cause overflows (if extra bits are needed), and right shifts cause bits to 'drop off' the end. Bits dropping off or overflowing can lead to a loss of accuracy/data.

Examples of Binary Shifts

Perform a 3 place left shift on the 8-bit binary number 0010 1001.
Explain the effect this will have on the number and problems that may occur.

1) Write down the original binary number, then shift all digits 3 places to the left.

2) Fill in the gaps on the right with 0s.

   The number has been doubled three times, so it has been multiplied by $2^3 = 8$.

These bits have overflowed.

If there are only 8 bits available to store the number then there is an overflow.
Some data/accuracy may be lost and an overflow flag will be displayed.

Perform a 2 place right shift on the binary number 0011 1100.
What effect will this have on the number?

1) Write down the original binary number, then shift all digits 2 places to the right.

2) Fill in the gaps on the left with 0s.

A 2 place right shift gives the binary number 0000 1111.
As this is a 2 place shift, the original number will have been halved twice (so divided by $2^2 = 4$).

Dividing using a right binary shift has the same effect as using the DIV operator (p.64) — your answer would not take into account any remainders.

Shift left to multiply and shift right to divide...

Binary shifts are really good for doing fast multiplication and division by powers of 2. Watch out for bits overflowing or dropping off the end — if this happens then you'll lose accuracy in your answer.

Hexadecimal Numbers

Hexadecimal (hex) is another number system used regularly in programming.
Hex uses a combination of digits and letters in order to represent a number.

Hexadecimal numbers are Shorter than Binary

1) Hexadecimal (or base-16) uses sixteen different digits.

2) A single hex character can represent any denary number from 0-15. To represent 0-15 in binary would require 4 bits (a nibble), so each hex character equates to a nibble in binary.

3) The table shows the denary and binary value of each hex character.

4) Programmers often prefer hex when coding, because:

- It's simpler to remember large numbers in hex — they're far shorter than binary numbers.
- Due to hex numbers being shorter, there's less chance of input errors.
- It's easier to convert between binary and hex than binary and denary.

Computers themselves do not use hex — they still have to convert everything to binary to process it.

Denary	Hex	Binary	Denary	Hex	Binary
0	0	0000	8	8	1000
1	1	0001	9	9	1001
2	2	0010	10	A	1010
3	3	0011	11	B	1011
4	4	0100	12	C	1100
5	5	0101	13	D	1101
6	6	0110	14	E	1110
7	7	0111	15	F	1111

Convert Hex to Denary by Multiplying each Character

In hex, moving right to left, place values increase in powers of 16.

4096	256	16	1

To convert from hex to denary, draw up a table, fill in the boxes, then multiply — just like in this example:

EXAMPLES:

1. Convert the hexadecimal number 87 into denary.

Luckily in the exam you'll only have to convert two digit hex numbers like in these examples.

1) First, draw this table, then write in your hex number.

16	1
8	7

2) Multiply the numbers in each column.

$8 \times 16 = 128$ $7 \times 1 = 7$

3) Add up the results: 128 + 7 = 135

So the hex number 87 is **135 in denary.**

To convert from denary to hex, draw the table but use division to fill it in.

2. Convert the denary number 106 into hexadecimal.

Remember, hex goes from 0-9, then A to F.

1) Start at the left. Divide 106 by 16, then hold onto the remainder.

16	1
6	A

106 ÷ 16 = 6 r 10

2) Divide the remainder from the last calculation by 1.

10 ÷ 1 = 10 = A

So the denary number 106 is **6A in hexadecimal.**

Hex can be a blessing and a curse...

Hex and denary can look fairly similar (as they both contain 0-9), so make sure you've got them the right way round when converting — 65 in hexadecimal is NOT the same as 65 in denary. Memorise the hex table and its advantages, then cover it up and write everything you remember.

Hexadecimal Numbers

Convert **Binary** to **Hex** by splitting it into **Nibbles**

1) Each hex character is equal to a <u>nibble</u> in binary, so it is possible to convert from binary to hex by splitting the binary code into <u>4-bit chunks</u>.

2) Binary to hex conversions can be much <u>easier</u> than converting from binary to denary, as you only have to deal with the nibbles <u>one at a time</u>.

EXAMPLE: **Convert the binary number 1011 1001 to hexadecimal.**

Remember, hex only uses letters for denary values between 10-15.

1) Firstly, <u>split</u> the binary number into <u>nibbles</u>:   1011 1001

2) Draw a table with columns labelled 1, 2, 4, 8, then <u>repeat</u> the values for as many nibbles as you require.

3) Fill in the table with your binary number.

8	4	2	1	8	4	2	1
1	0	1	1	1	0	0	1

4) For <u>each nibble</u>, add up the numbers with a 1 in the column, then convert this value to hex.

8 + 2 + 1 = 11
= B

8 + 1 = 9

5) Finally put the hex values <u>together</u>.   The binary number 10111001 is B9 in hexadecimal.

If the binary number can't be split into nibbles, you'll have to stick some zeros on the front.

EXAMPLE: **Convert the binary number 11 1110 1000 to hexadecimal.**

1) Add <u>zeros</u> to the <u>front</u> of the binary number, so that you can split it into nibbles.   0011 1110 1000

2) Draw a repeating table of 1, 2, 4 and 8, as above.

3) Write your binary number in the table.

8	4	2	1	8	4	2	1	8	4	2	1
0	0	1	1	1	1	1	0	1	0	0	0

4) Add up <u>each nibble</u> and <u>convert</u> each value to <u>hex</u>.

2 + 1 = 3

8 + 4 + 2 = 14
= E

8 = 8

5) Put the hex values together.   The binary number 1111101000 is 3E8 in hexadecimal.

For **Hex** to **Binary**, use each **Character's Denary Value**

To convert the <u>opposite</u> way (from <u>hex</u> to <u>binary</u>) convert each hex character into binary, then just put the binary numbers together.

EXAMPLE: **Convert the hexadecimal number 8C to binary.**

1) First, find the denary value of each character: 8 = 8 in denary   C = 12 in denary

2) Find the binary value of each denary number:

8	4	2	1
1	0	0	0

8	4	2	1
1	1	0	0

8 = 1000 in binary   12 = 1100 in binary

3) Put the nibbles together to get the equivalent binary number.   The hexadecimal number 8C is 10001100 in binary.

This page has so many nibbles it could spoil your lunch...

When converting binary to hex just remember to split the binary up into chunks of 4 bits, each with columns labelled 1, 2, 4 and 8. Then work out the individual hex values and put them together.

Warm-Up and Worked Exam Questions

Converting between binary, denary and hexadecimal tests your maths skills just as much as your computing knowledge. Have a go at these warm-up questions before diving into the exam questions on the next page.

Warm-Up Questions

1) Convert:
   a) 01011001 from binary to denary
   b) 69 from denary to binary

2) Add the following 8-bit binary numbers together: 01101000 and 10001010

3) Explain how overflow errors occur.

4) Perform a 3 place right shift on 10111000. Give your answer as an 8-bit number.

5) What is the effect of a 1 place left shift?

6) Convert:
   a) 48 from denary to hex
   b) C6 from hex to denary
   c) 10100010 from binary to hex
   d) 3D from hex to binary

Worked Exam Questions

1 Work out these conversions.

a) Convert the 8-bit binary number 10010011 into a denary number.

$$128 + 16 + 2 + 1 = 147$$

............147............
[1 mark]

b) Convert the denary number 252 into an 8-bit binary number.

Drawing an 8-bit table can help.

128	64	32	16	8	4	2	1
1	1	1	1	1	1	0	0

$252 - 128 = 124$
$124 - 64 = 60$
$60 - 32 = 28$
$28 - 16 = 12$
$12 - 8 = 4$
$4 - 4 = 0$

............11111100............
[1 mark]

2 Daniel is a programmer. He makes the following two claims about hex numbers.

Claim 1: "Hex is much easier to work with than binary."

Claim 2: "Converting from denary to hex is easier than converting from binary to hex."

Would other programmers agree with Daniel's claims? Explain your answers.

Claim 1: They're likely to agree with claim 1. Hex numbers are shorter so are easier to identify, remember, edit and share than binary codes.

Claim 2: They're likely to disagree with claim 2. Converting binary to hex is easier as binary numbers can be split into nibbles to quickly read off the hex values.

[4 marks]

Exam Questions

3 Binary shifts can be used to quickly multiply and divide binary numbers.

  a) Complete a 3 place left shift on the binary number 00011010.

....
[1 mark]

  b) State an appropriate binary shift to divide a binary number by 4 and use it on 11010100.

....
[2 marks]

  c) Yasha says "Adding a binary number to itself is the same as a 2 place left shift."
  Is he correct? Explain your answer.

....

....
[2 marks]

4 A security program encrypts passwords using a hexadecimal conversion.
The binary code of each letter for the password 'CAT' is shown below.
01000011 01000001 01010100

  a) Convert each binary number above to a hexadecimal number to encrypt the password 'CAT'.

....
[3 marks]

  b) The password 'DOG' is encrypted as 44 4F 47.
    i) Convert the first encrypted letter to binary.

....
[1 mark]

    ii) What password would be encrypted as 43 4F 44 45?

Look back at previous
    question parts.

....
[2 marks]

5 The function denary() converts one hexadecimal character to denary. (e.g. denary(F) = 15).

  a) Calculate the value of denary(A) + denary(C).

....
[2 marks]

  b) Write an algorithm using denary() to convert any 2-digit hexadecimal into denary.

Think about splitting the 2-digit hexadecimal into separate characters.

[4 marks]

Characters

Almost everything can be represented as binary code — words, images and sound can all be turned into bits and processed by a computer. Firstly let's look at words, which are made up of different characters.

Binary can be used to represent Characters

1) Alphanumeric characters are used to make words and strings (see p.67). They include uppercase and lowercase letters, the digits 0-9, and symbols like ? + and £.

2) Computers are unable to process these characters directly as they only process binary code. So they need a way of converting these characters to binary code and vice versa. They can do this using character sets.

> Character sets are collections of characters that a computer recognises from their binary representation.

Don't mistake a character set for a font. A character set is what determines the letter — the font you use just displays that letter in a certain way.

3) As well as the alphanumeric characters mentioned above, character sets also contain special characters which do certain commands (e.g. space, enter and delete).

4) So when you press a button on your keyboard it sends a binary signal to the computer telling it which key you pressed. The computer then uses the character set to translate the binary code into a particular character.

The number of Bits you'll need is based on the Character Set

Different character sets can have different amounts of characters. The number of characters in a character set determines how many bits you'll need. Here are some standard character sets you should know about:

ASCII

- ASCII is the most commonly-used character set in the English-speaking world. Each ASCII character is given a 7-bit binary code — this means it can represent a total of 128 different characters, including all the letters in the English alphabet, numbers, symbols and commands.

- An extra bit (0) is added to the start of the binary code for each ASCII character (see the table on the right). This means each ASCII character fits nicely into 1 byte.

Character	Binary	Hex	Denary
Backspace	00001000	8	8
+	00101011	2B	43
3	00110011	33	51
B	01000010	42	66
b	01100010	62	98

Some examples of ASCII characters.

Extended ASCII

- Extended ASCII is a character set which gives each character an 8-bit binary code, allowing for 256 characters to be represented. The first 128 characters are in exactly the same order as the ASCII characters.

- Extended ASCII is particularly useful for many European languages like French and German which include accents on some of the vowels, like é, ô and ü.

Unicode®

- Unicode® comes in several different forms and tries to cover every possible character that might be written. In its most common forms it uses 16-bit and 32-bit binary codes.

- The best thing about Unicode® is that it covers all major languages, even those that use a completely different alphabet like Greek, Russian and Chinese.

Character sets are used to turn binary data into characters...

Extended ASCII comes in several different forms. The first 128 characters are always the same, but the ones after that can change to suit the language you're writing in. E.g. the "Latin 1 Western European" character set is used for languages like French and German, while another is better suited to Eastern European languages.

Storing Images

Images and sounds are pieces of data stored on computers — so, naturally, they're made of bits (p.100).

Images are stored as a series of Pixels

1) The type of images you use most often are called <u>bitmap</u> images — they're mainly used for photos. Bitmap images are made up of lots of tiny dots, called <u>pixels</u>.

2) The <u>colour</u> of each pixel is represented by a <u>binary</u> code. The number of colours available in an image is related to the number of <u>bits</u> the code has.

3) <u>Black-and-white</u> images only use two colours, meaning they only need <u>1-bit</u> to represent each pixel — <u>0 for white</u> and <u>1 for black</u>.

4) <u>2-bit images</u> can be made up of four colours. Each pixel can be one of four binary values — <u>00</u>, <u>01</u>, <u>10</u> and <u>11</u>.

5) You can make a <u>greater range</u> of shades and colours by <u>increasing the number of bits</u> for each pixel.

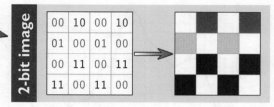

Increasing Colour Depth and Resolution increases the File Size

1) The <u>colour depth</u> is the <u>number of bits</u> used for <u>each pixel</u>.

2) Given the colour depth you can work out <u>how many colours</u> can be made using this <u>formula</u>:

Total number of colours = 2^n (where n = number of bits per pixel, or bpp)

| 1-bit image: 2^1 = 2 colours | 4-bit image: 2^4 = 16 colours | 24-bit image: 2^{24} = 16 777 216 colours |

3) Most devices use a <u>24-bit colour depth</u>, with 8 bits used to indicate the levels of <u>red</u>, <u>green</u> and <u>blue</u> needed for each pixel. It's estimated that the human eye can see around 10 million different colours, so a 24-bit colour depth should cover every colour that you could possibly see.

4) The <u>resolution</u> is the <u>density</u> of pixels in an image, i.e. how many pixels are within a certain area. It's normally measured in <u>dots per inch</u> (dpi).

5) The <u>higher the resolution</u>, the more pixels in a certain area and so the <u>better quality</u> of image. E.g. if an image has a resolution of 60 dpi, it means that a one-inch square contains a grid that is 60 pixels wide and 60 pixels high. So there are 60 x 60 = 3600 pixels in that square inch. If we increased the resolution to 90 dpi, it would mean 8100 pixels in that square inch, so a better image quality.

6) <u>Increasing</u> the resolution or the colour depth means that there are <u>more bits</u> in the image. This improves the <u>image quality</u>, but also increases the <u>file size</u>.

Devices need Metadata to display the images

1) <u>Metadata</u> is the <u>information</u> stored in an image file which helps the computer recreate the image on screen from the binary data in each pixel.

2) Metadata usually includes the image's <u>file format</u>, <u>height</u>, <u>width</u>, <u>colour depth</u> and <u>resolution</u>. It can also include extra information, like the time and date that the image was created or last edited.

3) Without metadata, devices would not be able to <u>display</u> the image on screen as intended.

Images are stored as long strings of bits...

You might see the term resolution used to mean the dimensions of an image in pixels (e.g. 720 × 1280), but don't get misled — if you're asked about it in the exam, they'll be talking about pixel density in dpi.

Storing Sound

Sound is made up of bits and stored in files on a computer. Or rather, digital sound is — the other type of sound, analogue, doesn't get on well with computers very much, so we've got to turn it into digital first.

Sound is Sampled and stored Digitally

1) Sound is recorded by a microphone as an <u>analogue</u> signal.
Analogue signals are pieces of <u>continually changing</u> data.

2) Analogue signals need to be converted into <u>digital</u> data so that computers can read and store sound files. This is done by <u>analogue to digital converters</u>, which are found in most modern recording devices.

3) The process of converting analogue to digital is called <u>sampling</u>:

The blue line shows the analogue sound wave — it's one <u>continuous</u> piece of data which <u>keeps changing</u>.

To convert the analogue recording to digital data, we <u>sample</u> the <u>amplitude</u> of the wave at <u>regular intervals</u> (shown by the dots on the graph). The <u>amplitude</u> can only take certain values depending on the <u>bit rate</u> (see below).

Once the device has sampled the recording, it creates the curve <u>digitally</u> like this.

Each block of data matches where each sample was taken.

The digital data is about the same shape as the analogue wave, but it's <u>not continuous</u>. It's <u>lost</u> a lot of data — e.g. the last peak in the analogue wave is much flatter in the digital data.

The digital data can be improved by taking samples <u>more regularly</u> — most music isn't sampled every second but every couple of <u>milliseconds</u>.

Several factors affect the Size and Quality of Sound Files

1) <u>Sampling intervals</u> are the gaps between each of the points where the analogue recording is sampled. E.g. the audio file might be sampled every 5 milliseconds (ms) — the sampling interval would be 5 ms.

2) <u>Sampling frequency</u> (or <u>sample rate</u>) is how many samples you take in a second — it's usually measured in kilohertz (kHz). E.g. a common sampling frequency is 44,100 samples per second (44.1 kHz).

3) <u>Sample size</u> is the number of bits available for each sample (like colour depth but for sound samples).

4) <u>Bit rate</u> is the number of bits used per second of audio — it's calculated using this <u>formula</u>:

> **Bit rate = Sampling frequency × sample size**

The bit rate is usually measured in kilobits per second (kbit/s).

5) <u>Increasing</u> the sampling frequency means the analogue recording is sampled more often. The sampled sound will be <u>better quality</u> and will more <u>closely match</u> the original recording.

6) <u>Increasing</u> the sample size means the digital file picks up <u>quieter sounds</u>, even if they're happening at the same time as louder ones. This will also result in a sampled sound that is closer to the <u>quality</u> of the original recording.

7) However, increasing the sampling frequency and sample size will <u>increase the bit rate</u>. This will increase the <u>number of bits</u> in the sound file, which means a <u>larger file size</u>.

You can change the size and quality of sound files...

The factors which impact the size and quality of sound files are all related — e.g. increasing the sampling frequency means more samples are taken per second, which decreases the sampling interval. Similarly, the sampling frequency and sample size are multiplied together to calculate the bit rate, so increasing either of them will increase the bit rate, and the file size too.

Compression

In the modern world, we're practically swimming in badly lit photos and subpar pop songs — so many, in fact, that you'd start to wonder how we can possibly store them all. The answer is down to data compression.

Sometimes we need to **Compress** files

1) <u>Data compression</u> is when we make <u>file sizes smaller</u>, while trying to make the compressed file as <u>true to the original</u> as possible.

2) Compressing data files has many <u>uses</u>:

- Smaller files take up <u>less storage space</u> on a device.
- <u>Streaming</u> and <u>downloading</u> files from the Internet is quicker as they take up less <u>bandwidth</u> (p.20).
- It allows <u>web pages</u> to <u>load more quickly</u> in web browsers.
- <u>Email</u> services normally have restrictions on the size of the attachment you can send — compressing the file allows you to send the same content with a much smaller file size.

There are **Two Types** of compression — **Lossy** and **Lossless**

1) <u>Lossy compression</u> works by permanently <u>removing data</u> from the file — this limits the number of bits the file needs and so reduces its size.

2) <u>Lossless compression</u> makes the file smaller by <u>temporarily</u> removing data to store the file and then restores it to its <u>original state</u> when it's opened.

	Pros	Cons	E.g. of File Types
Lossy	• Greatly <u>reduced file size</u>, meaning more files can be stored. • Lossy files take up <u>less bandwidth</u> so can be downloaded and streamed more quickly. • <u>Commonly used</u> — lots of software can read lossy files.	• Lossy compression <u>loses</u> data — the file can't be turned back into the original. • Lossy compression <u>can't be used</u> on text or software files as these files need to retain all the information of the original. • Lossy files are <u>worse quality</u> than the original. But, this loss in quality is normally <u>unnoticeable</u>.	• MP3 (audio) • AAC (audio) • JPEG (image)
Lossless	• Data is only removed temporarily so there is <u>no reduction in quality</u> — the compressed file should look or sound like the original. • Lossless files can be <u>decompressed</u> — turned back into the original. • Lossless compression can be used on <u>text</u> and software <u>files</u>.	• Only a <u>slight reduction</u> in file size, so lossless files still take up quite a bit of space on your device. E.g. a lossless song may have a file size of around 30 MB, while the same song with lossy compression may be 5 MB.	• FLAC (audio) • TIFF (image) • PNG (image)

 Phil has just heard a new band on the radio. He wants to download fifty of their songs from the Internet and store them on his smartphone to take on holiday. State which type of compression would be most appropriate in this situation and explain why.

<u>Lossy</u> compression would be the most appropriate. Lossy files are <u>smaller</u> so they would take up less bandwidth, meaning Phil could <u>download</u> the songs more quickly. Their smaller file size would also allow him to <u>store</u> them all on his smartphone without taking up too much storage space.

The best compression type? I'm afraid I'm at a loss...

Lossy files aren't as high quality as the originals, but the difference is normally unnoticeable to us unperceptive humans. This helps to explain why lossy file formats like JPEG (for photos) and MP3 (for music) are so popular — they save a lot of storage space and their inferior quality is hardly noticeable.

Warm-Up and Worked Exam Questions

That's the last of the stuff you have to learn, but you're not finished yet — there are a whole bunch of questions to answer. For the final time, test what you've learnt with these warm-up and exam questions.

Warm-Up Questions

1) What is the difference between the character sets ASCII and Unicode®?

2) How many different colours are possible with a colour depth of 4?

3) What would be the effect on the file size of an image if:
   a) the colour depth was increased? b) the resolution was decreased?

4) What is the bit rate of an audio file with a sampling frequency of 50 kHz and a sample size of 4 bits?

5) What would be the effect on the file size and quality of an audio sample if:
   a) the bit rate was increased? b) the sampling interval was increased?

6) Name the two types of compression and give one reason why each one is useful.

Worked Exam Questions

1   Sound is converted from an analogue sound wave to a digital format using sampling. Complete the flow diagram below to show the process of sampling.

The key thing to get across is that analogue waves are sampled to be turned into digital (or binary) data.

[4 marks]

2   State and explain which type of compression would be most appropriate in these examples.

a) Uploading 100 holiday photographs to a social media account.

Make sure the explanation relates to the context of the question.

Type Of Compression: ..... Lossy compression .....

Explanation: ..... Lossy compression will greatly reduce the size of ..... the files so uploading them will be quicker. .....

[2 marks]

b) Uploading a photograph of a model for a fashion magazine.

Type Of Compression: ..... Lossless compression .....

Explanation: ..... An image with all original detail may be preferred so they ..... can edit it and print it at the best possible resolution. .....

[2 marks]

Exam Questions

3 Helena is writing a news article using a word processor.

a) Define the term 'character set'.

....

....

[1 mark]

b) Complete the flowchart to explain how Helena's computer recognises characters she enters.

Start → Key pressed → [   ] → [   ] → Character displayed → Stop

[2 marks]

4 Jade records herself reading two extracts from a novel to use in an audiobook.
The bit rates and sampling frequencies of each recording are shown below.

	Length	Bit Rate	Sampling Frequency
Extract 1	2 minutes	128 kbit/s	32 kHz
Extract 2	2 minutes	320 kbit/s	44.1 kHz

a) Explain which extract would have the better sound quality.

....

....

[2 marks]

b) Give **one** drawback of using extract 2 rather than extract 1 for the audiobook.

....

[1 mark]

5 Duncan prints a 10 × 10 inch photograph with a resolution of 60 DPI.

a) Calculate the total number of pixels in Duncan's photograph.

Remember that you're not allowed to use a calculator.

....

[2 marks]

b) Explain how decreasing the DPI would affect the image quality.

....

....

[2 marks]

c) Explain the purpose of metadata in an image file.

....

....

[2 marks]

Revision Questions for Section Seven

That's the end of the content. Get through these questions, then it's time to have a go at the practice papers.

- Try these questions and <u>tick off each one</u> when you <u>get it right</u>.
- When you've done <u>all the questions</u> for a topic and are <u>completely happy</u> with it, tick off the topic.

Logic and Units (p.98-100) ☐

1) For each of the 3 main logic gates: a) Draw its symbol.
                                   b) State how many inputs and outputs it has.

2)* Draw the truth table for the logic diagram on the right.   c) Draw its truth table.

3) Why is binary used by computers?

4) Put these units in order of size: Terabyte, Petabyte, Kilobyte, Gigabyte, Megabyte

5)* A hard drive has a storage capacity of 2000 gigabytes.
    a) How many terabytes is this?   b) How many megabytes is this?

Binary and Hexadecimal (p.103-107) ☑

6)* Convert the following denary numbers to: a) binary   b) hexadecimal
                                     (i) 17   (ii) 148   (iii) 240

7)* Convert the following binary numbers to: a) denary   b) hexadecimal
                                   (i) 0011 1000 (ii) 1001 1111 (iii) 10 1011

8)* Convert these hexadecimal numbers to: a) denary   b) binary
                                  (i) 4A   (ii) 75   (iii) BD9

9)* Add the binary numbers 0101 1101 and 0011 0010.

10) What is an overflow error?

11) What effect do left and right shifts have on binary numbers?

12) Give three reasons why programmers prefer hexadecimal over binary and denary.

Characters (p.110) ☐

13) What is the definition of a character set?

14) Give the four types of character that are included in a character set.

15) a) What are the three main character sets?
    b) For each of your answers to part a) state how many bits it takes to represent each character.

Images, Sound & Compression (p.111-113) ☐

16) What is meant by a bitmap image?

17) Define colour depth.

18) What is an image's resolution and what units do we use to measure it?

19) Name two ways in which increasing the resolution or colour depth will affect the image.

20) What is metadata and what is it used for?

21) In no more than four bullet points, explain how audio sampling works.

22) Give a definition for each of the following and explain what happens when you increase each of them:
    a) sampling frequency   b) sampling interval   c) sample size   d) bit rate

23) Give four reasons why you might want to compress data.

24) What is the difference between lossy compression and lossless compression?

25) Give three reasons why you might want to use: a) lossy compression   b) lossless compression

*Answers on p.147

GCSE OCR Computer Science

Practice Paper 1
Computer Systems

Centre name				
Centre number				
Candidate number				

Time allowed:
- 1 hour 30 minutes

Surname	
Other names	
Candidate signature	

You **may not** use a calculator

Instructions to candidates
- Write your name and other details in the spaces provided above.
- Answer **all** questions in the spaces provided.
- Do all rough work in this book. Cross through any work you do not want to be marked.

Information for candidates
- There are 80 marks available on this paper.
- The marks available are given in brackets at the end of each question.
- Quality of extended responses will be assessed in this paper in questions marked with an asterisk (*).

For examiner's use				
Q	Attempt Nº	Q	Attempt Nº	
1		5		
2		6		
3		7		
4				
	Total			

Answer **all** questions in the spaces provided

1. Annie has a three year old laptop. She is giving it a full service before selling it on.

(a) Annie runs some 'Disk Health' utility software to check for any problems with her HDD.

(i) Define what is meant by utility software.

....

[1 mark]

(ii) Give **two** other examples of utility software.

1 ....

2 ....

[2 marks]

(b) The utility reports that Annie's hard disk is 25% fragmented.

(i) Explain **one** problem caused by a fragmented hard disk.

....

....

[2 marks]

(ii) Briefly describe the defragmentation process.

....

....

....

[3 marks]

(c) Annie also plans to perform a disk clean-up. Suggest why it could be better to do the disk clean-up before defragmentation, rather than afterwards.

....

....

[1 mark]

(d) Annie is considering getting a new laptop with an SSD rather than an HDD. Give **three** advantages of choosing an SSD over an HDD.

1 ....

2 ....

3 ....

[3 marks]

2. Karen stores her holiday pictures in the cloud. She decides to download an image from the cloud to her laptop.

(a) Define what is meant by the cloud.

....

[1 mark]

(b) Karen's laptop and the cloud server have a client-server relationship.
Describe the communication that takes place between the cloud server and Karen's laptop when she downloads the image.

....

....

[2 marks]

(c) The image is transferred from the cloud server to Karen's laptop using packets.

(i) Explain how packets are used to transfer the image over the Internet to Karen's laptop.

....

....

....

....

....

....

....

[6 marks]

(ii) Explain why packet switching is an efficient way to send data over large networks.

....

....

[2 marks]

(iii) State the name of the network protocol that is responsible for directing packets during the packet switching process.

....

[1 mark]

Turn over ▶

(d) The cloud hosting company uses a system of network forensics as part of its network policy.

(i) Define the term network policy.

....

[1 mark]

(ii) Explain what is meant by network forensics and how they are used.

....

....

....

....

[3 marks]

3. A Yorkshire-based television company has two studios, one based in Leeds and the other based in York. The company's computer network is shown in the diagram below.

Leeds — Local Area Network (LAN)   York — Local Area Network (LAN)

CAT5e cables

Wide Area Network (WAN) between the two sites using leased fibre optic cables.

Switch

Router   Router

Wireless Access Point (WAP)

(a) The Leeds studio uses wired connections, whereas the York studio uses wireless connections.

(i) Select words from the following list to complete the sentences below:

Ethernet   **WPA2**   **WAP**   **Coaxial**   **SQL**   **Frame**

.... is a network protocol used on wired networks.

.... is a security protocol used on wireless LANs.

[2 marks]

(ii) Describe **one** difference between a CAT5e twisted pair cable and a coaxial cable.

....

....

[2 marks]

(iii) Outline the advantages and disadvantages of each LAN setup.

The Leeds studio's wired setup: ....

....

....

The York studio's wireless setup: ....

....

....

[4 marks]

(b) The studios are connected in a Wide Area Network (WAN) using fibre optic cables.

(i) State **one** advantage of using fibre optic cables rather than copper cables in a WAN.

....

[1 mark]

(ii) Identify **one** reason why the company uses leased lines for its WAN.

....

[1 mark]

4.* Recent years have seen the increasing use of computer technology to distribute and view digital media content (music, movies and books).

Discuss the impact of the increasing use of digital media.

In your answer, you might consider:

- stakeholders
- technology
- environmental issues
- legal issues

....

....

....

....

....

....

....

....

....

....

....

....

....

....

....

....

....

....

....

....

....

....

....

....

....

....

....

....

[8 marks]

5. Hardeep wants to try a new operating system on his computer.
The new operating system is optimised for use with a touchscreen.

	Hardeep's PC	OS Minimum Requirements
Processor:	2.1 GHz, 4 cores	1.0 GHz, 4 cores
RAM:	2 GB	2 GB
Storage:	256 GB, 125 MB free	19 GB free space
GPU:	Integrated 256 MB	Dedicated 512 MB

(a) Hardeep needs to upgrade some of the components in his computer before the new operating system can be installed. State which components must be upgraded.

1 ....

2 ....

[2 marks]

(b) Would you recommend that Hardeep upgrades any other components in his computer? Explain your answer.

....

....

[2 marks]

(c) Explain why an operating system requires a certain amount of RAM.

....

....

[2 marks]

(d) The new operating system's GUI is optimised for touchscreen use. Describe **two** features that a GUI may include to take advantage of touchscreen technology.

1 ....

....

2 ....

....

[4 marks]

Turn over ▶

124

6. Dishley Academy stores personal information about pupils, such as name, age, address and phone number, on their network.

(a) For the following actions, tick the corresponding box to show whether or not they would be allowed under the Data Protection Act 1998.

	Allowed	Not Allowed
Giving each teacher a USB flash drive containing the personal information of all the pupils who have attended the school.		
Transferring pupils' personal information to their new school when they leave.		
Refusing to tell a parent what information is being stored about their son/daughter.		
Backing up pupils' personal information on a drive that is stored in a locked safe.		
Using pupils' personal information to get in contact with their parents.		
Putting pupils' personal information on the school website to make it easier for teachers and parents to access.		

[6 marks]

(b) The IT technicians at the academy want to protect pupils' data against possible network attacks. Describe **two** different types of network attack, and suggest a method that could be used to protect against it.

Type of attack: ....

Description: ....

....

Method of protection: ....

Type of attack: ....

Description: ....

....

Method of protection: ....

[6 marks]

7. A company has its employees' computers spread across four floors.
The computers on each floor are connected to that floor's server in a star network.
Employees need to access files on all of the servers, so each of the four servers are connected in another star network, with a central switch located on the ground floor.

(a) Describe the effect that the central switch failing would have on the rest of the network.

....

....
[2 marks]

(b) The company decides to remove the switch from the network and instead connect the four servers in a full mesh network, as shown in this diagram.

Explain the advantages and disadvantages to the company of connecting the servers together in a full mesh network instead of a star network.

....

....

....

....

....
[4 marks]

Turn over ▶

(c) At the end of every day, the servers run a backup utility to decide whether to do an incremental backup, full backup or no backup. The utility uses two different variables:

- `incTotal` stores the number of edited files since the last backup of any kind.
- `fullTotal` stores the number of edited files since the last full backup.

The number of files that have been edited each day are added to both variables. If the value of `incTotal` reaches 200, then the utility takes an incremental backup, and `incTotal` is set to 0. However, if the value of `fullTotal` reaches 1000, then a full backup is taken **instead**, and `fullTotal` and `incTotal` are set to 0.

Write an algorithm to demonstrate the function of the backup utility.

....

....

....

....

....

....

....

....

....

....

....

....

....

....

[6 marks]

END OF QUESTIONS

Practice Paper 2

This practice paper will test you on Sections 4-7 of this book and features more algorithm-based questions than Practice Paper 1 — this will be the case in the real exams as well.

GCSE OCR Computer Science

Practice Paper 2
Computational Thinking, Algorithms and Programming

Centre name				
Centre number				
Candidate number				

Time allowed:
*   1 hour 30 minutes

Surname	
Other names	
Candidate signature	

You **may not** use a calculator

Instructions to candidates
*   Write your name and other details in the spaces provided above.
*   Answer **all** questions in the spaces provided.
*   Do all rough work in this book. Cross through any work you do not want to be marked.

Information for candidates
*   There are 80 marks available on this paper.
*   The marks available are given in brackets at the end of each question.

For examiner's use

Q	Attempt Nº	Q	Attempt Nº
1		6	
2		7	
3		8	
4		9	
5			
		Total	

Answer **all** questions in the spaces provided

1. A petrol station needs a program to calculate the cost of fuel for each customer.

(a) Identify appropriate data types for:

(i) The name of the fuel that the customer used.

....

[1 mark]

(ii) The total cost of the customer's fuel.

....

[1 mark]

(b) Explain why it's important to use the correct data type to store information.

....

....

....

[2 marks]

(c) Describe, with an example, how the function str() might be used
when printing the receipt.

....

....

....

[2 marks]

(d) The source code for the program needs to be translated into machine code.
Outline **two** differences in the way a compiler and interpreter would translate
the program.

1 ....

....

2 ....

....

[4 marks]

2. **(a)** Convert the binary number 10101000 into denary.

....

....
[2 marks]

(b) Convert the binary number 10110101 into hexadecimal.

....

....
[2 marks]

(c) Calculate the sum of the binary numbers 10101000 and 10110101.

....

....
[1 mark]

(d) When a computer tried to add the binary numbers in part (c) together,
an overflow error occurred. What is meant by the term 'overflow error'?

....

....
[1 mark]

3. Lenny is writing a program for an exercise bike that adjusts the difficulty
based on information about the user.

(a) One of Lenny's sub programs takes `weight` as a parameter.

(i) Define what is meant by a 'parameter'.

....
[1 mark]

(ii) What is the scope of a parameter?

....
[1 mark]

(iii) Outline how arguments are different from parameters.

....
[1 mark]

Turn over ▶

(b) The code below appears near the start of Lenny's program.

```
global difficulty
input weight
procedure setInitialDifficulty(weight)
    difficulty = weight DIV 6
endprocedure
```

(i) Explain what the first line of this code does.

....

....

[2 marks]

(ii) Describe what the `setInitialDifficulty` procedure does.

....

....

[2 marks]

(c) Lenny wants a sub program that adjusts the difficulty depending on the user's heart rate.

- If their heart rate is below 90 then the difficulty level should be increased by 1.
- If their heart rate is over 140 then the difficulty level should be decreased by 1.
- If their heart rate is over 160 then the difficulty level should be set to 0 and the warning message "Slow Down!" should appear.

Write a sub program that takes heart rate as a parameter and adjusts the difficulty level as stated above.

....

....

....

....

....

....

....

....

[4 marks]

4. A car uses a logic circuit to decide whether to start the engine or not.

- The car has two buttons, labelled **S** (START) and **D** (DRIVE). If both buttons are on, the engine will start.

- The engine also starts if the ignition switch **I** is turned on.

(a) Draw the logic circuit diagram for this system, with **Z** as an output.

[3 marks]

(b) Fill in the missing values in the truth table for the logic circuit above.

S	D	I	Z
0	1		0
		0	1
1			0

[3 marks]

5. Every 5 minutes, an app on a mobile phone records the electrical current (in mA) passing through a pair of connected headphones. A sample of the readings is shown in the table below.

| 10 mA | 15 mA | 12 mA | 18 mA | 20 mA |

(a) Show the stages of a linear search to find the value '12 mA' in the list above.

....

....

....

....

....

....

[2 marks]

(b) If a reading is greater than 30 mA, the mobile phone will buzz and the program will stop. If not, the program will wait 5 minutes before taking another reading. Draw a flow diagram to show this program.

[6 marks]

6. Florence is a graphic designer for a publishing company. The image editing software that she uses represents each unique colour as a six digit hex code.

(a) As a power of 16, how many possible unique colours could Florence use?

....

[1 mark]

(b) Explain **one** benefit to programmers of using hex codes to represent the different colours.

....

....

....

[2 marks]

Florence saves the same image as three different file types (shown in the table below).

File Type	JPEG	PNG	TIFF
Size	0.2 MB	1 MB	0.9 MB

(c) One of the file types uses lossy compression. State and explain which file type is most likely to be an example of lossy compression.

....

....

....

[2 marks]

(d) Evaluate the impact if Florence always used lossless compression to store all her images.

....

....

....

....

....

[4 marks]

(e) Give **two** pieces of metadata that are often included in image files.

1 ....

2 ....

[2 marks]

Turn over ▶

7. Tony is writing a program to calculate a player's score in a dice game.
A player starts with a score of 0 and rolls a six-sided dice as many times as they want.
After each roll they add the number the dice lands on to their score. The aim is to get
as close to 21 as possible. If you go over 21 you get a score of 0.

The flow diagram below shows an initial design for his program.

(a) Tony designs a test plan for his program.
Explain why it's important for the test plan to include erroneous test data.

....

....

[2 marks]

(b) Tony tests each of the following sequences of inputs in his program.
For each test, state the type of test data, the intended outcome,
and what the actual outcome will be with his program's current design.

(i) 5, 6, 4, 3, 2

Type of data: ....

Intended Outcome: ....

Actual Outcome: ....

[3 marks]

(ii) 5, 9, 3, 2

Type of data: ....

Intended Outcome: ....

Actual Outcome: ....

[3 marks]

(c) Identify **two** ways that Tony could use input validation in his program.

1 ....

2 ....

[2 marks]

8. A comic book shop stores information about each of its comics in records.
The table below shows two records stored in the comics table.

ID No.	Title	Date published	Length	Genre	Rating
0001	Hike of Hope	04-05-2015	82	Adventure	5
0002	Space Voyage	05-09-2015	65	Science Fiction	4

(a) Explain why the comic book shop has chosen to store this information in records rather than an array.

....

....

....
[2 marks]

(b) Write an SQL query to return:

(i) the titles of all Science Fiction comics.

....
[2 marks]

(ii) the titles and lengths of all the comics that have fewer than 50 pages and a rating of 3.

....
[2 marks]

(iii) all the fields for comics with titles that begin with the letter H.

....
[2 marks]

9. The Prime Koalas are a band consisting of four members:
John on guitar, Paul on bass, Cheryl on vocals and Ida on drums.

(a) Complete the code below to generate a 2D array containing the names and instruments of all the band members.

```
array primeKoalas[4, 2]
primeKoalas[0, 0] = "John"
primeKoalas[1, 0] = "Paul"
primeKoalas[2, 0] = "Cheryl"
primeKoalas[3, 0] = "Ida"
```

[2 marks]

Turn over ▶

(b) John wants to open the empty text file called musicians.txt and write to it.
Each line of the file should contain a different band member and their instrument.
Write an algorithm that uses your array in part (a) to write this information to the text file.

....

....

....

....

....

....

....

....

[3 marks]

(c) The sub program toSpeech() takes a string as a parameter, turns the string into audio data and reads it out loud. Write a procedure using toSpeech() that takes a file name as a parameter and reads out all the data in the file.

....

....

....

....

....

....

....

....

....

....

....

....

[5 marks]

END OF QUESTIONS

Section One —
Components of a Computer System

Page 4 (Warm-Up Questions)

1 E.g.
- Power supply
- Case cooling fan
- CPU
- Heat sink
- Optical drive
- RAM
- Hard Disk Drive/HDD
- Graphics card/GPU
- Motherboard

2

Central Processing Unit

Control Unit
Program Counter

Other Registers
MAR

ALU
Accumulator

MDR

3 a) The accumulator stores the results of calculations done by the ALU.

   b) The MAR holds any memory address about to be used by the CPU.

   c) The MDR holds data or instructions that have been fetched from / are about to be written to memory.

Page 5 (Exam Questions)

3 a) A computer system built into another device. *[1 mark]*

   b) Any **two** devices, e.g.
   - Dishwasher *[1 mark]*
   - MP3 player *[1 mark]*
   - Digital thermometer *[1 mark]*
   - Washing machine *[1 mark]*
   - Manufacturing machinery *[1 mark]*
   [2 marks available in total]

   c) Any **two** benefits explained, e.g.
   - Embedded systems are far smaller than general purpose computers *[1 mark]* which means microwaves can be made more compact. *[1 mark]*
   - Embedded systems are cheaper to produce than general purpose computers *[1 mark]* which can reduce the costs / sale price of microwaves. *[1 mark]*
   - Embedded systems tend to be more reliable than general purpose computers *[1 mark]* which means that microwaves are less likely to break. *[1 mark]*
   [4 marks available in total]

4 a) Any **two** functions, e.g.
   - The control unit executes instructions. *[1 mark]*
   - It follows the fetch-decode-execute cycle. *[1 mark]*
   - It controls the flow of data within the CPU. *[1 mark]*
   - It controls the flow of data between the CPU and other parts of the computer system (such as memory, and input and output devices). *[1 mark]*
   [2 marks available in total]

   b) E.g. The ALU carries out arithmetic operations, e.g. addition, subtraction and multiplication (using repeated addition). *[1 mark]* It performs logic operations on binary data, such as AND, NOT, and OR. *[1 mark]*

   c) E.g. The cache is extremely fast memory in the CPU. *[1 mark]* It stores regularly used data or instructions. *[1 mark]* The CPU can access data stored in the cache much faster than retrieving it from RAM. *[1 mark]*

Page 10 (Warm-Up Questions)

1 RAM is volatile memory that can be read from and written to, used to store files and applications while they are in use. ROM is non-volatile memory that can generally only be read, which contains the startup instructions for the computer.

2 A clock speed of 3 GHz means that the single-core processor can process 3 billion instructions per second.

3 a) Magnetic tape

   b) E.g. Optical disk / CD / DVD / Blu-Ray™

   c) Hard disk drive (HDD)

4 E.g.
   - Optical disks tend to have lower capacity.
   - USB pen drives have faster read/write speeds.
   - Optical disks are easily scratched.
   - USB pen drives are more reliable for repeatedly rewriting to.
   - USB pen drives are pocket-size so are easier to carry.

Page 11 (Exam Questions)

3 a) E.g.
   - Secondary storage is needed to store data and software in the long term. *[1 mark]*
   - Secondary storage is non-volatile memory, so retains data when there is no power. *[1 mark]*
   - Computers could not function without permanent data storage, as all software and data would be lost when switched off. *[1 mark]*
   - Secondary storage has a high capacity, so you can store a lot more data. *[1 mark]*
   [3 marks available in total]

   b) Any **two** advantages, e.g.
   - Optical discs have a low cost per GB. *[1 mark]*
   - They are highly portable. *[1 mark]*
   - They are durable against shock and water damage. *[1 mark]*
   Any **two** disadvantages, e.g.
   - They are very slow to write to. *[1 mark]*
   - They require an optical drive to be read / written. *[1 mark]*
   - They can be scratched easily. *[1 mark]*
   - They have a low capacity compared to other forms of storage, e.g. flash memory cards. *[1 mark]*
   [4 marks available in total]

4 a) Cache is much faster than RAM. *[1 mark]* The larger the cache, the more data can be stored for quick access by the CPU, meaning the CPU should perform better. *[1 mark]*

   b) E.g. Jackson's CPU has more cores than Will's CPU, which should mean better performance. *[1 mark]* It also has a larger cache than Will's, which should again lead to better CPU performance. *[1 mark]* On the other hand Will's CPU has a higher clock speed than Jackson's, so there is a chance that Will's may give better performance than Jackson's. *[1 mark]* Overall, it is hard to tell whether Will's CPU will offer better performance, therefore it seems unwise to buy Will's CPU, as it may be no better than Jackson's current one. *[1 mark]*
   If you'd decided that Will's CPU was the best option, you'd still get the marks as long as you'd put together a sensible argument based on comparisons of the CPU specs.

   c) E.g. Increasing the amount of RAM increases the amount of data / number of applications that the computer can hold in memory. *[1 mark]* Jackson may not use all of the current RAM in his computer, as he may use undemanding software or he may not open many programs at once *[1 mark]* so adding more RAM will not improve performance. *[1 mark]*
   [2 marks available in total]

Page 17 (Warm-Up Questions)

1 E.g.
- User account control
- Password/pin protection
- Pattern locking
- Fingerprint/retina scanning

2 A compression utility reduces the size of a file so that it takes up less disk space/transfers quicker/etc.

3

	Open Source	Proprietary
OS	Linux	macOS®
Utility		Windows® Firewall
Other	VLC Media Player	Adobe® Photoshop®

Page 18 (Exam Questions)

3 a) E.g.
- Open source software is software where the source code is made freely available. *[1 mark]*
- Users can legally modify the source code to make their own version of the software. *[1 mark]*
- Modified versions of the original source code can be shared under the same license as the original software. *[1 mark]*
[2 marks available in total]

  b) Any **one** advantage, e.g.
- It's usually free of charge. *[1 mark]* Free software can be used as a marketing tool — once the device is paid for, the user won't need to pay for any more software. *[1 mark]*
- The software's source code can be adapted by users *[1 mark]* which may increase the functions of the TV-PC. *[1 mark]*
- Popular open source software can be very reliable as problems may be quickly fixed by the community or developers *[1 mark]* meaning Ioteck may not need to work on / push out their own updates. *[1 mark]*
Any **one** disadvantage, e.g.
- They may have unpatched holes in security *[1 mark]*, which could worry customers and reduce sales of the product. *[1 mark]*
- If there are problems with the open source software *[1 mark]* Ioteck may not have any support from the software developers. *[1 mark]*
- Ioteck won't be able to make money by selling their own proprietary software, *[1 mark]* so they may make less profit from the product overall. *[1 mark]*
[4 marks available in total]

4 a) A full backup is where a copy is taken of every file on the system. *[1 mark]* An incremental backup is where only the files modified or created since the last backup are copied. *[1 mark]*

  b) E.g. The company could do full backups once a fortnight, *[1 mark]* but do incremental backups twice a day. *[1 mark]* Every 6 months, the company could use data compression software to compress the previous 6 month's backups in order to reduce the file size. *[1 mark]* Backup disks / tapes can then be placed in a fireproof box / locked safe or kept on a different site to protect against fire / flood / theft. *[1 mark]*

5 E.g.
- When applications / programs / files are opened, the OS moves the necessary parts to memory. *[1 mark]*
- The OS will remove unneeded data from memory, e.g. when programs or files are closed. *[1 mark]*
- The OS divides memory into segments. When different programs are used, their data is placed into different segments so that running applications can not write over or interfere with each other. *[1 mark]*
- The OS organises the movement of data to and from virtual memory. *[1 mark]*
- The OS divides CPU time between running applications / programs / processes, as it can only process one at a time. *[1 mark]*
- The OS can prioritise CPU time for different programs in order for them to be processed in the most efficient order. *[1 mark]*
[6 marks available in total — award a maximum of 4 marks for points about RAM or CPU time]

Section Two — Networks

Page 25 (Warm-Up Questions)

1 E.g.
- Network Interface Controller (NIC)
- Switch
- Ethernet cables
- Wireless Access Point (WAP)

2 Clients send requests for data/services to the server, which processes the requests and then replies.

3 E.g. video calling/file sharing/etc.

4

No. of devices	Star	Partial Mesh	Full Mesh
4			
5			
6			

For the partial mesh topology, there are lots of possible answers — all you need is for all nodes to be indirectly linked to each other and for there to be more than one way to get between some of the nodes.

Page 26 (Exam Questions)

2 a) Ethernet is wired, Wi-Fi® is wireless *[1 mark]*

  b) Switch: directs data between devices in a LAN. *[1 mark]*
  Router: transmits data between separate networks / across a WAN / across the Internet. *[1 mark]*
  WAP: allows devices to connect to a LAN wirelessly. *[1 mark]*

3 Any **one** advantage,
E.g. If a single device or connection fails on a mesh network, the network still functions as data can go along a different route. *[1 mark]* In a star network, central switch failure will cause the whole network to fail / a single connection failure will cut that device off from the network. *[1 mark]*

Any **one** disadvantage,
E.g. Devices in a mesh network need many more connections than in a star network. *[1 mark]* This requires a lot of cabling which can be expensive / impractical for networks with a large number of nodes. *[1 mark]*

4 a) A Peer-to-Peer network is a group of devices connected to share data with each other *[1 mark]* in which all devices are equal / connected without a server. *[1 mark]*
  A Client-Server network is a group of devices connected to a central computer (server) *[1 mark]* which manages the network / processes requests from devices (clients) / stores files centrally. *[1 mark]*

b) Any **two** benefits, e.g.
- User files are stored centrally so resources are used more efficiently / files are less likely to be duplicated. *[1 mark]*
- Software is easier to install / update because it is centrally stored. *[1 mark]*
- Servers are more reliable than peer machines. *[1 mark]*
- It is easier to backup data centrally. *[1 mark]*
- There is greater security as anti-malware software can be installed centrally / user access to files can be controlled. *[1 mark]*

Any **two** drawbacks, e.g.
- Client-Server networks are expensive to set up. *[1 mark]*
- The business would need to employ an IT specialist to maintain the server / network. *[1 mark]*
- If the server fails then all the client computers lose access to their files / client computers are dependent on the server. *[1 mark]*
[4 marks available in total]

Page 34 (Warm-Up Questions)

1

Protocol	Function
TCP	Sets rules for how devices connect on the network / splits data into packets / reassembles packets into original data / checks data is sent and delivered.
IP	Responsible for packet switching.
HTTP	Used by web browsers to access websites / communicate with web servers.
HTTPS	A more secure version of HTTP.
FTP	Used to access, edit and move files on other devices.
SMTP	Used to send emails / transfer emails between servers.
IMAP	Used to retrieve emails from a server. The user downloads a copy of the email and the server holds the original email until the user deletes it.
POP3	Used to retrieve emails from a server. The server holds the email until the user downloads it, at which point the server deletes it.

2 a) Trojan
   b) Rootkit
   c) Worm
   d) Ransomware

Pages 35-36 (Exam Questions)

2 a) The Internet is a global network of networks. *[1 mark]* The World Wide Web is a collection of websites hosted on web servers. *[1 mark]*

   b) A Domain Name Server translates a website's domain name into its IP address / stores domain names of websites in a directory. *[1 mark]*

3 a) E.g.
   - IP addresses are used to identify devices on a network / on the Internet. *[1 mark]*
   - Routers use IP addresses to direct data packets to the correct destination. *[1 mark]*
   [2 marks available in total]

   b) E.g.
   - Holly's laptop checks periodically that all packets have been received. *[1 mark]*
   - If Holly's laptop does not receive all the packets in a certain amount of time it sends a timeout message back to the smartphone. *[1 mark]*
   - Mahindar's smartphone resends the email / packet. *[1 mark]*
   - Holly's laptop uses the packet numbers to reassemble them into the correct order. *[1 mark]*
   [3 marks available in total]

4 a) E.g.
   - Different user access levels prevent students from accessing the same data as teachers, including sensitive data like their peers' personal information. *[1 mark]*
   - Different user access levels prevent a student from maliciously deleting or editing data. *[1 mark]*
   - Different user access levels prevent students accidentally deleting or editing important files. *[1 mark]*
   - Different user access levels allow network administrators to flexibly change the amount of access students and staff have to certain files. *[1 mark]*
   [3 marks available in total]

   b) i) A brute force attack is a type of attack on a network which uses trial and error to crack passwords *[1 mark]* by employing automated software to produce hundreds of likely combinations. *[1 mark]*

      ii) Any **two** measures, e.g.
      - The school can lock access to user accounts after a certain number of password attempts. *[1 mark]*
      - The school can ensure that strong passwords are used / the school can ensure that passwords are long enough / the school can ensure that passwords are made of a mix of different types of character. *[1 mark]*
      - The school can add additional security checks, like using a secret question or CAPTCHA test. *[1 mark]*
      [2 marks available in total]

5 a) E.g.
   - A MAC address is a unique identifier. *[1 mark]*
   - A MAC address is assigned to the hardware of every network-enabled device. *[1 mark]*
   - MAC addresses are used to direct data to the right device on a network. *[1 mark]*
   [2 marks available in total]

   b) i) A layer of network protocols is a group of protocols with similar functions *[1 mark]* that cover one particular aspect of network communications. *[1 mark]*

      ii) E.g.
      - Data link layer *[1 mark]* Function: passing data over the physical network / sending data bits as electrical signals over cables, wireless and other hardware. *[1 mark]*
      - Network layer *[1 mark]* Function: making connections between networks / directing data packets / handling traffic. *[1 mark]*
      - Transport layer *[1 mark]* Function: controlling data flow / splitting data into packets / checking packets are correctly sent and delivered. *[1 mark]*
      - Application layer *[1 mark]* Function: turning data into websites and other applications / turning websites and other applications into data. *[1 mark]*
      [2 marks available in total]

      iii) Any **three** benefits, e.g.
      - Layers break network communication into manageable pieces. *[1 mark]*
      - Layers allow developers to focus on one area of the network without worrying about the others. *[1 mark]*
      - Layers are self-contained. *[1 mark]*
      - There are set rules for each layer. *[1 mark]*
      - Layers allow interoperability / layers make companies produce compatible, universal hardware and software. *[1 mark]*
      [3 marks available in total]

6 Points you might include:

Advantages of the cloud
- Users can access files from any location, so the company and authors can work on the same files without having to email or post manuscripts.
- Cloud storage is managed by the hosting company which will be a cheaper alternative to managing their own storage.
- The hosting company manages the security of data in the cloud, so the publishing company does not need to spend time securing its data.
- The hosting company is responsible for backing up data in the cloud, so the publishing company does not need to invest in any additional hardware to ensure data is backed up correctly.
- The publishing company could use cloud-based software rather than installing it on their machines and keeping it up to date. This could give writers access to the same software.

Disadvantages of the cloud
- An Internet connection is required to access the cloud, and maintaining a steady Internet connection can be difficult in rural areas.
- The publishing company is dependent on the hosting company for the security in the cloud, meaning the publishing company has very little control over the security of its data.
- The publishing company is dependent on the hosting company for backing up their data.
- Cloud software may require a monthly subscription which may be more expensive than buying computer licences.

How to mark your answer:
- Two or three brief points with very little explanation. *[1-2 marks]*
- Three or four detailed points covering both advantages and disadvantages. *[3-4 marks]*
- Five or more detailed points that form a well-written, balanced discussion, covering both advantages and disadvantages. *[5-6 marks]*
  Make sure your answer is relevant to the situation you're given — the company in the question has particular needs and qualities which you shouldn't ignore.

7 Points you might include:

The threats posed to the firm's network
- Hackers could use rootkits, spyware and other malware to steal confidential information.
- Employees unaware of the potential dangers could be tricked into giving criminals sensitive information through social engineering.
- Disgruntled employees could use their position to attack the network, e.g. by releasing malware onto the network from a USB drive.
- Hackers with packet sniffers or other similar tools could intercept and read information entering or leaving the company's network.
- Hackers could use a brute force attack to crack weak passwords.

What a good network policy would include
- Automatic encryption of all data leaving and entering the network.
- Installing anti-malware and firewall software.
- Regular penetration testing to find problems in the network security.
- Education of employees on the dangers of social engineering.
- Mandatory use of strong passwords / passwords that are changed regularly.
- An acceptable use policy that all employees must sign.
- Controlling physical access to hardware / the network, e.g. keeping servers in locked rooms.
- Different user access levels given to different groups of users.

How a good network policy would prevent potential attacks on the firm's network.
- A firewall would prevent harmful malware from entering the network.
- Education of employees could prevent social engineering.
- Different user access levels and physical security measures could limit the dangers of an insider attack.
- Encrypting data could prevent intercepted data from being read by hackers and criminals.
- Using strong passwords could prevent successful brute force attacks.

How to mark your answer:
- Two or three points with very little explanation. *[1-2 marks]*
- Three to five points with detailed explanation. *[3-5 marks]*
- Six or more detailed points that form a well-written, balanced discussion. *[6-8 marks]*

Section Three — Issues

Page 43 (Warm-Up Questions)

1

	Censorship	Surveillance
A business monitors what their employees view online.		✓
A country's government blocks access to Facebook®.	✓	
A government agency intercepts emails containing certain words.		✓
A school restricts access to harmful websites.	✓	
An Internet Service Provider collects data on browsing habits.		✓

2 E.g.
- Eyestrain — use suitable lighting / keep a good distance from the screen / take regular breaks.
- Repetitive Strain Injury (RSI) — ensure good posture / arrange your desk appropriately / take regular breaks.
- Back pain — ensure good posture / use adjustable equipment / sit at a suitable angle.

3 The digital divide is the separation between people who have ready access to technology and those who don't, who tend to be at a disadvantage because of this.

Page 44 (Exam Questions)

2 a) An individual or group of people with an interest in a particular decision / are affected by a particular outcome. *[1 mark]*

   b) Any **two** stakeholders, e.g.
   - Business owners / managers *[1 mark]* — positive *[1 mark]* because they receive increased profits and do not have to pay the staff. *[1 mark]*
   - Checkout staff *[1 mark]* — negative *[1 mark]* because they have lost their jobs. *[1 mark]*

3 a) E.g.
   - The Internet / social media / email mean Tom can be contacted at any time of day. *[1 mark]*
   - Tom may be expected to carry a smartphone so he can be contacted by his boss at all times. *[1 mark]*
   - Tom's smartphone may alert him when he receives work emails from clients. These can be hard to ignore. *[1 mark]*
   [2 marks available in total]

   b) E.g.
   - Companies try to influence people into using their new product, e.g. by using advertisements. *[1 mark]*
   - Many children may feel peer pressure to buy the new devices for fear of being bullied by their classmates. *[1 mark]*
   - Parents can feel pressured to buy the latest technology for their children. *[1 mark]*
   [2 marks available in total]

c) Any **one** reason, e.g.
- They might not have a lot of money *[1 mark]* so cannot afford to buy expensive electronic devices. *[1 mark]*
- They might live in a rural area *[1 mark]* so could have poor network coverage. *[1 mark]*
- They might have little knowledge of how to use the Internet or electronic devices *[1 mark]* so feel too intimidated to use them. *[1 mark]*

[2 marks available in total]

4 Points you might include:

Stakeholders
- Manufacturing businesses can cut costs by getting the same products made without having to pay any wages.
- Workers in the manufacturing sector could become unemployed, as robots take over their jobs.
- Consumers could be able to buy the same products for less, as the costs involved in making them could be lower.

Technology
- The hardware and software of robots may not be sophisticated enough to fully replicate the work of human employees.
- The increased use of robots in the workplace could help improve them as problems can be identified and fixed.
- Successful use of robots in manufacturing could lead to their application in other areas of work.

Ethical issues
- Manufacturing businesses could leave hundreds of people without jobs in order to pursue profit.
- There is currently a lack of awareness and rules around the use of robots in the workplace.
- By allowing robots to do the routine jobs, workers are free to do more interesting, creative and fulfilling work.
- New jobs are created to program, maintain and manufacture the robots.
- Robots can perform hazardous tasks, meaning there could be fewer injuries in the workplace.

How to mark your answer:
- Two or three brief points with very little explanation. *[1-2 marks]*
- Three or four detailed points covering at least two of: stakeholders, technology and ethical issues. *[3-4 marks]*
- Five or more detailed points that form a well-written, balanced discussion, covering all of: stakeholders, technology and ethical issues. *[5-6 marks]*

Page 48 (Warm-Up Questions)

1 Copper, platinum, plastic, mercury, gold and silver.

2 a) Data Protection Act 1998
  b) Computer Misuse Act 1990
  c) Freedom of Information Act 2000
  d) Data Protection Act 1998
  e) Computer Misuse Act 1990

3 a) The copyright holder must be given credit.
  b) The work cannot be used for financial or commercial gain.
  c) Modified works can only be distributed with the same terms as those applied to the original.
  d) The work cannot be modified or built upon.

Page 49 (Exam Questions)

3 a) A way of protecting intellectual property / a way of protecting something that has been created / a way of protecting written and recorded content, e.g. books, music, films, software and video games. *[1 mark]*
  b) Works in the public domain are those whose copyright has expired / works which do not have any copyright attached to them *[1 mark]* meaning they can be shared and copied without normal copyright rules being applied. *[1 mark]*

4 a) E-waste is discarded computer material / discarded electronic material. *[1 mark]*
  b) Any **two** reasons, e.g.
  - Smartphones are portable, so can be broken easily, for example by dropping them. *[1 mark]*
  - Smartphones are not built to last more than a few years. *[1 mark]*
  - It is often cheaper to replace a smartphone than it is to repair it. *[1 mark]*
  - Smartphone manufacturers release new devices on a regular basis and use advertisements to influence people into buying them. *[1 mark]*
  - People often want to buy the newest technology and are happy to discard their old smartphone regularly. *[1 mark]*
  - Retailers only provide short warranties on many smartphones. *[1 mark]*
  - Many people feel pressured by their peers to upgrade to the latest smartphone. *[1 mark]*

  [2 marks available in total]
  c) E.g.
  - E-waste is sent to landfill sites *[1 mark]* where toxic chemicals can enter groundwater / harm wildlife. *[1 mark]*
  - The short life span of devices also means more natural resources have to be extracted to make new devices *[1 mark]* which causes pollution and depletes scarce resources. *[1 mark]*
  - Manufacturing devices uses up a lot of electricity *[1 mark]* which is often generated using non-renewable resources. *[1 mark]*

  [4 marks available in total]
  d) E.g.
  - People can take devices to local collection facilities to be correctly disposed of according to WEEE regulations *[1 mark]* rather than throwing them out with general waste. *[1 mark]*
  - The government can put pressure on companies or local authorities to ensure WEEE regulations are being followed. *[1 mark]* The government can set recycling targets to increase the amount of e-waste that is recycled. *[1 mark]*
  - Old devices can be refurbished and reused *[1 mark]* and their raw materials can be recycled. *[1 mark]*

  [2 marks available in total]

5 Points you might include:
- The cinema should ask permission from the customer before storing their data.
- The cinema should ask the customer to sign an agreement as to how the information should be used.
- The cinema should only use the data to make it easier for customers to book seats and for contacting them for details on future films.
- The cinema should give customers the option to unsubscribe from their service, so that their data is removed from the cinema's computer system if they want.
- The cinema should be active in keeping its data up to date and allow their customers to change their details.
- The cinema should not give customers' data to third party organisations unless the customer permits it.
- The cinema should ensure that customers' data is held safely and securely, e.g. by using a firewall on its computer system and encrypting the data.

How to mark your answer:
- Two or three brief points with very little explanation. *[1-2 marks]*
- Three or four detailed points that show a good understanding of the Data Protection Act. *[3-4 marks]*
- Five or more detailed points that show a good understanding of the Data Protection Act and clearly apply it to the situation. *[5-6 marks]*

Think about each principle of the Data Protection Act and apply it to this situation.

Section Four — Algorithms

Page 54 (Warm-Up Questions)

1 Decomposition, Abstraction and Algorithmic Thinking

2 An algorithm is a process or set of instructions used to solve a problem or carry out a task.

3 B and D

4

Page 55 (Exam Questions)

2 a) It asks the user to input a height and width. *[1 mark]*
It then multiplies these values together *[1 mark]*
to get the area and prints the value of the area. *[1 mark]*

 b) $5 \times 10 = 50$ *[1 mark]*

3 a) E.g. Abstraction is picking out important details and ignoring irrelevant ones. The file uploading service will focus on the important details like the file name and ignore the unimportant details like the contents of each file.
 [3 marks available — 1 mark for a definition of abstraction, 1 mark for an example of a detail to ignore, 1 mark for an example of a detail to focus on]

 b) E.g. Decomposition breaks the programming task down into smaller problems. A programmer might focus on 'How will the service keep track of files already uploaded?' or 'How will the service compare file names?' and try to solve each programming problem individually.
 [3 marks available — 1 mark for a definition of decomposition, 1 mark for each example of decomposition up to a maximum of 2 marks]

4 Using Start / Begin. *[1 mark]*
Asking user to input x, y. *[1 mark]*
Using SqMove (with correct subroutine box). *[1 mark]*
Decision box with appropriate question. *[1 mark]*
Creating a loop to repeat SqMove. *[1 mark]*
Using Stop / End. *[1 mark]*
E.g.

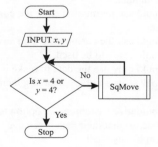

Page 60 (Warm-Up Questions)

1 a) Middle item = $(7 + 1) / 2$ = 4th item = 11
11 is bigger than 8 so take left hand side.
3, 6, 8
Middle item = $(3 + 1) / 2$ = 2nd item = 6
6 is smaller than 8 so take right hand side.
8
Middle item = $(1 + 1) / 2$ = 1st item = 8
Stop searching as 8 has been found.

 b) Check 1st item: $3 \neq 11$.
Check 2nd item: $6 \neq 11$.
Check 3rd item: $8 \neq 11$.
Check 4th item: $11 = 11$.
Stop searching as 11 has been found.

2 See page 57.

3 a) *1st pass (2 swaps):*

Chris	Beth	Dalia	Ahmed
Beth	Chris	Dalia	Ahmed
Beth	Chris	Ahmed	Dalia

 2nd pass (1 swap):

| Beth | Chris | Ahmed | Dalia |
| Beth | Ahmed | Chris | Dalia |

 3rd pass (1 swap):

| Beth | Ahmed | Chris | Dalia |
| Ahmed | Beth | Chris | Dalia |

 4th pass (no swaps — list is in order):

| Ahmed | Beth | Chris | Dalia |

 You don't necessarily need to do the last pass — since there are four items in the list, the algorithm will only take at most three passes to get the list in order.

 b)

 c)

Chris	Beth	Dalia	Ahmed
Beth	Chris	Dalia	Ahmed
Beth	Chris	Dalia	Ahmed
Ahmed	Beth	Chris	Dalia

4 Merge Sort

Page 61 (Exam Questions)

3 *1st pass (3 swaps):*

5.32	5.50	5.39	6.50	6.28	6.14
5.32	5.39	5.50	6.50	6.28	6.14
5.32	5.39	5.50	6.28	6.50	6.14
5.32	5.39	5.50	6.28	6.14	6.50

 2nd pass (1 swap):

| 5.32 | 5.39 | 5.50 | 6.28 | 6.14 | 6.50 |
| 5.32 | 5.39 | 5.50 | 6.14 | 6.28 | 6.50 |

 3rd pass (no swaps — list is in order):

| 5.32 | 5.39 | 5.50 | 6.14 | 6.28 | 6.50 |

 [4 marks available — 1 mark for each correct swap, 1 mark for correct ordered list]

4 a) Compare butterscotch to mint. *[1 mark]*
Mint is greater so split and take the left side. *[1 mark]*
A further comparison. *[1 mark]*
Correct identification of butterscotch. *[1 mark]*
E.g.
Middle item = $(5 + 1) / 2$ = 3rd item = mint.
Compare mint with butterscotch.
Butterscotch comes before mint, so take left hand side.
The list is: Butterscotch, Chocolate.
Middle item = $(2 + 1) / 2$ = 1.5 = 2nd item = chocolate.
Compare chocolate to butterscotch.
Butterscotch comes before chocolate, so take left hand side.
Middle item = $(1 + 1) / 2$ = 1st item = butterscotch.
Stop searching as butterscotch has been found.

 b) It is much more efficient / takes fewer steps for large lists of items. *[1 mark]*
You won't get the mark for just saying it's quicker or more efficient.

5 a) i)

3	7	6	2	5
7	3	6	2	5
7	6	3	2	5
7	6	3	2	5
7	6	5	3	2

 [4 marks available — 1 mark for each row from rows 2-5]

Answers

ii) E.g.

3	7	6	2	5

3	7	6		2	5

3	7		6		2	5

3	7		6	2	5

7	3	6		5	2

7	3	6	5	2

7	6	5	3	2

[4 marks available — 1 mark for correctly splitting the list into single items, 1 mark for each correct merging row]
The list doesn't split evenly so there is more than one way to get the right answer depending on how you split the items.

b) Any **one** benefit of insertion sort contrasted to merge sort, e.g.
- Insertion sort uses less memory *[1 mark]* as, unlike a merge sort, all the sorting is done on the original list. *[1 mark]*
- Insertion sort is quicker to check if a list is in order *[1 mark]* as a merge sort would still need to go through the splitting–merging process. *[1 mark]*

[2 marks available in total]

Page 62 (Revision Questions)

8 E.g.

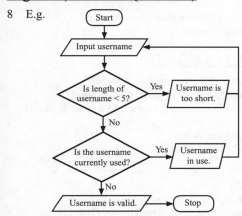

11 a) <u>Binary Search</u>:
The middle item is the 4th item, *Dagenham,* which comes before *Morpeth.* So <u>lose first half of list</u> to leave:
Morpeth, Usk, Watford
The middle item of the new list is the 2nd item, *Usk,* which comes after *Morpeth* so <u>lose second half of list</u> to leave:
Morpeth
The middle item of the new list is the 1st item, which is *Morpeth,* so you've found the correct item.
Even when there is one entry left you still have to carry on with the algorithm to check that it is the correct entry.

b) <u>Linear Search</u>:
Ashington ≠ Morpeth
Brecon ≠ Morpeth
Chester ≠ Morpeth
Dagenham ≠ Morpeth
Morpeth = Morpeth
You've found the correct item.

13 b) *1st pass (4 swaps)*:
<u>O, B</u>, A, P, G, L
B, <u>O, A</u>, P, G, L
B, A, O, <u>P, G</u>, L
B, A, O, G, <u>P, L</u>
B, A, O, G, L, P

2nd pass (3 swaps):
<u>B, A</u>, O, G, L, P
A, B, <u>O, G</u>, L, P
A, B, G, <u>O, L</u>, P
A, B, G, L, O, P

3rd pass (no swaps — list is in order):
A, B, G, L, O, P

16 a)

8	7	5	1	3	6	4	2

8	7	5	1		3	6	4	2

8	7		5	1		3	6		4	2

8	7	5	1	3	6	4	2

8	7	5	1		6	3	4	2

8	7	5	1		6	4	3	2

8	7	6	5	4	3	2	1

b) 8 <u>7</u> 5 1 3 6 4 2
    7 8 <u>5</u> 1 3 6 4 2
    5 7 8 <u>1</u> 3 6 4 2
    1 5 7 8 <u>3</u> 6 4 2
    1 3 5 7 8 <u>6</u> 4 2
    1 3 5 6 7 8 <u>4</u> 2
    1 3 4 5 6 7 8 <u>2</u>
    1 2 3 4 5 6 7 8

Section Five — Programming

Page 68 (Warm-Up Questions)

1 a) String   b) Integer   c) Real/Float   d) Boolean

2 a) 40   b) 1   c) 4   d) 19

3 a) True   b) True   c) False   d) True

4 E.g. The value of a constant is set at design time and does not change as the program is running. The value of a variable might change as the program is running.

5 a) 7   b) lob   c) LOBSTER   d) bst

Page 69 (Exam Questions)

3 a) Boolean *[1 mark]* — the variable can only take two values, either pressed or not pressed, i.e. true or false. *[1 mark]*

  b) Integer *[1 mark]* — it's measuring the number of whole seconds and whole numbers are best stored as integers. *[1 mark]*

4 Investment is declared as a constant but its value changes / it is not assigned a value when it is declared. *[1 mark]*
Interest is declared as an integer but it should be able to take non-integer values. *[1 mark]*

5 a) Joining together two or more strings. *[1 mark]*

  b) ORA2000 *[1 mark]*

  c) 05 fruit = fruit.upper *[1 mark]*
      06 prodID = fruit.subString(0, 3) *[1 mark]*
                  + str(volume) *[1 mark]*

Page 74 (Warm-Up Questions)

1 a) Iteration   b) Selection   c) Selection
  d) Iteration   e) Selection   f) Iteration

2 E.g. A SWITCH-CASE statement makes selections based solely on the value of one variable, an if-elseif statement makes selections based on any conditions that are true or false.

3 a) Count-controlled loop: FOR loop
Condition-controlled loop: E.g. DO UNTIL loop

  b) A FOR loop will iterate a specified number of times.
A DO UNTIL loop will keep iterating until a specific condition is satisfied.

4 a) False   b) True   c) True   d) True

Page 75 (Exam Questions)

3   a)   Sequence *[1 mark]*

    b)   2 hours and 30 minutes *[1 mark]*

4   a)   Using an IF-ELSE or nested IF statement. *[1 mark]*
         Using the correct conditions to check all settings. *[1 mark]*
         Changing the temperature correctly for each setting. *[1 mark]*
         E.g.
         int setting, temperature
         if setting == 3 then
            temperature = 50
         elseif setting == 2 then
            temperature = 30
         elseif setting == 1 then
            temperature = 20
         else
            temperature = 0
         endif

    b)   Any **two** reasons, e.g.
         • You only need to check the value of one variable. *[1 mark]*
         • The setting variable only has a set number of possible values. *[1 mark]*

5   Using an appropriate selection statement. *[1 mark]*
    A Boolean condition that checks each of the conditions. *[1 mark]*
    Allowing the dryer to start if conditions are met. *[1 mark]*
    E.g.
    real weight
    bool allowStart, doorClosed
    if (weight > 1.5 AND weight < 15.0) AND doorClosed == true
    then
       allowStart = true
    else
       allowStart = false
    endif

6   Count controlled loop to allow 10 games. *[1 mark]*
    Asking for an input of the winner's name for each game. *[1 mark]*
    A selection statement for the winner of each game. *[1 mark]*
    Adding 1 to the winner's score. *[1 mark]*
    A selection statement to find the overall winner. *[1 mark]*
    Printing the correct message depending on the scores. *[1 mark]*
    E.g.
    int karlWin = 0
    int johnWin = 0
    string winner
    for i = 1 to 10
       winner = input("Enter the winner's name")
       switch winner:
       case "Karl":
          karlWin = karlWin + 1
       case "John":
          johnWin = johnWin + 1
       endswitch
    next i
    if karlWin > johnWin then
       print("The winner is Karl.")
    elseif johnWin > karlWin then
       print("The winner is John.")
    else
       print("The game is a draw.")
    endif
    To make your algorithm more robust you could have used input
    validation to make sure winner was either "Karl" or "John". You could
    also have named the variables differently so that the game could be
    played by any two players regardless of their name.

Page 83 (Warm-Up Questions)

1   a)   Assigns the 4th element in the array to the variable 'player'.

    b)   Replaces the 6th element of the array with the string "Pele".

2   a)   openRead()   b) openWrite()   c) close()   d) readLine()

3   E.g.
    • A record can store different data types.
    • Names can be given to the different fields.
    • Record structures cannot accidently be changed later on.

4   a)   SELECT — the fields you want to return.

    b)   FROM — the table you want to get the data from.

    c)   WHERE — A condition that has to be true for a record to be returned.

    d)   LIKE — A pattern of data to look for.

5   Any **three** benefits, e.g.
    • You only have to write them once so you don't have to repeat blocks of code.
    • You can call them from anywhere in the program.
    • You only have to debug them once.
    • They will improve the readability / maintainability of the code.
    • They break the program down into smaller more manageable chunks.

6   Arguments are the actual values that parameters take when the sub program is called.

Pages 84-85 (Exam Questions)

2   A function that takes a single parameter. *[1 mark]*
    Finding the cube and square of the parameter. *[1 mark]*
    Returning the difference between the cube and square. *[1 mark]*
    E.g.
    function cubeSquare(numberInt)
       return(numberInt^3 – numberInt^2)
    endfunction

3   a)   String *[1 mark]*

    b)   Any **three** reasons, e.g.
         • Multiple items of data need to be stored. *[1 mark]*
         • All the data being stored has the same data type. *[1 mark]*
         • The data is split by two categories / can be represented in a table so a 2D array is useful for storing it. *[1 mark]*
         • Stores the data together under one variable name. *[1 mark]*
         • Accessing the information is more efficient. A single command, e.g. *sportsDay[position, event]* can be used to access any name from the array. *[1 mark]*
         [3 marks available in total — at least one reason must specifically mention 2D arrays.]

4   a)   5 *[1 mark]*

    b)   A record is a data structure used to store multiple pieces of data about one thing together (e.g. information about a particular car). *[1 mark]* A field is one of the items in a record that contains a particular piece of data (e.g. car registration or car make). *[1 mark]*
         Just saying that records are rows of the table and fields are columns will not be awarded any marks.

    c)

Make	Type
Stanton	Hatchback
Stanton	Saloon

         [2 marks available — 1 mark for each correct record]

5 a) *print(distanceRun[4, 3]) [1 mark]*

   b) Asking the user to input the runner number. *[1 mark]*
       Using a FOR loop. *[1 mark]*
       Adding all elements correctly. *[1 mark]*
       Printing the total distance. *[1 mark]*
       E.g.
       int totalDistance = 0
       int runner
       runner = input("Choose a runner number from 0-3")
       for i = 0 to 6
       *   totalDistance = totalDistance + distanceRun[i, runner]*
       next i
       print(totalDistance)

   c) A FOR loop going from 0 to 3. *[1 mark]*
       A FOR loop going from 0 to 6. *[1 mark]*
       Using milesConvert() on each element of the array. *[1 mark]*
       E.g.
       for i = 0 to 3
       *   for j = 0 to 6*
       *   distanceRun[i, j] = milesConvert(distanceRun[i, j])*
       *   next j*
       next i

6 Opening the story in read mode. *[1 mark]*
   A condition-controlled loop to stop at the end of the file. *[1 mark]*
   Waiting for a keypress input. *[1 mark]*
   Using a selection statement to check the user's input. *[1 mark]*
   Printing the next line of the story. *[1 mark]*
   E.g.
   char keypress
   story = openRead("adventure.txt")
   while NOT story.endOfFile()
   *   input keypress*
   *   if keypress == "y" then*
   *   print(story.readLine())*
   *   endif*
   endwhile
   story.close()

7 a) Any **two** differences, e.g.
       • Local variables can only be changed and accessed from
         within the part of the program they're declared in. *[1 mark]*
         Global variables can be changed and accessed from anywhere
         in the program. *[1 mark]*
       • The same local variable name can be used in different
         sub programs and declared differently each time. *[1 mark]*
         Global variable names can only be declared once. *[1 mark]*
       • Local variables are declared inside part of a program (e.g.
         in a sub program). *[1 mark]* Global variables are usually
         declared at the start of the main program. *[1 mark]*
       [4 marks available in total]

   b) A function that takes the number of sides the dice
       have as a parameter. *[1 mark]*
       Using a condition controlled loop. *[1 mark]*
       Simulating two dice rolls. *[1 mark]*
       Increasing the score by 1 after each roll. *[1 mark]*
       Returning the score. *[1 mark]*
       E.g.
       function rollDouble(side)
       *   int score = 0*
       *   int x, y*
       *   do*
       *   x = roll(side)*
       *   y = roll(side)*
       *   score = score + 1*
       *   until x == y*
       *   return(score)*
       endfunction

Page 86 (Revision Questions)

9 *string first_day*
   first_day = input("Enter the first day of the month")
   if first_day == "Sunday" OR first_day == "Monday" then
   *   print("The month has 5 Mondays")*
   else
   *   print("The month has 4 Mondays")*
   endif

11 a) *print(chars[4])*

   b) *chars[2] = "D"*
       print(chars)

   c) *for i = 0 to 9*
       *   chars[i] = "N"*
       next i
       print(chars)

12 *array multiply[10, 10]*
   for i = 0 to 9
   *   for j = 0 to 9*
   *   multiply[i, j] = i * j*
   *   next j*
   next i

15 The query will return every field of the world_records table.
   A record will be returned if the sport is athletics and the surname
   begins with an "M".

Section Six — Design, Testing and IDEs

Page 94 (Warm-Up Questions)

1 Validation checks make sure that data meets certain criteria
   before passing it into the program, while sanitisation is used
   to remove unwanted characters from data before passing it
   through the program.

2 a) Presence check

   b) Look-up table

3 E.g.
   • Clear comments
   • Indentation
   • Properly named variables/subprograms
   • Use of local (rather than global) variables where possible

4 a) False   b) True   c) True   d) False

5 Iterative testing puts the program through multiple development
   cycles, adjusting the requirements after each cycle to make the
   software closer to what the customer really wants.

6 A compiler translates all of a program's source code
   into one executable file of machine code.

7 Code Editor: used for writing code.
   Breakpoints: a debugging tool that stops the program
   at certain points.
   Error Diagnostics: highlight errors in the program.

Pages 95-96 (Exam Questions)

2 A translator turns the source code into machine code *[1 mark]*
   allowing Cynthia to run the application. *[1 mark]*

   Error Diagnostics highlight errors in the code *[1 mark]* allowing
   Cynthia to easily find and fix errors in her application. *[1 mark]*

   A Code editor allows the user to enter code and includes features
   like indenting, auto-correct, line numbering and colour coding
   [1 mark] making it a lot easier for Cynthia to write and maintain
   her application. *[1 mark]*

3 a) E.g. a test plan should take the user down all possible paths
       of the program. *[1 mark]* It should use normal, extreme and
       erroneous test data. *[1 mark]* If any of the tests get a result not
       equal to the expected outcome then the user knows there is a
       logic error. *[1 mark]*

b)

Test Data	Expected Outcome	Reasons for test
Group_Size = 4	210	Check program with data user is likely to input.
Group_Size = 9	460	Check program works with values on the limit.
Group_Size = 12	Display an error message	Check what happens if input is too large.

[5 marks available — 1 mark per box]

4 a) Any **two** reasons, e.g.
- They may need to have a greater control over the program in order to make a program with lower memory use. *[1 mark]*
- They may need to have a greater control over what the CPU does in order to make a program run quicker. *[1 mark]*
- They may be trying to maintain old code or hardware. *[1 mark]*

[2 marks available in total]

b) Assembly languages are more readable for humans than machine code *[1 mark]* so can be programmed/edited more easily. *[1 mark]*

c) Assembler *[1 mark]*

5 a) Error: Missing bracket on line 4. *[1 mark]*
Correction: *print("Valid pincode")* *[1 mark]*

b) Error: Wrong Boolean operator in line 3. *[1 mark]*
Correction:
if pincode.length >= 4 AND pincode.length <= 6 then
[1 mark]
Tiffany's code currently allows any pincode length. Changing OR to AND makes sure only pincodes with lengths from 4 to 6 characters are allowed.

6 E.g.
- Input validation could make sure that only appropriate data was entered. *[1 mark]* E.g. only allowing numbers to be entered for the card number. *[1 mark]*
- Input validation would ensure the input data matches certain criteria or is of a certain format. *[1 mark]* E.g. it can make sure that the expiration month is between 1 and 12. *[1 mark]*
- Input validation alone will not prevent all errors. *[1 mark]* E.g. it cannot check that a customer's card number matches their name. *[1 mark]*
- Using input sanitisation alongside validation would improve the defensive design *[1 mark]* as you'd be able to remove unwanted parts of an input before validating it. *[1 mark]*

[6 marks available in total]

7 E.g.
- The code editor might include an auto-indentation feature *[1 mark]* which will make the code clearer to read. *[1 mark]*
- The code editor might include an auto-colour feature *[1 mark]* which makes it easier to distinguish between different features of the code, e.g. variables and comments. *[1 mark]*
- Finding logic errors requires a lot of work by the user — the IDE has debugging tools to help *[1 mark]* but most of the work is done through testing. *[1 mark]*
- The IDE won't be able to tell if clear variable names and comments have been used *[1 mark]* so it won't be able to help with this, it's up to the developer. *[1 mark]*
- The IDE can't check if programmers have used a consistent approach in different parts of the program *[1 mark]* so it will be up to the developers to maintain good practice. *[1 mark]*

[6 marks available in total]

Page 97 (Revision Questions)

4 Input validation — the program checks if the user has entered a valid year before breaking out of the DO UNTIL loop.

10 The code doesn't do anything if the age is exactly 16. Either change the first condition to "*x >= 16*" or the second condition to "*x <= 16*".

On line 3 of the code, the variable x should be cast as a string before being concatenated with the other strings. Instead of "*x*", it should read "*str(x)*".

15 E.g.

Test Data	Reason for Testing	Expected Outcome
"tra"	Normal usage of the program.	"art", "rat", "tar"
No input	No input is entered.	Prompt to enter something.
"stm"	Input can't be made into a word.	Returns no words.
"AtN"	Input contains upper and lower case letters.	"tan", "ant", "nat"
"2t1?"	Input contains numbers and symbols.	Error: Unknown character.

Section Seven — Data Representation

Page 101 (Warm-Up Questions)

1 a)

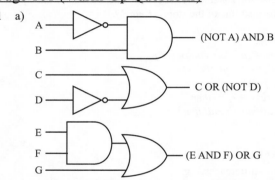

b)

A	B	NOT A	(NOT A) AND B
0	0	1	0
0	1	1	1
1	0	0	0
1	1	0	0

C	D	NOT D	C OR (NOT D)
0	0	1	1
0	1	0	0
1	0	1	1
1	1	0	1

E	F	G	E AND F	(E AND F) OR G
0	0	0	0	0
0	0	1	0	1
0	1	0	0	0
0	1	1	0	1
1	0	0	0	0
1	0	1	0	1
1	1	0	1	1
1	1	1	1	1

2 Nibble, Byte, Kilobyte, Megabyte, Gigabyte

3 a) String A: 0110101**0**
String B: 0100101**1**
String C: 011010010100101**1**

b) String A: 0110101**1**
String B: 0100101**0**
String C: 011010010100101**0**

Page 102 (Exam Questions)

3 a)

A	B	C	NOT A	B AND C	(NOT A) AND (B AND C)
0	0	0	1	0	0
0	0	1	1	0	0
0	1	0	1	0	0
0	1	1	1	1	1
1	0	0	0	0	0
1	0	1	0	0	0
1	1	0	0	0	0
1	1	1	0	1	0

[3 marks available — 1 mark for each correct column]

b)

(NOT A) AND B AND C

[3 marks available — 1 mark for input A going into a NOT gate, 1 mark for inputs B and C going into an AND gate, 1 mark for outputs going into an AND gate with one output]

4 a) A digit added to the end of a string of numbers / data to check that data has been entered and received correctly. *[1 mark]* The value is calculated from the digits in the string. *[1 mark]*

b) Computers are made up of logic circuits *[1 mark]* which use 1 and 0 to show high and low voltage. *[1 mark]*

c) String 1 contains an error *[1 mark]* because it has an odd number of 1s. *[1 mark]*

d) In the case where an even number of bits are read incorrectly *[1 mark]* a parity bit will not detect an error. *[1 mark]*

Page 108 (Warm-Up Questions)

1 a) 89   b) 1000101

2 11110010

3 Overflow errors occur when binary operations produce results that have more bits than the CPU is expecting to store/process.

4 00010111

5 Multiplying the number by 2.

6 a) 30   b) 198   c) A2   d) 111101

Page 109 (Exam Questions)

3 a) 11010000 *[1 mark]*

b) A 2 place right shift *[1 mark]* gives 00110101. *[1 mark]*

c) He is not correct.
E.g. 0001 + 0001 = 0010 is a 1 place left shift.
[2 marks available — 1 mark for not correct, 1 mark for a valid explanation]

4 a) Split bytes into nibbles and convert to hexadecimal.
0100 = 4, 0011 = 3, so 01000011 = C = 43. *[1 mark]*
0100 = 4, 0001 = 1, so 01000001 = A = 41. *[1 mark]*
0101 = 5, 0100 = 4, so 01010100 = T = 54. *[1 mark]*

b) i) D = 44 = 01000100 *[1 mark]*

ii) From CAT, 43 = C and from DOG, 44 = D and 4F = O.
E is 1 more than D (= 44) so 45 = E. *[1 mark]*
The password is CODE. *[1 mark]*

5 a) denary(A) = 10 and denary(C) = 12 *[1 mark]*
So, denary(A) + denary(C) = 10 + 12 = 22 *[1 mark]*

b) Taking a hexadecimal as an input. *[1 mark]*
Splitting hexadecimal into characters. *[1 mark]*
Multiplying first character in denary by 16. *[1 mark]*
Adding the second character in denary to the first. *[1 mark]*
E.g.
hexadecimal = input("Enter a two digit hexadecimal")
char1 = hexadecimal[0]
char2 = hexadecimal[1]
*ans = 16 * denary(char1) + denary(char2)*
print(ans)

Page 114 (Warm-Up Questions)

1 ASCII uses fewer bits to represent each character but is a much smaller character set.

2 16

3 a) The file size would increase.

b) The file size would decrease.

4 200 kbit/s

5 a) The file size and quality would both increase.

b) The file size and quality would both decrease.

6 E.g. Lossy compression will make file sizes a lot smaller. Lossless compression will maintain the quality of the original file.

Page 115 (Exam Questions)

3 a) A character set is a collection of characters a computer recognises from their binary representation. *[1 mark]*

b) E.g. Binary code sent to computer. *[1 mark]*
Character set used to translate binary code. *[1 mark]*

4 a) Extract 2 would have a better sound quality *[1 mark]* because it has a larger bit rate and sampling frequency, both of which are indications of better overall sound quality. *[1 mark]*

b) The file size would be larger. *[1 mark]*

5 a) 60 × 60 × 10 × 10 *[1 mark]* = 360 000 *[1 mark]*

b) A lower DPI would reduce the quality of the image *[1 mark]* because the number of pixels in a given area decreases. *[1 mark]*

c) Metadata is 'data about data' / information about a file. *[1 mark]* Metadata includes information about height, width, resolution etc. so the image is displayed properly. *[1 mark]*

Page 116 (Revision Questions)

2

A	B	C	A OR B	(A OR B) AND C
0	0	0	0	0
0	0	1	0	0
0	1	0	1	0
0	1	1	1	1
1	0	0	1	0
1	0	1	1	1
1	1	0	1	0
1	1	1	1	1

5 a) 2 terabytes

b) 2 000 000 megabytes

6 a) i) 10001   ii) 10010100   iii) 11110000

b) i) 11   ii) 94   iii) F0

7 a) i) 56   ii) 159   iii) 43

b) i) 38   ii) 9F   iii) 2B

8 a) i) 74   ii) 117   iii) 3033

b) i) 1001010   ii) 1110101   iii) 101111011001

9 10001111

Practice Paper 1 — Computer Systems

1 a) i) Utility software is software that helps to configure, optimise or maintain a computer. *[1 mark]*

   ii) Any **two** examples of utility software, e.g.
   - Disk defragmentation software *[1 mark]*
   - System diagnostic tools *[1 mark]*
   - Anti-virus / anti-spyware *[1 mark]*
   - Backup software *[1 mark]*
   - Compression software *[1 mark]*
   - File management software *[1 mark]*
   [2 marks available in total]

   b) i) E.g. When the hard disk is fragmented, it will take longer to read/write data on the hard disk. *[1 mark]* This in turn may slow down the computer. *[1 mark]*

   ii) E.g.
   - Defragmentation software reduces fragmentation by moving files on the hard disk. *[1 mark]*
   - The empty spaces/gaps are collected together. *[1 mark]*
   - Different bits of the same file are moved to be stored together. *[1 mark]*
   - This means the read/write heads won't need to move as far across the disk, so the read/write speed should improve. *[1 mark]*
   [3 marks available in total]

   c) E.g. Disk clean-up will remove a number of files, so it will immediately leave gaps in the data stored on the hard disk, leading to fragmentation. *[1 mark]*

   d) Any **three** advantages, e.g.
   - SSDs are faster than HDDs. *[1 mark]*
   - SSDs do not need to be defragmented. *[1 mark]*
   - SSDs do not make any noise. *[1 mark]*
   - SSDs are more shock-proof than HDDs. *[1 mark]*
   [3 marks available in total]

2 a) The use of online servers provided by a hosting company to store files and software. *[1 mark]*

   b) E.g.
   - Laptop/web browser sends a request to the cloud server, to send the image. *[1 mark]*
   - The cloud server processes the request. *[1 mark]*
   - The cloud server replies with the image. *[1 mark]*
   [2 marks available in total]

   c) i) E.g.
   - The cloud server splits the image into packets. *[1 mark]*
   - Each packet is given control information, including the IP addresses of the server and the laptop. *[1 mark]*
   - The server calculates a checksum number for each packet. *[1 mark]*
   - Each packet is given a packet number to show the order of the data. *[1 mark]*
   - Each router reads the control information of the packet and decides which way to send the data. *[1 mark]*
   - IP protocol governs packet switching. *[1 mark]*
   - The way the data is sent changes according to network traffic so packets take different routes to their destination. *[1 mark]*
   - Packets arrive at their destination in the wrong order. *[1 mark]*
   - The receiving device puts the packets in the right order using the packet numbers on each packet. *[1 mark]*
   - The receiving device recalculates the checksum. *[1 mark]*
   - If all packets are successfully delivered and the checksums match, a receipt confirmation is sent back to the sending device. *[1 mark]*
   [6 marks available in total]

   ii) E.g.
   - There are many possible routes the data can take *[1 mark]* so the data can reach the destination even if there is heavy network traffic. *[1 mark]*
   - Splitting data into small packets allows different parts of the data to be routed separately *[1 mark]* which is more flexible than sending the whole file in one go. *[1 mark]*
   [2 marks available in total]

   iii) Internet Protocol (IP) *[1 mark]*

   d) i) A set of rules and procedures the organisation will follow to ensure their network is protected against attacks and unauthorised access. *[1 mark]*

   ii) E.g.
   - Network forensics are investigations undertaken to find the cause of attacks on a network. *[1 mark]*
   - To conduct network forensics, an organisation needs to have a system of capturing data packets as they enter their network. *[1 mark]*
   - After the network is attacked, data packets can be analysed to discover how the network was attacked. *[1 mark]*
   - The information gained from network forensics can be used to decide how to prevent future attacks. *[1 mark]*
   [3 marks available in total]

3 a) i) Ethernet is a network protocol used on wired networks. *[1 mark]*
   WPA2 is a security protocol used on wireless LANs. *[1 mark]*

   ii) Any **one** difference, e.g.
   - CAT5e twisted pair cables use four twisted copper wires *[1 mark]* whereas coaxial cable uses one single copper wire. *[1 mark]*
   - CAT5e cables prevent interference by twisting the wires together *[1 mark]* whereas coaxial cable uses a braided metallic shield to prevent interference. *[1 mark]*
   [2 marks available in total]

   iii) E.g.
   The Leeds studio's wired setup:
   - Wired connections have a more reliable performance as there is no loss of signal no matter where the devices are in the building. *[1 mark]*
   - Wired connections are more restrictive as it is harder to add new devices / access the network while moving through the building. *[1 mark]*

   The York studio's wireless setup:
   - Wireless connections are easier for the employees to connect to (e.g. no need for cables to add a laptop or mobile device to the network). *[1 mark]*
   - Wireless connections can suffer from signal problems caused by building interference or interference from other wireless signals nearby. *[1 mark]*

   To get all four marks, you'll need one advantage and one disadvantage for wired connections, as well as one advantage and one disadvantage for wireless connections.

   b) i) Any **one** advantage, e.g.
   - Fibre optic cables tend to have greater bandwidth / can carry more data than copper cables. *[1 mark]*
   - Fibre optic cables can carry data over longer distances / don't suffer signal degradation or interference. *[1 mark]*
   - Fibre optic cables are easier to maintain than copper cables so cost less in the long term. *[1 mark]*
   [1 mark available in total]

   ii) E.g.
   - Laying its own cables between Leeds and York could be too expensive for the company. *[1 mark]*
   - Leased lines are likely to be more reliable and faster than other WAN connections. *[1 mark]*
   [1 mark available in total]

4 Points you might include:

Stakeholders
- Consumers will be able to access a greater variety of books, films and music. They will be able to purchase them at their own convenience without having to go to a shop. The books, films and music should also be cheaper as the costs are much lower to produce digital copies than physical copies.
- Traditional bookshops, CD shops and film retailers will have to adapt to distributing their stock digitally or face a decline in profits.
- Content creators will be able to distribute their media more cheaply, as they no longer have to pay for a record label, production team or publisher.
- New businesses that distribute books, music and films digitally could flourish as they gain some of the traditional stores' market share. New business models have been founded to distribute digital media, e.g. subscription-based services or streaming services where money is made through advertising.

Technology
- Use of digital media has encouraged the development and improvement in technology. E.g. e-readers introduced a new type of display technology that looks and feels more like a printed book. In the future, displays which are even more paper-like may be used.
- The use of digital media has placed extra demands on communication networks. This creates a cycle of improvement, e.g. watching high-quality films increases demand for better broadband speeds, which in turn encourages people to watch higher quality films, increasing demand for good broadband.
- The use of digital media is changing TVs from devices that receive broadcasted transmissions to Internet-enabled devices used to stream media from the Internet.

Environmental issues
- Less use of physical media means there could be less physical waste from packaging and discarded books, CDs and DVDs.
- No need for packaging or physical media, so fewer natural resources required in the distribution of the media.
- Greater use of digital media means increased use of electricity, as well as increased e-waste if hardware is discarded.

Legal issues
- Use of digital media could increase the amount of illegal file sharing.
- It is often unclear who owns the copyright to the original piece of work, and how profit from the book / music / film should be shared. E.g. how much money should a musician receive from their music being listened to on a free streaming service.
- It is often unclear who owns the digital file. E.g. should someone be able to pass their movie files onto their children, or does the ownership over them go back to the original distributor.

How to mark your answer:
- Two or three brief points with very little explanation. *[1-2 marks]*
- Three to five detailed points covering at least two of: stakeholders, technology, environmental issues and legal issues. *[3-5 marks]*
- Six or more detailed points that form a well-written, balanced discussion, covering all of: stakeholders, technology, environmental issues and legal issues. *[6-8 marks]*

5 a) Storage *[1 mark]*, GPU *[1 mark]*

b) E.g. Hardeep should upgrade the RAM in his computer, *[1 mark]* as he only just has enough RAM to cover the minimum requirements, so the OS may not run very smoothly. *[1 mark]*

   It's fine to answer 'no', as long as you've justified your answer.

c) RAM stores applications and data that is currently in use. *[1 mark]* As operating systems are running all the time, a large amount of the OS is kept in RAM. *[1 mark]*

d) Any **two** features, e.g.
- Large buttons and icons *[1 mark]* that can be pressed to open applications and windows. *[1 mark]*
- Screens and menus *[1 mark]* that can be navigated / controlled by swiping or dragging with a finger. *[1 mark]*
- Support for finger gestures *[1 mark]* such as pinching to zoom out / tap and hold to open additional options / four finger swipes to swap between apps etc. *[1 mark]*
- Virtual on-screen keyboard *[1 mark]* to allow the user to type without attaching an external keyboard. *[1 mark]*

[4 marks available in total]

6 a)

	Allowed	Not Allowed
Giving each teacher a USB flash drive containing the personal information of all the pupils who have attended the school.		✓
Transferring pupils' personal information to their new school when they leave.	✓	
Refusing to tell a parent what information is being stored about their son/daughter.		✓
Backing up pupils' personal information on a drive that is stored in a locked safe.	✓	
Using pupils' personal information to get in contact with their parents.	✓	
Putting pupils' personal information on the school website to make it easier for teachers and parents to access.		✓

[6 marks available — 1 for each correct row]

b) Any **two** forms of network attack and a suitable method of protection, e.g.
- Passive attack *[1 mark]* — using tools such as network-monitoring devices and packets sniffers to intercept sensitive information. *[1 mark]* Can be protected against by encrypting data on the network. *[1 mark]*
- Active attack *[1 mark]* — using malware or other means to break into a network and steal data. *[1 mark]* Can be protected against by using a firewall. *[1 mark]*
- Insider attack *[1 mark]* — exploiting a person's position within the organisation to gain access to data on the network. *[1 mark]* Can be protected against by using user access levels to restrict access to people that are trusted. *[1 mark]*
- Brute force attack *[1 mark]* — using automated software and trial-and-error to find a password that will allow access to the network. *[1 mark]* Can be protected against by locking accounts after a certain number of failed attempts. *[1 mark]*

[6 marks available in total]

7 a) If the central switch fails, users will be unable to access files on other servers *[1 mark]* because there will be no connections between any of the servers. *[1 mark]*

b) E.g.
- Connecting servers in a mesh network means that if one connection fails, there are other routes to connect the servers. *[1 mark]* This means the network can still operate fully and all the computers can access data on all servers. *[1 mark]*
- Adding an extra server to a mesh network would be more complicated *[1 mark]* because it would need to be connected to all of the other servers rather than just the switch. *[1 mark]*
- Some connections would be redundant most of the time *[1 mark]* as the servers would communicate using the quickest or most direct route. *[1 mark]*

[4 marks available in total — at least one advantage and one disadvantage required for full marks]

c) Increasing incTotal and fullTotal by the number of files edited on that day. *[1 mark]*
Conditional statement based on the values of fullTotal and incTotal. *[1 mark]*
Taking full backup if fullTotal reaches 1000 (regardless of the value of incTotal). *[1 mark]*
Resetting fullTotal and incTotal to 0 after full backup. *[1 mark]*
Taking incremental backup if incTotal reaches 200 (unless fullTotal ≥ 1000). *[1 mark]*
Resetting only incTotal to 0 after incremental backup. *[1 mark]*
E.g.
dailyTotal = number of files edited today
incTotal = incTotal + dailyTotal
fullTotal = fullTotal + dailyTotal
if fullTotal >= 1000 then
    take full backup
    fullTotal = 0, incTotal = 0
elseif incTotal >= 200 then
    take incremental backup
    incTotal = 0
endif

Practice Paper 2 — Computational Thinking, Algorithms and Programming

1 a) i)   String *[1 mark]*
    ii) Real/Float *[1 mark]*

b) Using the correct data type will make your programs more memory efficient. *[1 mark]* It will also make your programs more robust and predictable. *[1 mark]*

c) E.g. All the different data values might be converted to strings using the str() function so string concatenation can be used to join them together on the receipt. *[1 mark]* For example the cost of fuel might be converted from a real / float to a string so it can be printed in a sentence, e.g. "The cost of fuel was £20.76". *[1 mark]*

d) Any **two** differences, e.g.
• A compiler would produce an executable file *[1 mark]* while an interpreter would not. *[1 mark]*
• A compiler would list any errors at the end of the translation *[1 mark]* while an interpreter would return the first error it found then stop. *[1 mark]*
• A compiler would translate the code all at once *[1 mark]* while an interpreter would translate and run the code line by line. *[1 mark]*
[4 marks available in total]

2 a) 10101000 = 128 + 32 + 8 = 168
[2 marks available — 1 for correct working and 1 for correct final answer]

b) Split 10110101 into nibbles:
1011 = B, 0101 = 5, so 10110101 = B5
[2 marks available — 1 for correct working and 1 for correct final answer]

c)   1 0 1 0 1 0 0 0
   + 1 0 1 1 0 1 0 1
   ‾‾‾‾‾‾‾‾‾‾‾‾‾‾‾‾‾‾‾
   1 0 1 0 1 1 1 0 1 *[1 mark]*
          1

d) An overflow error is where the result of a calculation requires more bits than are available and some of the data is lost. *[1 mark]*

3 a) i)   A parameter is a special variable that passes data into a sub program. *[1 mark]*
    ii) Parameters have a local scope to the sub program they're defined in. *[1 mark]*
    iii) Arguments are the actual values that parameters take when the sub program is called. *[1 mark]*

b) i)   Declares a new variable, difficulty, *[1 mark]* which has global scope so it can be used anywhere in the program. *[1 mark]*
    ii) It takes weight as a parameter *[1 mark]* and sets the variable difficulty equal to the integer (quotient) part when weight is divided by 6. *[1 mark]*

c) A sub program that takes heart rate as a parameter. *[1 mark]*
Using a selection statement. *[1 mark]*
Having correct conditions on the selection statement. *[1 mark]*
Setting the difficulty depending on the conditions. *[1 mark]*
E.g.
procedure adjustLevel(heartrate)
    if heartrate > 160 then
        difficulty = 0
        print("Slow Down!")
    elseif heartrate < 90 then
        difficulty = difficulty + 1
    elseif heartrate > 140 then
        difficulty = difficulty – 1
    endif
endprocedure

4 a)

[3 marks available — 1 for inputs S and D going into an AND gate, 1 for the output of AND gate and input I going into an OR gate and 1 for Z being the OR gate output]

b)
S	D	I	Z
0	1	0	0
1	1	0	1
1	0	0	0

[3 marks available — 1 for each correct row]

5 a) Check each item in order.
Check the first item: 10 mA ≠ 12 mA
Check the second item: 15 mA ≠ 12 mA
Check the third item: 12 mA = 12 mA.
Stop searching as the item has been found.
[2 marks available — 1 for starting with 10 mA and 1 for checking items in order until you find 12 mA]

b) Using Start / Begin. *[1 mark]*
Input to check reading. *[1 mark]*
Decision box with appropriate question. *[1 mark]*
'Buzz' as an output. *[1 mark]*
Wait 5 minutes as a process. *[1 mark]*
Using Stop / End. *[1 mark]*
E.g.

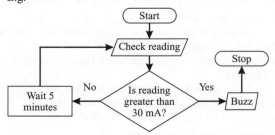

6 a) 16^6 *[1 mark]*

b) E.g. It would be easier to remember the hex code for a particular colour *[1 mark]* because the hex code would be shorter than the binary or denary equivalents. *[1 mark]*

c) JPEG is an example of lossy compression *[1 mark]* — it produces a much smaller file size than the other formats. *[1 mark]*

d) E.g.
- No data is lost when compressed *[1 mark]* so graphics can be reverted back to the original — this is essential to ensure graphics are always high quality. *[1 mark]*
- File sizes are only slightly reduced *[1 mark]* so there would be an impact on storage requirements to the company. *[1 mark]*
- Not all software is compatible with lossless file types *[1 mark]* so clients may not be able to open graphics. *[1 mark]*
- File sizes are large *[1 mark]* so the images will take longer to upload or attach to emails for clients. *[1 mark]*

[4 marks available in total]

e) Any **two** pieces of metadata, e.g.
- File format *[1 mark]*
- Height/width in pixels *[1 mark]*
- Colour depth *[1 mark]*
- Resolution *[1 mark]*
- Date created/date modified *[1 mark]*
- Creator's name *[1 mark]*

[2 marks available in total]

7 a) Erroneous test data contains values that the program should not accept. *[1 mark]* Using them in testing will make sure that the user can enter any data without breaking the program. *[1 mark]*

b) i) Type of data: Normal *[1 mark]*
Intended Outcome: 20 *[1 mark]*
Actual Outcome: 20 *[1 mark]*

ii) Type of data: Erroneous *[1 mark]*
Intended Outcome: User receives an error message, e.g. "Invalid dice score, please re-enter." *[1 mark]*
Actual Outcome: 19 *[1 mark]*
The game uses a six-sided dice, so if the user inputs a 9 they should receive an error message. However, Tony's program does not check for this.

c) Any **two** ways, e.g.
- He could make sure only integers are accepted. *[1 mark]*
- He could make sure only the numbers from 1 to 6 are accepted. *[1 mark]*
- He could ensure that the input is only one character long. *[1 mark]*
- He could make sure that only Yes/No, yes/no, Y/N, y/n, etc. are accepted for the "Roll again" prompt. *[1 mark]*

[2 marks available in total]

8 a) E.g. Storing the data in records allows the different fields to have different data types *[1 mark]* while if they used an array, they would all have to be the same data type. *[1 mark]*

b) i) SELECT Title FROM comics
WHERE Genre = "Science Fiction"
[2 marks available — 1 for selecting the correct fields from the comics table and 1 for a correct 'where' statement]

ii) SELECT Title, Length FROM comics
WHERE Length < 50 AND Rating = 3
[2 marks available — 1 for selecting the correct fields from the comics table and 1 for a correct 'where' statement]

iii) SELECT * FROM comics WHERE Title LIKE "H%"
[2 marks available — 1 for selecting all fields from the comics table and 1 for a correct 'where' statement]

9 a) array primeKoalas[4, 2]
primeKoalas[0, 0] = "John"
primeKoalas[1, 0] = "Paul"
primeKoalas[2, 0] = "Cheryl"
primeKoalas[3, 0] = "Ida"
primeKoalas[0, 1] = "guitar"
primeKoalas[1, 1] = "bass"
primeKoalas[2, 1] = "vocals"
primeKoalas[3, 1] = "drums"
[2 marks available — award 2 for all 4 correct lines of code, otherwise award 1 for at least two correct lines of code]

b) Opening and closing the file properly. *[1 mark]*
Using a loop. *[1 mark]*
Writing the name and instrument of each band member to the file. *[1 mark]*
E.g.
band = openWrite("musicians.txt")
for i = 0 to 3
  band.writeLine(primeKoalas[i, 0] + " " + primeKoalas[i, 1])
next i
band.close()

c) A procedure taking a file name as a parameter. *[1 mark]*
Opening the file in read mode. *[1 mark]*
A condition-controlled loop to stop at the end of the file. *[1 mark]*
Using the toSpeech() procedure to read out each line. *[1 mark]*
Closing the file. *[1 mark]*
E.g.
procedure readAll(fileName)
  file = openRead(fileName)
  while NOT file.endOfFile()
    toSpeech(file.readLine())
  endwhile
  file.close()
endprocedure
It's important that you always remember to close a file once you're finished reading from it or writing to it.

Glossary and Index

Glossary and Index

Glossary and Index

Glossary and Index

Glossary and Index

COS41